E. F. Sampson

Christ Church Sermons

with an introductory essay

E. F. Sampson

Christ Church Sermons

with an introductory essay

ISBN/EAN: 9783337264598

Printed in Europe, USA, Canada, Australia, Japan

Cover: Foto ©Lupo / pixelio.de

More available books at **www.hansebooks.com**

CHRIST CHURCH SERMONS

a

CHRIST CHURCH SERMONS

WITH AN INTRODUCTORY ESSAY

BY THE REV.

E. F. SAMPSON, M.A.

STUDENT TUTOR AND FORMERLY CENSOR OF CHRIST CHURCH, OXFORD

LONGMANS, GREEN, & CO.
LONDON, NEW YORK, AND BOMBAY
1896

PATRI REVERENDISSIMO IN DEO

EDWARDO

EPISCOPO LINCOLNIENSI

ÆDIS CHRISTI PER DUODECIM ANNOS CANONICO

SUORUM SI QUIS ALIUS

AMICO PASTORI MAGISTRO

PREFACE

THE sermons printed here were preached at considerable intervals in the course of the last twenty-one years; during seventeen of these years the author held the office of Censor of Christ Church. They were written without any idea of publication, and it has consequently been necessary to correct them in details; they are, however, substantially unchanged. Care has been taken to give, as far as possible, references to any books of which use was made; but as, with very few exceptions, the manuscripts were never looked at from the dates at which they were preached, until they were re-read for the purpose of this book, it is possible that some of the references have been lost sight of and forgotten: for any such accidental omission the author wishes to apologize. In one or two cases it is obvious that the sermons are considerably indebted to particular writers. The first sermon would never have been written as it stands, if it had not been suggested by a book on "Mental Physiology," by Dr. W. B. Carpenter.[1]

---

[1] "Principles of Mental Physiology," by W. B. Carpenter, M.D., F.R.S. London: Kegan Paul & Co.

On re-reading it, there appeared to be difficulty in marking the particular references that should be made; the author, however, wishes to acknowledge fully his general indebtedness to this very interesting book. Two other Sermons (VIII. and XVIII.) draw very largely upon the standard work on "The Doctrine of the Incarnation," by Archdeacon Wilberforce.[1] Their publication here seems to need no apology; any one well acquainted with the book will recognize at once how large the author's debt to it is; any one who does not know the book, and has his attention directed to it by one of these sermons, will be grateful for the introduction to so instructive and suggestive a treatise.

There is difficulty—perhaps generally, certainly under the conditions in which sermons have to be written—in distinguishing between what may and what may not be held to be original. Ideas are suggested in conversation as well as in magazines and books; they take their place in the mind, germinate there and reappear, sometimes without any recollection on the part of the writer of the origin from which they spring. The author is perfectly conscious how much he owes to such indirect sources for guidance and stimulus, in all sorts of ways. It is, of course,

---

[1] "The Doctrine of the Incarnation," by Archdeacon R. I. Wilberforce. London, Murray, 1849.

only possible to acknowledge this debt in general terms; but the debt is none the less real, and the acknowledgment of it none the less sincere. As these words are being penned, there rise up before the writer memories of friends and colleagues—among them some who have now passed "from out our bourne of Time and Place"—who have given, and still give, to life in Oxford its peculiar happiness. This is the special reward that Christ Church has been able to bestow so lavishly upon those who have worked for the House; and it is in the help given by this friendship, that the author finds the source of all that there may be of any value in what he has written, while he accepts as his own the full responsibility for any failure or shortcoming.

CHRIST CHURCH,
September, 1896.

CONTENTS

	PAGE
INTRODUCTION	xvii

I.
Sowing and Reaping.

"Whatsoever a man soweth, that shall he also reap."—GAL. vi. 7   1
(*The First Sunday after Trinity, May* 30, 1875.)

II.
The Things that are Unseen.

"For now we see through a glass, darkly; but then face to face: now I know in part; but then shall I know even as also I am known."—1 COR. xiii. 12 11
(*Quinquagesima Sunday, February 8*, 1880.)

III.
The Kingdom of Christ.

"My kingdom is not of this world."—ST. JOHN xviii. 36 . . 23
(*Twenty-sixth Sunday after Trinity, November 21*, 1880.)

IV.
The Finite Intellect.

"We know in part."—1 COR. xiii. 9 33
(*Sunday after Ascension-day, May 29*, 1881.)

V.
Worship.

"This is none other but the house of God, and this is the gate of Heaven."—GEN. xxviii. 17 44
(*Twenty-fifth Sunday after Trinity, November 26*, 1882.)

VI.

The Church and Wealth.

"Son, remember that thou in thy lifetime receivedst thy good
things."—ST. LUKE xvi. 25   55

(*First Sunday after Trinity, May 27, 1883.*)

VII.

Faith and Knowledge.

"Except a man be born again, he cannot see the kingdom of
God."—ST. JOHN iii. 3   67

(*Quinquagesima Sunday, February 24, 1884.*)

VIII.

The Church the Body of Christ.

"The Church which is His Body."—EPH. i. 23   78

(*Twentieth Sunday after Trinity, October 26, 1884.*)

IX.

Penitence.

"My sin is ever before me."—PSALM li. 3   87

(*Sexagesima Sunday, February 8, 1885.*)

X.

The Holy Trinity.

"Blessed are the pure in heart: for they shall see God."—ST.
MATT. v. 8   95

(*Trinity Sunday, May 31, 1885.*)

XI.

Christian Self-assertion.

"I can do all things through Christ which strengtheneth me."
—PHIL. iv. 13   105

(*Twenty-fifth Sunday after Trinity, November 22, 1885.*)

XII.

Self-purification.

"We know that, when He shall appear, we shall be like Him; for we shall see Him as He is. And every man that hath this hope in him purifieth himself, even as He is pure."—1 St. John iii. 2, 3 114

(*Sixth Sunday after Epiphany, February 14, 1886.*)

XIII.

The Work of Life.

"Their eyes were holden that they should not know Him."— St. Luke xxiv. 16 121

(*Fifth Sunday after Easter, May 30, 1886.*)

XIV.

Truthfulness.

"Speak every man truth with his neighbour: for we are members one of another."—Eph. iv. 25 131

(*Nineteenth Sunday after Trinity, October 31, 1886.*)

XV.

Love towards God.

"Charity never faileth."—1 Cor. xiii. 8 140

(*Quinquagesima Sunday, February 20, 1887.*)

XVI.

The Anxieties of Life no Excuse for Failure of Courage.

"He that observeth the wind shall not sow; and he that regardeth the clouds shall not reap."—Eccles. xi. 4 . . 150

(*Twenty-first Sunday after Trinity, October 30, 1887.*)

XVII.
The Life of the World to come.

"I saw a new heaven and a new earth."—Rev. xxi. 1 . . 159

(*Septuagesima Sunday, January 29, 1888.*)

XVIII.
Faith.

"Then opened He their understanding, that they might understand the scriptures."—St. Luke xxiv. 45 170

(*Sunday after Ascension Day, May 13, 1888.*)

XIX.
The Wise and the Foolish Virgins.

"Then shall the kingdom of heaven be likened unto ten virgins, which took their lamps, and went forth to meet the Bridegroom. And five of them were wise, and five were foolish."—St. Matt. xxv. 1, 2 180

(*Fifth Sunday after Epiphany, February 10, 1889.*)

XX.
The Resurrection.

"Then went in also that other disciple . . . and he saw, and believed."—St. John xx. 8 188

(*Fourth Sunday after Easter, May 19, 1889.*)

XXI.
The Dangers of Externalism.

"These have no root in themselves, and so endure but for a time."—St. Mark iv. 17 198

(*First Sunday in Lent, February 23, 1890.*)

XXII.

Excuses.

"They all with one consent began to make excuse."—St. Luke xiv. 18 207

(Second Sunday after Trinity, June 15, 1890.)

XXIII.

Esau and Jacob.

"Jacob have I loved, but Esau have I hated."—Rom. ix. 13 . 218

(Second Sunday in Lent, February 22, 1891.)

XXIV.

God's Voice must be Heard in the Claims of Present Duties.

"And he said, Nay, father Abraham: but if one went unto them from the dead, they will repent. And he said unto him, If they hear not Moses and the prophets, neither will they be persuaded, though one rose from the dead."—St. Luke xvi. 30, 31 227

(First Sunday after Trinity, May 31, 1891.)

XXV.

The One Lord.

"Jesus Christ is the same yesterday and to-day, yea and for ever."—Heb. xiii. 8 (R.V.) 236

(Second Sunday in Lent, March 13, 1892.)

XXVI.

The Love of God.

"As the Father hath loved Me, so have I loved you."—St. John xv. 9 247

(Twentieth Sunday after Trinity, October 30, 1892.)

XXVII.

Thanksgiving.

"O all ye works of the Lord, bless ye the Lord: praise Him and exalt Him above all for ever."—Song of the Three Holy Children, 35 257

(*Twenty-second Sunday after Trinity, October* 29, 1893.)

XXVIII.

The Bearing of the Cross.

"If any man will come after Me, let him deny himself, and take up his cross, and follow Me."—St. Matt. xvi. 24 . . . 265

(*Second Sunday in Lent, February* 18, 1894.)

XXIX.

Covetousness.

"Take heed, and beware of covetousness: for a man's life consisteth not in the abundance of the things which he possesseth."—St. Luke xii. 15 274

(*Quinquagesima Sunday, February* 16, 1896.)

XXX.

Covetousness.

"Take heed, and beware of covetousness: for a man's life consisteth not in the abundance of the things which he possesseth."—St. Luke xii. 15 283

(*First Sunday in Lent, February* 23, 1896.)

INTRODUCTION

The following sermons, with the exception of the last two, have no immediate link of connection with each other; yet, from the fact that they were all preached to a College audience, there are naturally special points that recur more than once. On two of these it may be well to make a few preliminary remarks.

I.

In the sensitive atmosphere of Oxford, where during the last half century everything that is generally included under the term faith has had almost of necessity a very hard struggle for existence, it is natural that in speaking to younger men a preacher should be anxious in every way he can to lay stress upon the reality of the things that belong to the unseen world. And, if he ventures to touch on such questions as this, he must deal with them, as best he can, from the purely intellectual side. A University is a place of books, of people who are reading widely, and whose chief duty is either learning or teaching—one or both of these.

Men are outside the stream of general life; they are theorists, some would perhaps say dreamers, rather than practical men dealing with everyday life in all its many-sidedness. The "academic mind" is a well understood phrase; and it is under conditions dominated by it that the maintenance or defence of so intensely practical a thing as the Christian Creed has to be undertaken. Hence comes the tendency to insist on the fact, that the ultimate intellectual difficulties of the reason, when it acknowledges its allegiance to the Creed, are not in reality seriously greater than those it has to meet if it refuses this allegiance; that in the end, if a man persistently examines and probes and cross-examines his first principles, he must find questions put to him to which he can give no complete and satisfactory answer; and this quite as certainly on non-Christian as on Christian lines of thought.

The writer matriculated in 1865; the Conservatism of the older Oxford had by that time done its best— or its worst—in the way of restraining or stifling the growth of new ideas, and in compelling thought to move, if it moved at all, only along lines traced out and fixed unchangeably by prevalent ideas and opinions. The Tractarian Party was supposed to be crushed, or if not quite crushed, yet to be reduced to so completely a quiescent condition, that those who had been living in terror at the idea of the possible re-establishment of Papal authority in these kingdoms were able to sleep in peace. Really they had won their imaginary peace only by the proverbial method of creating a solitude. By the suspension of Dr. Pusey some twenty years earlier, the leaders of the old Oxford party had struck a fatal blow at Church life; followed as this suspension was within a few years by the Gorham judgment and by renewed secessions to Rome, all possibility of steady influence was for the time taken away from the group of men, who, whatever their faults might have been supposed to be, were the leading thinkers within the Church. From the beginning of the movement they had steadily maintained a very high ideal of what life in Oxford should be, in its simplicity of manners as well as in its intellectual eagerness and industry. It is easy to understand how entirely distasteful such enthusiasms must have been to the old-fashioned academic mind. It, indeed, would have none of these innovations, and in the end it practically carried its point. Dr. Pusey himself was undismayed; he held his ground, set like a great rock in the corner of "Tom Quad," unmoved and unmovable; years hence men will, perhaps, be able to estimate what the Church of England owes to his courage and tenacity. Here and there were one or two —notably the late Dr. Liddon, then one of the younger Students of Christ Church—who kept the flame that had been kindled in the earlier days from entirely dying out; but in the main, at that date, the victory rested with those who desired to keep down the New Movement. Enthusiasm was checked, and Church life was left to be represented by the traditional ideals of conformity, by College services which were compulsory, with little attempt to infuse life or reality or glow into them, and by monthly celebrations of the Holy Communion, which, strange as it seems to us, were also practically compulsory. It is scarcely necessary to criticize principles which could produce such results as these. At a time when the ferment of a newly awakened life was spreading through the nation, when, after the passing of the Reform Bill of 1832, new ideas were making themselves felt and were beginning to tell in every direction—Tractarianism, after all, was no isolated phenomenon; it had its place in and its relation to the general movement of the day—the University, under the guidance of the then dominant party, made its attempt to stand aside and to remain uninfluenced by the forces that were working in the world; it tried to do this, and it failed as it was bound to fail. The author is entirely convinced that the reforms which have been carried out during the last fifty years were reforms that ought in any case to have been made, and that it was right, as well as inevitable, to deprive the Church of England of the exclusive position it held in Oxford. It is, however, certainly worthy of remark, that the first serious blows at the Church were struck, not in the House of Commons or by a political party, but within the University itself, and by the hands of some who claimed to be among its most faithful sons.

The success which attended the old Hebdomadal Board in dealing with the religious movement within the University, did not follow them in other and, from their point of view, quite as important struggles. While they were doing what they could to suppress the Tractarians, new and, so far as they were concerned, entirely unforeseen forces were beginning to assert themselves and to complicate the problems that pressed for solution. In the sixties the question of the religious tests on the M.A. and superior degrees (tests on the undergraduates and on the bachelors' degrees, except Theology, had been removed by Parliament in 1854) had become a burning question; and this question, troublesome enough in itself, was further complicated by the fact, that almost all the Headships and a considerable majority of the Fellowships were confined to only a minority of those who were members of the Church of England—that is, to those who either were already in Holy Orders, or who were prepared to promise to be ordained within a few years of the date of their election or appointment. Further, as this minority was a steadily diminishing one, owing to the growing reluctance of the younger men to become clergymen, it became difficult to keep up a sufficiently high standard of attainments for the clerical Fellowships. No doubt there were many causes at work tending to produce this result. The political and social developments of the preceding half century had been marvellously rapid, and it was consequently impossible to remain within the old lines of thought and to look at life in the old way. The regular Oxford career—a fellowship, then a tutorship, then a College Living—could no longer be regarded as the normal one. New interests and ideas had made their way into life; the growth of the natural sciences and the opening out of new fields of knowledge made it impossible that ordination should continue to be a necessary condition of holding positions of learning and education. Men wished to be students and teachers without becoming clergymen; we nowadays, perhaps, find it difficult to understand how it was possible seriously to oppose wishes that appear to us so entirely rational. This appears to be the plain matter-of-fact truth of things that underlay much passionate rhetoric that was used on both sides in the years during which the struggle lasted. Common sense said this change must be made; experience proved that the clerical restrictions did much to make the idea of ordination repugnant to men, and in this way increased the hesitation some felt in making up their minds whether to become clergymen or not; in a word, the restrictions were positively harmful to those who were bent on retaining them.

It will be readily understood that this did not make

it easier to discuss the general imposition of tests on the full degree—that is, on all degrees that admitted men to a share in the government of the University. The question, however, dragged on, and meanwhile the work of the University had to be done. The natural outcome was the growth of opinions which were directed towards the minimizing of the tests in every possible way; and modes of explanation and interpretation began to be current that made them an almost unmixed evil. It is not intended to criticize these opinions in themselves, or to find fault with those who advocated them; they were an almost necessary consequence of the point at which matters stood at the time; but, in this at least all must agree, when perfectly conscientious people were found to argue seriously that in signing the Articles a man did no more than promise not to controvert them publicly in his position as a University graduate or teacher—that the subscription in no way committed him to any positive belief in them, the position of those who adhered to the tests became very difficult. For it is clear that the tests, so interpreted, excluded mainly Roman Catholics and Nonconformists, who, conscientiously and on religious grounds, dissented from the Church of England: other men, on the theory largely advocated that Englishmen as such were members of the State Church, and in presence of a very liberal interpretation of the tests, were able without any great strain on their consciences to affix their signatures to the Thirty-nine Articles. It is quite obvious that under such conditions as these subscription could not be long retained.

The controversies that arose from these circumstances would, if long continued, have been little less than disastrous to Oxford. On the one hand they certainly were full of danger for all that was best in the religious life of the University, while on the other hand they checked and impeded the intellectual development of the place. They divided men into two hostile bodies, sharply opposed to each other, either section inclined to judge their opponents' ability and power of usefulness solely by the attitude they took on the one question of the tests. Fortunately the passing of the Act of 1871 by the Government of Mr. Gladstone, followed as it was a few years later by the work of the last University Commission—a necessary consequence of the Bill of 1871—settled effectively what may be spoken of as the political side of the question. There are, it is true, some clerical offices still in existence; but as they are now constituted they exist with a definite object, namely, the instruction of members of the Church of England, and the maintenance of the College services. They thus have special duties attached to them: incidentally also they are very useful as a connecting link between the present and the past life of the University; and

Oxford thus escapes that sudden and entire break with its past which is always to be deprecated in the case of a great historic society. None, it is imagined, will object to this statement except those, if there are any, who consider revolution preferable to evolution.

Hitherto the points referred to have been mainly what may be called political points. They could not be wholly omitted; but there are other considerations that touch religious life and thought much more closely than they do. As a matter of fact intellectual difficulties in regard to the Christian Creed had a very large influence in determining men's attitude to ordination and to clerical restrictions. These difficulties were made much more acute by the modes of thought which at that time dominated the Oxford Schools. The teaching of Mr. J. S. Mill was at the zenith of its popularity; the positions which he maintained, and the methods that underlay all Mr. Herbert Spencer's work, were regarded as in a very real sense final and conclusive; they were supposed to contain within themselves the last word that could be said on all subjects.[1] In the methods of these teachers there was but small place to be found for any of the ideas usually associated with the Creeds. The truths of

---

[1] It is only intended here to enter a protest against the absolute autocracy that Oxford allowed these teachers thirty years ago. The author always feels that he himself owes Mr. Herbert Spencer a debt of real gratitude for the "First Principles."

Christianity were not denied; they were rather left on one side; partly perhaps because they were not understood, partly because, so far as they were thought about at all, they were not regarded as worth attacking: they were no doubt welcome to survive, if they were able to do so, on the condition that they accepted the principles that underlay the prevailing school of thought. This was of course impossible; and consequently men began to discover that there was gradually forming round them a mental atmosphere in which, on intellectual grounds, it ceased to be possible to remain Christians in belief. The conceptions of the Creeds could only drag on a precarious existence for imaginative minds as a kind of vague and mystic poetry; as facts, in any usual sense of the word, they had ceased to be intelligible; they could no longer be made subjects of serious study.

For some years this school was absolutely dominant in Oxford, and then a great change began to make itself felt. A writer would require very special qualifications to be able to justly estimate the work done in the University by Professor T. H. Green; it was, however, impossible to live there, while he was teaching, without having some idea how deep and wide was the influence exercised by him over his pupils and his contemporaries. Among the former were a number of able men who seized on his teaching with avidity, and made it the basis of their own work, and became afterwards the pioneers of the younger High Church party. It has happened to them, as it often does in such cases, to be denounced most strongly by some of those whose lineal successors they undoubtedly were. This was perhaps unavoidable; for the work of the earlier Tractarians had lain in the past; they were compelled by circumstances, first to prove,—and they certainly proved it,—that the line of teaching they maintained had existed continuously within the Church of England since the Reformation; and next, to restore the study of the fathers and early Church literature, with a view to showing the practical identity of this teaching with that prevailing in the Church before quarrels and schisms had broken it up and disunited it. This work done, it was done once for all, and the problems that then demanded solution were entirely different. The relations of Christianity to modern modes of thought had to be considered; in view of the changed conceptions which were becoming part of the ordinary mental furniture of every thinking man, some re-statement of Christian doctrine was absolutely unavoidable. This duty the younger High Church party undertook, and they did their work under the inspiration of Professor Green's teaching.

It is not, of course, for one moment implied— the mere suggestion of such an idea is grotesque to any one who knows anything of the Professor and his work—that in doing this they were simply putting into a different shape what they learned from him. The point is, not that he taught them exactly what to say, but that he opened the way into methods of thought that made their line of teaching a possibility. He broke the chains by which, during the immediately preceding years, men's minds had been held in bondage, and kept shut up within the limits of principles that were ultimately—however little some perhaps of those who accepted them would allow it—naturalistic, materialistic, or agnostic. The late Rector of Lincoln College—who was a brilliant representative of the thought of the Oxford of thirty years ago—saw clearly what was going on, and spoke with cynical bitterness of the way in which High Churchmen were carrying off to their own hives the honey created by the new school of thought.[1] The great work of Professor Green from an outsider's point of view—and it is superfluous to say that the writer speaks only as an outsider—was that he brought us freedom, cleared the air and made it more breatheable. His influence was fortunately greatest in the University in the seventies, the years immediately following the passing of the Tests Act, by which—strange as some may think the admission to be—Parliament had removed one of the greatest obstacles that stood in the way of the restoration of religious life in Oxford. How far the successors of the Tractarians have done their work it is

---

[1] Cf. "Mark Pattison's Memoirs," p. 167.

too soon to estimate; but it is certain that Oxford has passed out of the phase of thought in which it had become practically impossible for many men to accept the Creeds. It is not now an axiomatic truth that to be frankly Christian is incompatible with the possession of any intellectual power; this change the author believes to be due in a very real sense to the teaching of Professor Green.

It is not suggested for one moment that under these new conditions a complete and final system has been, or is being evolved, which will supply a sufficient *vade mecum* to all the mysteries that lie about our lives. But, and it is this that is important, it is now possible to think that there are some things which are true and which must be reckoned with, that are not discoverable in the laboratories of the physiologist and the chemist; that there are facts of the soul and spirit as certain and as urgent as those of the body; and that any attempt to analyze or explain humanity, which ignores or denies the former, dooms itself to failure. In a word, it is possible once more to say with Pascal, "*Le cœur a ses raisons que la raison ne connait point.*"[1] This is not, as is sometimes suggested, equivalent to denying or dethroning reason. The attempt to give reason—reason, that is, as the term is understood in its relation to positive knowledge—a supreme and commanding position in regard to every side of life and

[1] "Pascal's Pensées," Ed. Faugère, ii. 172.

thought, appears to the writer equivalent to the attempt, if such an attempt can be imagined, to drag the skeleton out of the human body, and then, because life cannot get on without it, to assume that it is the principle of life, and that the rest of the body may be ignored. It is a sheer impossibility, except as an intellectual *tour de force,* to separate the reason from the moral and spiritual sides of man—from all that belongs to the heart and the affections. To deny the latter their due place is to confuse and perplex the former, and so to make the reason quite unable to fulfil its function in guiding and directing life as a whole.

There is, then, no intention to argue that the change that has taken place in the way in which all such questions as these are regarded, makes it possible to offer a mathematical demonstration of the truth of the Creed. Most certainly it does nothing of the sort; but it does grant conditions in which it is no longer little less than an intellectual impossibility to accept the Creed. This is the important point. In many cases, and especially with younger men, much of the difficulty felt in remaining true to the Creed of the Church is taken out of the way, when they begin to understand that the ultimate intellectual difficulties, which have to be met on all lines of thought, present problems that are practically insoluble; that the pre-suppositions of materialistic systems are pre-suppositions just as surely as those of Christianity; less objectionable, perhaps, and less difficult of acceptance to particular minds, but none the less for all that pre-suppositions; that all systems ultimately ask questions to which it is quite impossible for men, constituted as they are, to give final answers. When this is admitted, and it is seen that the way is open to listen to the appeal of the heart, to pay attention to the claims of the moral and spiritual sides of man's complex nature, the Creed can command a hearing; it is no longer as a matter of course set aside and rejected. Certainly there is no steady pressure of continuous and unassailable argument, as in the case of the Propositions of Euclid, compelling men to accept its conclusions; certainty of this order is only possible in the most exact of the exact sciences. But the road along which the lines of thought demanded by Christian dogmatic teaching invite men to travel, is no longer hidden from sight, or blocked up and rendered wholly impassable; the path is open and clear, and those who will may follow its track. This is all that can be wished or expected. Anything more than this would annihilate all conception of the present life as a time of trial and probation, in which it is possible for men to choose and accept, but in which also it is possible to refuse and to deny.

Any system that aims at completeness and self-sufficiency appears to the present writer unintelligible in this relation. That the whole must remain too vast for human grasp, that it must at times seem hopelessly tangled, that there must be apparent contradictions, apparent impossibilities, is to him certain. All completely reasoned out theories, all complete pocket charts, whose authors claim to have sounded every depth and climbed to every height of the mysteries that lie about us, appear to him to be of less than no value. "Whatever may be true, it is quite certain that cannot be, it is far too simple," is a remark made to him one day by a friend, which practically puts in a single sentence the position here maintained. The paradox "credo quia impossibile" contains a profound truth, since all that is the subject matter of faith cannot by its peculiar conditions be verified by immediate experiment; as soon as it can be so verified, it passes into the domain of positive knowledge, and must be judged by its methods. That which is not possible under the conditions we can experimentally measure and verify may become the object of faith; nothing else can. There seems no reason why we should hold ourselves permanently committed to the dualism involved in this way of speaking; things no doubt will be made clearer as more is known of the world of phenomena; something probably of the same mystery that surrounds life everywhere else will be found, as men go back more steadily to first principles, to underlie, in the sphere of positive knowledge, a great deal that is now regarded as perfectly known and understood.

Meanwhile it is convenient to accept common phraseology, not as dividing knowledge into two sections that are wholly different, and therefore stand quite apart from each other, but as representing two widely contrasted aspects of it, under one or other of which our ideas are compelled to range themselves.

It may seem that the end aimed at here is of small advantage, even if it is attained; that the purpose is, as indeed it is, simply to prepare the way for the teaching of the Creed, and to do something, if it may be so, to remove or lessen difficulties which go so far in many cases to make the acceptance of Christian doctrine a simple impossibility. If, however, this end could be gained, a position of great importance would have been won. We cannot live with our intellect and our heart permanently divided against each other; and among thinking men, with whatever sorrowful reluctance and even pain, the intellect is sure sooner or later to assert itself, and become the master. Therefore, to win the concession of the full right to appeal to the moral facts of life and to the claims of the affections, to secure attention to the logic of the heart, is to win what may be, in some cases, the one thing necessary to ensure a hearing for the truths, which the Church of Christ is commissioned to proclaim and teach; and thus some, at all events, may be delivered from the painful necessity of choosing between the dreary alternatives, of either gradually giving up the

Creed, in which they have found full satisfaction for all the needs of their hearts and consciences, or of living in a state of continual warfare with the growing strength of their intellectual life.

II.

Wealth, its dangers and its responsibilities, is, all must allow, one of the most serious questions that could be spoken about to an Oxford undergraduate audience. The existence among the younger members of the University of a considerable number of men who have command of large sums of money, and who live and are used to living, to use the regular phrase, up to their means, forces on those who know anything of the manner of life of multitudes of men and women in this country, the anxious problems connected with the rich and the poor, and makes it impossible for them to remain altogether silent.

It is an astonishing fact that, after so many centuries of Christian teaching, Christian conceptions of wealth and poverty should seem so very strange to us. Christianity is the gospel of poverty; it continually blesses the poor as poor; it always treats riches as a danger and a responsibility; it never speaks of them as a blessing. Men still choose steadily to shut their eyes to this fact, although it forces itself upon their attention in almost every page of the Gospels. "There seems to me," the late master of Balliol once said,[1] "to be much more in the New Testament in praise of poverty than we like to acknowledge." These words exactly hit the point; men do not like to admit the fact, and therefore purposely ignore it. It would, perhaps, be well if they were contented only not to think of it; unfortunately they sometimes deliberately set themselves to teach the exact contrary of the New Testament lessons. Our Lord taught that men should seek first the kingdom of God and His righteousness, and that all other things should then be added to them. This precept is now generally reversed; men seek everything else first and His righteousness last of all; if indeed they do seek it even last. Look well ahead, a young man is told; make sure of a due share of wealth and comfort—each one interpreting the phrase by the standard of his immediate surroundings—win for yourself a decent income and an assured position; and then, as to the rest —since the doctrine of "good works" has a somewhat "Romish" flavour about it, and is therefore to be abhorred by all sound Protestants,—it is quite easy to be religious and moral if you have money; religious and moral, that is, in the estimation of a world that does not trouble itself to look below the surface; that is always prepared to stamp with its approval all who conform to its customs and accept its conventions,

[1] "Benjamin Jowett, Master of Balliol," by Hon. L. A. Tollemache, p. 4.

while it regards with a certain suspicion ideal standards of life and conduct. In such a world as this it certainly is not good to be poor; the "Northern Farmer" does not stand quite alone in his decision that "the poor in a loomp is bad."[1] It is not indeed generally said quite so bluntly as this; yet wealth is practically looked upon as a guarantee of moral worth, and although the complementary proposition regarding poverty is not openly stated, there is an undercurrent of belief in something very like it. And so it comes about that, in one form or another, wealth is the great object that men are taught to set before themselves in life.

Money, without doubt, can buy social consideration; and to appear as a supporter of charitable institutions or as a liberal subscriber to works connected with churches and church organization, is one very well recognized way of spending it with a view to the purchase of this most desirable possession. This is sometimes euphemistically spoken of as "giving away" money. It is really nothing of the sort; money so spent is not "given away" at all; it is laid out in the purchase of a much-sought-after article of merchandize. And, besides this, it buys also power, a far more valuable commodity, and one that has great attractions for many who do not think about social consideration. In truth, none of us ever "give," who

[1] Tennyson's "Northern Farmer, New Style."

dispose of our surplus pounds here and there in charity, under conditions which involve no self-denial and cost us absolutely nothing. To know what "giving" means, it is necessary to be poor. The man who, out of hundreds or thousands, subscribes a five-pound note to feed hungry children "gives" nothing; the woman who shares her loaf with a starving neighbour, not knowing where to-morrow's meal is to come from for herself, "gives." This is the real thing; she is the representative of the widow with her two mites who won our Lord's emphatic approval. Political economy of course objects. One overhears cautious people murmuring to themselves something about recklessness and improvidence. Had these cautious people been at Jerusalem, no doubt they would have condemned the woman our Lord blessed. At the same time—there is no reason to deny it—it is probable enough that the poor are often both reckless and improvident; nothing is more saddening than to hear them lauded, as they sometimes are by people who want their votes, as if because they were poor they had no vices. Of course they have their vices, those to which, as poor, they are more liable than the rich are; but the fact remains eternally true that the vices that belong to the rich as such, shut and bar for them the gates of the kingdom of heaven, in a way that the vices of the poor never bar them against the poor. We cannot say this too decidedly; we have our Lord's own warrant for the statement.[1]

Covetousness, greed—the desire of amassing wealth and the comforts that belong to wealth—is a sin that attaches itself to societies no less than to individuals; it is spoken of in the last but one of these sermons as a national sin. No doubt it may be objected that Englishmen are not more covetous than other nations. This is possibly true; there are, it is certain, what may

---

[1] There is nothing new in this way of looking at things. A very quaint old book was printed in 1862 by J. B. Nichols and Sons, London, for the Roxburghe Club, called "Roberd of Brunnè's Handlyng Synne;" it was written in 1303. In it the claims, almost the rights, of poverty are set out in no halting phrases (*e.g.* pp. 210, 215); the slothfulness and self-indulgence of the rich are denounced (p. 135); it is said they even grudge the poor man the little he gets (p. 187). It is impossible not to feel that some of these old mediæval people had a firm grip of sides of truth that we have forgotten. We need not be astonished at this; the human race does not move forwards and upwards in a perfectly straight line; the course is at best zigzag and irregular; there is always loss as well as gain; it must be enough for us that the total result is advance. Since the sixteenth century English Christianity has been tainted with what has been well called "practical pelagianism:" this has re-acted on and increased our national self-sufficiency, and so made us blind to the beauty of the more humble virtues. It is curious to note (p. 131) that in these old days the characteristic sin of England was "envy"—the feeling of regret or grudge at a neighbour's success or prosperity. This is not unknown in the present day; witness the assumption which underlies many questions asked and many answers given in Parliament, that any change in international relations or agreements must of necessity be wrong, unless it results in some practical gain to ourselves. The envy of a neighbour's prosperity is only another aspect of covetousness. The author is indebted for his knowledge of this book to his friend and colleague the Rev. T. B. Strong.

be called "world" sins as well as national sins, and, constituted as men are, it is only too likely that greed is such a sin. But this does not help matters much. As nations can only be made better by mending the morals of individuals among them, so the world can only be made better by raising the moral tone of the different nationalities; and, therefore, the call to national repentance and national amendment becomes only more pressing and more urgent, in the case of each separate people, as the area of the sin is widened. The world is a very sorry sight; every nation of Europe is armed to the teeth. Japan, on entering into relations with the western nations, finds itself compelled to tread the same fatal path. Our own country can no longer keep out of European complications; and consequently our war burdens, or, as one would fain regard them, our defence burdens, must become heavier and heavier year by year. The root of all this misery entailed upon the silent, suffering populations is to be found in international envy, suspicion, and greed. Certainly he must be a bold man who is prepared to claim that we as a nation are guiltless of these sins; almost as bold as if he were to say that the "patriotic" songs of our theatres and music-halls were Christian hymns.

It is sometimes said that democracies will be found to be as warlike as the most autocratic governments. It is to be feared that there may be truth in this statement; if so, it is not because the masses of the people are eager for war, but because men are as sheep, and readily follow any leader who presents himself: the consequence is that noisy self-assertive militant factions, whose advantage is found in fishing in troubled waters, readily pose as the representatives of the whole nation, and before the great majority know what is happening some irrevocable step is taken, some reckless challenge given and accepted. It is open to question whether a true democratic government has yet been seen; men as men seem to ask to be governed, and up to the present time democracies have shown no special capacity for developing really national leaders, or indeed leaders at all in any noble sense of the word. If this be indeed so, and if democracies cannot rise to the level of the duties which political evolution has assigned them, then they must continue to pay the penalty of their failure, until by suffering they have learned how to govern themselves, how to do justly and to live unselfishly.

It is not intended to suggest for one moment—it is scarcely necessary to say it—that the defence of our own homes, our own country, our own kith and kin in our colonies, is not a primary duty, and one that must be fulfilled under any difficulties and at any cost. But the entire acknowledgment of this duty is perfectly compatible with a decided refusal to accept theories of national growth and national expansion, which constitute a declared policy of national greed. The civilized nations of the world appear to be engaged just now in what can only be called a "game of grab" on a gigantic scale; and men assume that all must to the extent of their power and opportunity follow out this policy of greed; that any nation which attempted to adapt international relations to the principles of the Gospels would be at once blotted out of existence. Is this quite so certain? If the present intolerable strain of militarism is ever to be relaxed, such release can only come about by the adoption of a code of international ethics that is in accord with, or, to put it quite modestly, is not wholly incompatible with the ethics of Christianity. As it is, the nations of the world have denied God; they have consecrated greed and set up the great golden image as the object of popular worship, and men are consequently beginning to groan under the weight of burdens they find too heavy to be borne. National sins, no less than individual sins, involve suffering; and sooner or later the crash must come, the penalty of the sin must inevitably be paid. One war, however, will not see the end of it, neither will two, nor three; the end can only come when the idols men have hitherto been taught to worship are ground to powder and cast to the four winds of heaven. But this can never be; perhaps so, as we men look at things: that, however, which is impossible with men is possible with God;

the work Christianity has to do in the world is not yet finished; on some sides, indeed, it is true to say it has never even been begun.

There are two principles which, if clearly and steadily held, may guide men through present anxieties, and also bring hope to any who are beginning to despair, as they think of what may be in store for their children. They are these:—

1. A firm belief in God revealed in the Bible as a God of Love; with a steady conviction that the Movement of the Ages, in spite of human perversity, is the expression of His will for man.

2. A clear recognition that the present distribution of property is not of divine ordinance, and may be amended or entirely changed without mortal sin.

The second proposition does not involve the corollary that, although the present arrangement of property is not ordained of God, some new one that will hereafter be set up as a consequence of franchises, palavers, and parliaments, will be of divine ordinance. No system is or ever will be divine; the New Testament cares nothing about these things; "Who made Me a divider over you?"[1] is the expression of its inmost thought. It does, indeed, care infinitely what manner of beings the men are, who have to bear the

[1] St. Luke xii. 14.

grave responsibility that attaches to earthly possessions. When men are governed by the Christian law of Charity the conditions of the distribution of wealth are not of primary importance. Where the law of Charity is unknown, and so far as it is denied in practice, no system can be devised that will not, sooner or later, become a grinding tyranny.

The great difficulty for any preacher lies in this, that he has to make statements and to enunciate truths, which must appear to his audience to put forward a claim on the part of the speaker to a steadfastness of belief, and to a lofty standard of life and action which, as he only too sadly knows, lie far away from anything that he has reached. This difficulty is not made less when the words are put out as printed words. But the message must be spoken, however weak or faulty he may be who has to deliver it; it cannot be dragged down to the level of his own life. In saying this there is no intention, either to suggest that the preacher may say what he does not believe, or to make any excuse for insincerity, exaggeration, or untruthfulness on his part. So far as the author is able to judge himself, all that is said here represents his sincerest convictions, which, through many years of work, under conditions always of the fullest interest, often of true happiness, at times too of real and pressing anxiety, have steadily grown and strengthened. The problem that such convictions can grow without at once over-mastering all other interests, and so putting an end once for all to the moral and spiritual struggles of our life, is, perhaps, one of those open contradictions by which we may, in some degree, measure how, in our probation here on earth, we live confused and tangled lives; so that, even when we see the better things and might lay hold upon the substance, we are nevertheless quite ready to pursue the shadow, and seek after the things that are worse. Arthur Hugh Clough felt, it may be, something of the truth that lies hidden here when he wrote the lines that have been so often quoted:—

> "It fortifies my soul to know
> That, though I perish, Truth is so:
> That, howsoe'er I stray and range,
> Whate'er I do, Thou dost not change.
> I steadier step when I recall
> That, if I slip, Thou dost not fall."

RESPICE IN SERVOS TUOS ET IN OPERA TUA. ET SIT SPLENDOR DOMINI DEI NOSTRI SUPER NOS: ET OPUS MANUUM NOSTRARUM DIRIGE.

I.

Sowing and Reaping.

"Whatsoever a man soweth, that shall he also reap."—GAL. vi. 7.

(THE FIRST SUNDAY AFTER TRINITY, MAY 30, 1875.)

OUR actions, we are sometimes told, are merely the resultants of the forces which act upon us; we take up, it is said, a particular line of conduct simply because we cannot help it; and as we exercise no sort of control over the forces, it is impossible to hold us to be morally responsible for their resultant. On the other hand, we hear some speak as if we were altogether free, as if everything that we did were the outcome of our own independent decision, as if nothing external to ourselves had any part at all in the direction or control of our actions; and hence the conclusion is naturally drawn that we are, in the widest sense of the term, responsible agents. Does not the real truth of the matter in this, as in many another question, lie between these extreme positions? On one side it is true we are free, on the other side it is also true that we are influenced by determining forces which are wholly beyond our control. We assume at once, as a question about which it is impossible to dispute, that the children of consumptive parents are very likely to be consumptive, that their bodily organism will probably show the same weaknesses as their parents' from whom it is inherited; but we apparently shrink from making the analogous assumption, for which there seems to be quite as good evidence, that the children of vicious parents are likely to inherit a tendency to vice, that moral tendencies as well as physical qualities pass down from father to son. We cannot, however, hesitate any longer to make this assumption, and consequently we find ourselves compelled to admit that we inherit with our physical organism inclinations towards good and evil which necessarily affect us when we come to make our choice between right and wrong, and therefore so far interfere with our freedom of action.

Again, consider the circumstances which have surrounded us since our birth. Over the majority of these we have had no control whatever; and yet can we venture to say that they have had no influence upon us? that we are in no way different from what we should have been had all our early years been passed, to take a very extreme instance, in the homes of vice and misery that are to be found in our great cities? What should we, who were shielded during our childhood from every breath of evil, have become had our lot been that of many who are born into this world? If ever we feel ourselves the least inclined to thank God with the Pharisee that we are not as other men, we might remember this. And if, as we think of it, the burden of sin seems to grow too heavy to bear—the burden, I mean, of human sin—the sense of the utter weakness of the vast brotherhood to which we belong, the feeling of man's wonderful capacity for good, and yet of his appalling failure; if we see one or another around us going farther and farther away from what is true and good, we shall fall on our knees to offer up our prayers to the great Father of all with no touch of the complacent self-satisfied feelings of those who, secure in the contemplation of their own rectitude, beg forgiveness for a brother who has fallen into sin; our prayer will not be "forgive him," but "forgive us." We do not know what his temptations were; we can only feel that perhaps had we been so severely tried, our failure would have been more completely disastrous than his. It is certain that the more we think of it, the more and more shall we be compelled to admit the very large influence which our lot in life, the various conditions of our environment, exercise upon us both for good and for evil. Thus, in a second direction, our freedom is curtailed, since it is true up to a certain point that we are what circumstances make us.

Is man, then, the slave of circumstance? Emphatically no. We have souls as well as bodies. No doubt the soul is in this life irrevocably tied to the body, and consequently it must be conditioned and even hampered by it. To each one is given a body, acted upon within and without by many influences, some for good, but only too many for evil; and out of this weary and tuneless discord the soul is bidden to beat out the music of a holy life. Men have done this in the past by the grace of God, and in the same strength we in our turn may do it if we will. If we will; for the will of man is in itself free. It matters little what hard logic may sometimes seem to demand from us; we need only appeal to experience. We know that we are free. We may make the experiment at any moment. We know that we can and do make our choice between two courses of action, that we reject the first and choose the second, when it was just as much in our power to have rejected the second and chosen the first. We may indeed rest content with this one fact, that those who on intellectual grounds reject the freedom of the will, are compelled in practical life to act as if they believed in it. We find, therefore, that there is within us one force which is the expression of our inmost selves, which may beat down all opposition, may make all the opposing forces that we have to meet its subjects and its slaves; or which may, on the other hand—we must never forget it—be itself overpowered and crushed, until the man ceases to be, in any sense of the words, a responsible being, and is tossed like a rudderless boat on every wave of passion.

Here, then, is a third direction in which we may lose our freedom. In this case, however, there is the great difference that now the loss comes upon us through our own fault. We constantly speak of the formation of habits; what do we mean? We mean that any action we continually repeat, after every repetition we are more likely to do again, when the opportunity occurs; that is, we more and more lose our freedom of choice as to whether we will or will not do that particular thing. Thus, as life goes on, those influences over which in the first case we had no control and our will are continually modifying each other; each time we sin we are giving our inherited tendencies to evil, and all other opposing forces that surround us greater power, and at last we may give them such an advantage that we can no longer be considered to be responsible for what we do; not responsible for our actions, but responsible for the loss of our responsibility; we are guilty of having allowed and encouraged some sin while it was yet in our power to have resisted it, and we have continued this encouragement until we have lost our chance of escaping from it.

Physiology tells us the same story. Every time we do anything we modify our brain; we strengthen the nervous forces which continually impel us to the reproduction of that particular action whether it be good or bad. It cannot, of course, be allowed for one moment that the little bit of brain tissue is the habit, is the force that holds us in its grasp; but still we are told that the soul, as it were, stamps on the brain the evidence of all that has been done, and consequently we bear about with us, graven on our living selves, the records of our past. The particles of matter which make up the body are continually changing, yet a scar will retain its old shape throughout life, the new material taking exactly the same shape as the old; in the same way, the modifications we have introduced into the brain tend to perpetuate themselves, in other words, habits are formed. Thus it is no idle metaphor to say that "we are tied and bound with the chain of our sins." And then there is the possibility of the complete paralysis of our will, the absolute loss of our responsibility; in the words of the Bible, it is possible to quench the Spirit of God, to drive Him altogether from our hearts; it is possible to create within ourselves such strong forces for evil that the soul, numbed and deadened, can no longer hear the voice of God. We dare not set limits to the power of God; but we have no right to expect Him to work miracles for us, and nothing short of a miracle can help one whose will, whose power over himself, is entirely destroyed.

"As a man soweth so also shall he reap." Even now, if you think a little, you know you are reaping in a very real sense as you sowed in the years of school life. But for you the seed time of life has not yet passed away; life is not yet a dreary contemplation of what might have been; it is full of hope, full of the boundless "may be's" that lie in an unknown future. What that future shall be depends, far more than you can understand now, on the way you spend the next few years. In the quiver and throb and excitement of your life in these Oxford years, your inner selves, like metal molten in a furnace, are imperceptibly but surely running away into the mould that will fix them fast for life. It is therefore of the very last importance that you should make some effort to train your wills now, when the task is comparatively easy: a few years hence it will have become almost impossible.

But there is no need to rest the question on what may after all seem to be only selfish grounds. St. Paul's words strike far deeper than we at first sight imagine them to do. If what we have been thinking about is at all true, then we are ourselves gathering in the harvest that has grown up from what our fathers have sown, and the next generation will reap as we, in our turn, sow for them. We may even go a step further still; we very often forget how many and how subtle are the actions and reactions which are continually going on in the social world; and yet it is certain that we are all day by day making each other better or worse. We cannot help it; it is one of the laws of our life. Our past actions have created around us a moral atmosphere which we must perforce carry with us wherever we go, which must, therefore, have its influence on all with whom we come in contact. If we have any "enthusiasm of humanity"—to borrow a well-known expression—any desire to do what we can to make men better, or to avoid doing our share towards making them worse, the only road is through patient self-discipline, not undertaken for merely selfish ends, not springing, as indeed it never could, from what has been called "other worldliness," but undertaken rather for the sake of those we love, or, as we should better say, from love to the good, to God, and through this, as the only sure basis for it, of love to men. It is only by being brave and pure and generous and true ourselves that we can do anything whatever to help to make others so. If we are impure, mean, and cowardly, then we must, we cannot help it, do our share in making those with whom we constantly live cowardly, mean, and impure too.

And this task of self-education laid upon each one of us as our life's work would be heavier than the bravest of us dare attempt, were it not that all the help we need for its fulfilment is within our reach.

Do not hesitate or draw back at the thought of prayer and of the things that belong to the religious life, because so much that is said and done in the name of religion is the reverse of manly, is weak and feeble and effeminate; because duty is sometimes insisted on till it seems as if men were called only to be slaves, slavishly doing a master's bidding, and not called to learn, it may be very slowly and very painfully, to become free men, masters and rulers of their own hearts and wills. Remember we are not bidden to destroy our wills, we are called on to assimilate these wills to the will of Almighty God. If, then, we realize the task set before us, if we believe, as we say we do, that—to quote words known to some of us—"the upper zones of human affection above the clouds of self and passion take us into the sphere of a Divine Communion,"[1] if we know, as we must, our deep need in our hour of weakness of that strength which only Divine sympathy and compassion can supply, then prayer becomes the natural outpouring of the heart, the constant means of intercourse of the soul with God, the speaking to Him face to face as to a friend; it is not, what it is often misrepresented as being, a succession of petitions for earthly comforts and selfish gratifications. In the light of such thoughts as these College services and College prayers will surely take

---

[1] Address at Manchester New College, London, on October 6, 1874, by Dr. James Martineau, Principal.

a new character; they can no longer be regarded as formal perfunctory or unwelcome duties; they become most essential factors in our life; the extent of their influence upon all that is best in us is, we may be sure of it, beyond our power to estimate.

Let me leave this with you. Here in these undergraduate days you have a unique opportunity of training yourselves that you may in after years do something to help on all that is true and of good report; if through indolence and self-indulgence you lose rather than gain in self-control and self-discipline now, you can only recover the lost ground in later life after many a weary struggle with yourselves, and it may be you will never win your way back again at all.

"Be not deceived; God is not mocked: for whatsoever a man soweth, that shall he also reap. For he that soweth to his flesh, shall of the flesh reap corruption: but he that soweth to the Spirit, shall of the Spirit reap life everlasting."

II.

The Things that are Unseen.

"For now we see through a glass, darkly; but then face to face: now I know in part; but then shall I know even as also I am known."
—1 Cor. xiii. 12.

(Quinquagesima Sunday, Feb. 8, 1880.)

Words are sometimes put into the mouth of God by the Bible, which are at first sight somewhat startling; He loves and hates, He is angry and jealous; no apology is made, no explanation is offered, it is all said in a matter-of-fact sort of way. If we begin to consider what these sentences really mean we are conscious at first of a feeling that they border on irreverence, since they appear to represent Almighty God as if He were a man of like passions with ourselves. And in support of this feeling comes the taunt that is at times levelled against Christian men, that the God they worship is only the creature of their own imagination, that He is, to quote well-known words, only "a magnified, non-natural man."

We need not be very careful to find an answer to this objection. It is impossible to doubt that if the brute creation had reason and were trying to picture to themselves God, unless they had accurate knowledge of some higher form of existence, they would picture Him under the symbolism of their own creature life—they could not do otherwise; nor is it possible for men to act differently. In those simpler days, now long gone from us, men saw God everywhere near them; "He made the clouds His chariots and walked upon the wings of the wind;"[1] it was "the Lord that thundered out of Heaven, the Highest gave His thunder: hailstones, and coals of fire;"[2] it was "the voice of the Lord that shook the wilderness."[3] But these days have passed away, it was God's will they should, and we have grown, as we think, wiser. We have measured the various activities of nature, and have to some extent learned to hold them in control; we have compelled the world around us to disclose her most secret workings; we have tabulated and labelled her forces, and have fallen into the error of supposing that because we have given a thing a name we know all about it; and sometimes the conclusion has been drawn that natural forces and natural development supply the key to all the problems of the universe.

But good and real as all this work is in relation to those questions that rightly belong to it, it cannot give us the complete interpretation of our lives. It leaves out of consideration facts as real, as irresistibly

---

[1] Ps. civ. 3. [2] Ps. xviii. 13. [3] Ps. xxix. 7.

cogent, as any that it includes. What can it say to all those vague wants we feel, to that wild unrest that nothing this world can give us is able to satisfy? What can it say to the sense of right and wrong, the certainty that, say what men may, there is a right and there is a wrong? Very little it seems, except to suggest that they are delusions, useful enough perhaps, and therefore to be maintained, if possible, as a sort of social police force. But whatever molecular theories may be possible it is hard to believe that morality can ever be securely founded on a molecular basis.

The truth is that we have not really moved so far away from that older life as the external conditions of existence in the nineteenth century suggest; the problems of life are as pressing now as in the Psalmist's days. Each one of us knows that there is some unknown power within him and around him in the world; if he ascends up to Heaven it is there, if he goes down into the depths it is there also; he cannot, do what he will, escape from its presence. What it may be he cannot understand; he gropes blindly after it if haply he may find it, and yet he can lay no hand upon it. He cannot keep silence, he must speak to one and another about him to ask them if they can help him to penetrate the mystery of life and thought—to ask them, as we Christians should put it, to help him to find out God. But how can he speak? In what words? How shall the finite grasp the infinite? How can he, but by comparing the infinite to what he can understand, by lowering it down to the highest and best that he knows, and what is that but man? He speaks of God under figure of a man; in no other way could he speak of Him at all, for the eye has not seen Him nor the ear listened to His voice.

But surely, it may be said, we have our Bibles, and in them we are given a direct revelation from God Himself. This is, indeed, true enough, and we may well thank God for the great gift so given to us. But if we think for a moment, what is it that the Bible teaches us? At once everything and nothing. It tells us that God is, that He is our Creator, our Redeemer, our Sanctifier; it brings us the story of a perfect life, and it bids us make that life our example; it tells us that "we see now through a glass, darkly," but that we shall "hereafter see face to face"; and it points us to that future, when we are crushed down by doubt or despair in the twilight and uncertainty of this present life, and declares that then all things shall be made clear, and that "we shall know even as we are known." But it does not answer all the questions we would so gladly put to it if we could. It does not, it could not, map out for us, as in a chart, a clear and definite plan of the mind and purpose of God; it could have no scheme of salvation reasoned out for us with all the accuracy of a mathematical proposition.

It speaks of God as man; it uses figures drawn from humanity, and in doing so it sanctions our use of them; it could not do more than this. If it showed us God as He is, it would at once make us more than men; a God scientifically understood would no longer be God at all. Thus the Bible can only use, as we can only use, language that stretches out as it were towards God, borrowed from the best and highest ideas which we can conceive, borrowed, that is, from the idea of a perfect man. And we cannot go wrong in following its guidance; unless, indeed, we forget that our formulæ are not scientifically accurate, unless we imagine that they give us the sum of the whole matter, that they represent to us in themselves the beginning and the ending, the first and the last of Him, of whom we can only say, in language that satisfies us simply because it goes beyond anything that we can completely know, and stretches far away from our tiny selves into the infinity around us, "Lord, Thou hast been our refuge from one generation to another. Before the mountains were brought forth, or ever the earth and the world were made, Thou art God from everlasting, and world without end."[1]

Thus, when with all the skill of the practised dialectician, with all the accuracy of the scientific laboratory, with all the cogency of a pitiless logic, men proceed to take to pieces the Christian Creed, and show

[1] Ps. xc. 1, 2.

us a contradiction here, an impossibility there, and tell us that on this side and on that what we profess to believe passes beyond the limits of their understanding, and then go on to draw the conclusion that, as our language cannot be technically accurate, the God whom we worship is a fiction, and our hopes and beliefs, at best the idle fancies of a dreamy mysticism—when they say all this, they are missing their mark completely. We never thought that we could hold the infinite in the hollow of our hand; we never thought that we could be given a clear picture, accurate in every detail, of all that it has never entered into the heart of man to understand; but God is, although we cannot see Him; if we will only listen to His voice, He speaks to our inmost souls, and no science and no logic need ever, if we will, take Him away from us.

> "Scarcely I catch the words of His revealing,
> Hardly I hear Him, dimly understand,
> Only the Power that is within me pealing
> Lives on my lips and beckons to my hand.
>
> "Whoso has felt the Spirit of the Highest,
> Cannot confound, nor doubt him, nor deny:
> Yea, with one voice, O world, though thou deniest,
> Stand thou on that side, for on this am I."[1]

It is useless, worse than useless, to tell men that there are no difficulties before them. Faith would be a word of absolutely no meaning at all, if all the present

[1] St. Paul. F. W. H. Myers.

and all the future were wholly within our ken. We only know, experience has proved it for us, that apart from God our lives cannot be complete. When we once clearly understand what is the alternative that is offered to us, the dreary wastes of endless criticism, the cold austerity of pure intellect, the hopeless attempts to build up man—body, soul, and spirit—out of the dry bones of the natural sciences, then we shall be satisfied with something short of mathematical certainty; we shall be content to see now through a glass darkly, and by God's grace we shall look on with a faith that, come what may, will not allow itself to be crushed, to that unseen life, "when we shall see face to face, and shall know even as also we are known."

It is hard enough, let us frankly admit it, to hold our ground, for the faith of many is growing cold. The fact is forced on our attention in endless ways; we see it, perhaps, most plainly in the great change that has come over men's minds in regard to ordination; for I fear there can be no doubt that Oxford is not giving, as she used to do, of her best-trained and most cultivated intellects to clerical work. The current opinions of the thinking world have created around us an atmosphere which appears to seriously influence even those who have the courage to hold fast to their own personal beliefs; they shrink back from undertaking to definitely maintain positions which they hear so often, and sometimes, as it may seem, so successfully assailed; and thus, although, even when the destructive criticism has appeared most complete, their whole soul refuses to accept the negative conclusion, yet they determine that just now the risk of ordination is too great—they will wait until things are more settled; and by this they mean, until some of the problems that perplex us have received a definite solution. If men must wait till this day comes, if they have not faith and courage to work on, seeing only "through a glass, darkly," the day will never come when they can work for the Church of Christ. No; certainty will never be given us in this life; but we are given sufficient satisfaction to make us really responsible for our failure in duty, if we elect to stand idly by, and let the days, when we might do some true work, pass from us without an effort to employ them in the service of Almighty God.

Meanwhile, the cry for men at home, in the colonies, and in the wide missionary field, is most urgent; the work that is put before us is noble work, it rises to the level of the heroic; it has in it enough to satisfy the most chivalrous spirits. There is a want of men of education, and of the breadth of sympathy that education gives, a want of men of physical and intellectual vigour, to work in the East End of London and among the teeming populations of our great manufacturing towns. Why should these wants remain unsatisfied? One often hears the complaint that men who have taken their degrees at Oxford have no idea what to do with themselves. Sometimes they have—it may be unfortunately for themselves—what is called an independent position; this is often supposed to mean that they have a right, if they please, to live merely for amusement. If they work at anything, it is really very much to their credit; such self-denial could scarcely have been expected from them. There is no opinion which is so entirely false as this: the man who does not work for his daily bread, it matters not whether he be rich or poor, has practically stolen it. Those men and women who live only to amuse themselves, who have never done any real honest work for God or for man, who at last have but one object in life left to them, the discovery of a new means of excitement—these are the authors of that social revolution which some tell us we shall see even before the end of this present century. If the wealthy classes of this country become as a body indolent and self-indulgent, then assuredly the crash will come, and the upper and not the lower strata of society will be mainly responsible for it. It is impossible to lay all the crimes of the French Revolution on the unhappy people who worked it out. We shall find its true source in the selfishness and the vices of the upper classes of France in the preceding century. History, it is said, repeats itself. We at least have what the French had not, a warning of what may be the consequences of cynical and careless self-indulgence.

Here, then, we have on the one hand a crying want, the want of educated men for the work of the Church, and on the other hand many in this University who have no idea what duties to look forward to in after life. Is there not in this one fact a direct call, at all events to some amongst us, to come forward and help? It is a great work to which men are called, and one that can only be done by accepting the responsibilities of the clerical office. It is indeed sorrowfully true that at times the clergy of the Church of England have woefully failed in their duty to the nation as a whole; but it is excusable to think that there is in some quarters a greater anxiety to note these failures, than to recognize the widespread influence for good that has been exercised by her ministers. It seems clear that, while they are drawn from very different classes of the community, the clergy must be specially qualified to bridge the gulf that some think to be daily widening between the upper and the lower classes, or rather, as it has now become, between the rich and the poor. They may, it is quite certain, do much to ensure that the social and political changes that must be brought about in the next century, shall not come in England in the wild gusts of revolutionary passion, but in the gradual evolution and development that has marked the growth of our present surroundings. If, however, for the future, members of the better-educated and of the wealthier classes are to hold aloof, the clergy as a body would no longer be fitted for this work. The loss will be our own. God's work for the salvation of souls will be done without help from any one of us; but we who might have shared in the work and have refused to do so, what of us?

We are now on the eve of Lent, a season when we all give some thought, not only to the past, but also to the future—to the work in life which we are doing, or are preparing ourselves to do. Let me suggest to any one before whose mind ordination floats as a vague possibility some few years hence, not to allow himself to drift either one way or the other, but rather to face the question at once, and to give thought and earnest prayer to it during the coming weeks. He may, indeed, ultimately refuse so great a responsibility; he cannot be wrong in doing so if he refuses it, with as deep a sense of the issues involved in his decision, as he would have felt had he accepted it.

It is no doubt excusable to hesitate; no thinking man could undertake the responsibilities of the ordination vows unless he knew that he did not stand alone: but never forget that, if you are truly called to this office and work, He who lays the burden upon you will, while you are true to Him, also give you strength to fulfil its duties. "Holy, holy, holy, is the Lord of Hosts: the whole earth is full of His glory. Then said I, Woe is me! for I am undone; because I am a man of unclean lips: for mine eyes have seen the King, the Lord of Hosts. Then flew one of the seraphims unto me, having a live coal in his hand: and he laid it on my mouth and said, Lo, this hath touched thy lips; and thine iniquity is taken away and thy sin purged." Then, and then only, when fire from God's altar has touched our lips, as the ever-recurring question sounds in our ears, "Whom shall I send, and who will go for us?" can we dare to answer, "Here am I; send me."[1]

[1] Isa. vi. 3-9.

III.

The Kingdom of Christ.

"My kingdom is not of this world."—St. John xviii. 36.

(Twenty-sixth Sunday after Trinity, November 21, 1880.)

When John the Baptist came preaching in the wilderness of Judæa, the burden of his teaching was contained in the words, "Repent ye, for the kingdom of Heaven is at hand," and the same summons was repeated by our Lord when He began His public ministry. This kingdom of God is an image that continually recurs in the New Testament; in parable after parable our Lord unfolds its laws, its constitution. He proclaims its universality, its spirituality; "Many shall come from the east and west, and shall sit down in the kingdom of Heaven;"[1] "Behold, the kingdom of God is within you."[2] Such teaching as this was quite unintelligible to Jews, and, therefore, the disciples and even the apostles themselves did not understand what the words implied. They could explain them in only one way; the kingdom of God,

[1] St. Matt. viii. 11.   [2] St. Luke xvii. 21.

what would that be but the house of Israel? What could their teacher be foreshadowing to them but the restoration of the Davidic kingdom in more than its ancient splendour, as a rival to the victorious and, as it seemed to men of that day, the indestructible greatness of the Roman Empire?

A kingdom that was not of this world was an idea even apostles could not entertain; they could only look for a magnificent temporal dynasty: and full of this thought, they began to dispute among themselves who among them should, when the day of triumph came, take rank after the new sovereign, and sit on his right hand and on his left. Our Lord made no immediate attempt to correct these mistaken fancies. He left it rather to the teaching of events, and contented Himself with enigmatical answers, and veiled reproofs of which, at the time, they could not see the meaning; these reproofs, however, were remembered and translated in the light of all that happened in later years. "Ye know not what manner of spirit ye are of;"[1] and again, "Can ye drink of the cup that I drink of? and be baptized with the baptism that I am baptized with?"[2]

If we understand this, we see at once why the disciples forsook our Lord at the crucifixion. There in a moment, and as it seemed to them for ever, all their hopes were shattered; the idol that they had set up

---

[1] St. Luke ix. 55. [2] St. Mark x. 38.

in their heart was crushed to pieces, and they fell away in complete despair. When, a few days later, they began to realize that the news brought to them from the sepulchre on the first Easter morning might be true, they could only regard the resurrection from one point of view; with the thought that Christ was again alive their old hopes revived; it was possible that even now the dream of their life was to have its fulfilment; "Lord, wilt Thou at this time restore again the kingdom to Israel?"[1] is the question they at once ask: and the answer given them is, "It is not for you to know the times or the seasons which the Father hath put in His own power. But ye shall receive power after that the Holy Ghost is come upon you."

The day of Pentecost came, and at once the whole meaning of what Christ had taught them broke in upon their minds. David is indeed dead and buried, but God has raised up Jesus to sit on David's throne, and made Him, whom the house of Israel had crucified, both Lord and Christ;[2] and the promise is not to the Jew only, but also to the Gentile, even to all that are afar off. They understood now the meaning of the prayer they had often prayed, "Thy kingdom come:" this kingdom was no earthly empire; it belonged to the unseen world within the veil, through which their Master and King had passed out of their sight; it knew no difference of race or of language, but all

---

[1] Acts i. 6-8.   [2] Acts i. 29-35.

nations of every tongue and people should be gathered into it.

Christ's kingdom, therefore, could not be founded as human kingdoms are; it owed nothing to human intrigue or violence; nor did armed enthusiasts raise up the standard of the cross and compel men to baptism by fear of death. A small company of men, some of them ignorant and unlettered, went from village to village, and from city to city proclaiming the gospel of the kingdom of God; they had indeed little in common with the conquerors of men; despised and rejected as their Master before them, treated with scorn and contempt by Jew and by Roman alike, imprisoned, beaten, stoned, they were as St. Paul says, "made a spectacle unto the world;"[1] but still they worked steadily on; no discouragement could quench their zeal, no pain or suffering could dim their faith; rather it grew stronger and clearer as they rejoiced that they were counted worthy to suffer for His sake; for they were inspired by the one enkindling enthusiasm to spread abroad among men the knowledge of the love of God in Christ. At first not many great or noble or wise were called; but the poor, the weak, the outcast,—the things, as St. Paul says, that were not—were the subjects of the Church's earliest triumphs; and beginning with these, it made its way, step by step, through all strata of society, until it claimed

---

[1] 1 Cor. iv. 9.

among its converts the occupant of the imperial throne. "Not by might, nor by power, but by the Spirit"[1] of the Lord Himself, was this great work done. All the powers of the world, all the energies of religions dying, and therefore desperate, were banded together to resist the growth of the kingdom of Christ; but, in spite of all, it grew into a mighty tree, and at last overshadowed the world.

Since the days of Constantine the civilized world, at least in its outward aspect, has been nominally Christian; and consequently the power of the government, which before that time had been used to resist the Faith of Christ, has since been used, only too often, to persecute in its behalf. Christianity had become an important factor in the world, and so of necessity was brought into relation with the ruling powers. This could not be avoided, and we can see how essential it was that, at the break-up of the Roman Empire, Christian influences should control those in authority. Still Christianity lost as well as gained by the alliance; in its new relation to society, it could not but be affected by State intrigues; it was bound to be used by political parties or by unscrupulous rulers or ministers for their own ends. And then the days came when the sword was drawn in its behalf, when armies were employed to extend its influence. In all this it suffered loss; its strength was not, and never could be, in the sword.

[1] Zech. iv. 6.

Again and again the old spirit revives; and men like Savonarola, and many of those who lived in the Reformation period, and to come nearer our own day, the last martyr Bishop of the English Church, Bishop Patteson, have restored, each in their own time, its old ideal of love and self-sacrifice, and have counted all things but loss, given up every earthly good, everything that we men hold dear, only that they may proclaim the faith of Jesus Christ, and help to establish His kingdom in the earth.

Here, where it has been since the day that the Holy Spirit was given to the infant Church, is still the one and only source of the Church's strength and life. Some would have us believe that this simple faith is a thing altogether of the past, and that men hold fast to the externals of Christianity, some from conservatism and because they cannot face the consequences involved in its rejection, others from the meaner motive of the present advantages which they get by their Christian profession; but we, living in this place, as we recall the lives and examples of those who have served Christ here, know that faith in a risen Saviour is a living force among us at this day as certainly as in the past ages of the Church; a force, too—our parish clergy know it—which can now, as in those days long ago, lift simple ordinary lives up to the level of real heroism.

Many of those who are listening to me this morning

will, I hope, some day be clergymen; let me venture to say a word on one aspect of this question in regard to which it seems to me to be our bounden duty to exercise the strictest self-control, although it may not be, and in the immediate future probably will not be, easy for us to do so. It is a really serious question for us how far we allow our political opinions to affect our relations to the people committed to our charge; how far we are inclined to act and speak as if our political cause, which is often enough only the expression of our own private or class interest, were really the cause of God Himself, and so to endeavour to gain additional weight for our opinions by identifying them with the name of Him who is the Truth Itself. We pay a heavy price for such a daring mistake: there can be little doubt that the alienation of the poorer classes from the Church of England is due in no small measure to the action of her clergy in the past: for example, the doctrine of the divine right of kings was sometimes taught by them as equally binding on the conscience of Churchmen with the doctrine of the Incarnation, and Englishmen, being somewhat matter-of-fact, took these teachers at their word and left a Church that appeared to impose upon them a political creed which they could not accept.

The Church as such has no knowledge of political parties, or even of forms of government. In the not very distant future we shall stand face to face with the Democracy; among them are, no doubt, many who are professedly Republicans; while we must not on the one hand abate one iota of our personal loyalty to our Sovereign, on the other hand we have no right to erect constitutional monarchy into an article of the Christian Faith; if we do, depend upon it we shall not convert men to our political ideals, but we may certainly do a great deal to make Christianity seem impossible to them. They will regard the Church as a state engine, which exists in the interests of the classes to which they do not belong, and for the propagation of social theories to which they are entirely opposed. If this country became a Republic to-morrow our duties as Christ's ministers would be unchanged; the message we are bidden to deliver to the world would be what it has always been, and we should not think of telling people that until they were prepared to support a Restoration they could not be loyal members of the Church of Christ. This is no doubt an extreme instance, and one in regard to which we may earnestly hope that none of us in our lifetime will be called upon to act. But there are other questions which come nearer to the sphere of practical politics, and through which the personal feelings of many amongst us may before long be very keenly tried. One such question is the political position of the Church of England.

It may help us, in what must at best be a most

difficult question, if we never forget that we are not primarily members of a department of the State, or officers in a wealthy corporation endowed with peerages and dignities and tithes and rent-rolls, but servants of Christ's spiritual kingdom, bound before all things to Him who is our Saviour and our King; sent by Him that we may hold up before men that Christlike life of self-sacrifice and gentleness and goodness to which He calls all the members of His great human family, to enable them to attain which He lived and died.

If we, unmindful of this duty laid on us, let our personal interests interfere with our teaching, if we tie up the message of repentance and forgiveness, which is committed to our charge, with particular phases of political thought, and thus render it practically impossible for those who do not accept our theories to do otherwise than suspect our motives when we speak to them of God and the soul, then we have betrayed our trust and shall hereafter be called to a terrible reckoning. The future of the visible Church we must leave in His hands; she has lived through ages of poverty and oppression, she has been, and here in England she is still, rich and powerful; but he must read her history thoughtlessly who thinks her days of greatest spiritual weakness have always coincided with her days of temporal depression. "Lo, I am with you alway, even unto the end of the world," are the last words she heard from her Master's lips. Nation shall rise against nation and kingdom against kingdom, empires shall be overthrown, forms of government shall change, but under all the ever-shifting scenes of the visible world, He continues to give His Presence, unchanged and unchanging, to the Church which is His Body. Christ's kingdom is not of this world; the Church does not draw her life from Establishment; she knows nothing of political conditions; in a world where pain and death are the common inheritance of all, she repeats and will repeat as long as time shall last, her one unvarying message—Repent, believe, and live.

The truest defence of the Church is to be found in the lives of her members—her surest bulwarks are unselfishness, purity, gentleness, goodness; if in the past she had always used her proud position to help the needy, to succour the oppressed, to protect those who could not protect themselves, the political outlook might be other than it is; but we are not responsible for the past; the present is ours, and we have a share in moulding the future; we shall fail miserably if our one or our main object is to support a great secular position; come what may, we cannot fail if we are loyal to our heavenly King.

IV.

The Finite Intellect.

"We know in part."—1 Cor. xiii. 9

(Sunday after Ascension-day, May 29, 1881.)

The leading principle which in our day dominates the world in matters of business or commerce as well as in the higher region of intellectual activity, is the principle of specialization or division of labour—in other words, the area of work whether in practical or intellectual matters is too wide and too varied for one man to cover the whole, or anything like the whole of it; and consequently we each have assigned to us one little corner in which we busy ourselves, in which we make, or try to make, ourselves complete masters of our subject, in relation to which our opinion may be asked and we may speak with some authority: but beyond and outside this narrow circle, our knowledge and attainments, however varied they may be, are at best uncertain and untrustworthy. This is the rule of modern life, we may almost take it as our definition of civilization.

As years go by the principle becomes more and more clearly marked; each of us becomes dependent on larger numbers of his fellowmen; more and more we are separated from our old isolation, our old self-centred life. We learn nowadays to do one thing, we work at one trade, or we get up one subject of study, and we do what we do marvellously well; but outside this small section we are practically helpless. It is almost miraculous what this special training can do; call to mind the marvellous readiness of the specially trained eye or ear; think for one moment of the delicate combinations of hand and eye to be found in our chemical and physical laboratories, or in our astronomical observatories; consider the wonderful sensitiveness of the musician's ear, who, as he stands before a great orchestra and chorus, can unravel its practically infinite intricacies, can follow each instrument, each voice, and knows at once, if there is any flaw in the harmony of the whole, where the fault is to be found. It is wonderful what this special training can do, what capacities it develops, what powers it confers. But we should do well to notice one point; the trained ear does not imply the trained eye—indeed to a great extent, since human life is short and human capacities limited, it would seem almost to exclude it. We, on the contrary, too often assume that eminence in one direction implies eminence in all, and that any one prominent in some art or science, or skilled in some delicate or artistic manipulation, is at once qualified to pronounce a sort of *ex cathedrâ* judgment on every conceivable question that may be brought before him. It is really amusing to notice sometimes how our daily newspapers chronicle, as of the last importance, an opinion which a man eminent in some one particular line of work, has been unfortunate enough to deliver on a subject that lies entirely outside his own special study.

This is a matter of far greater importance than we are likely at first sight to think it. On the intellectual side it has most important bearings on our whole attitude to knowledge. Take for a moment the student of the exact sciences, the mathematician, and to a certain extent the student of nature. He asks for positive evidence, all else is worthless; he does not deal with probabilities, he asks for an exactly accurate explanation of each different point, a clear unbroken sequence in each argument. It almost raises a smile to talk about a probable demonstration of a proposition of Euclid; if it is true it can be fully demonstrated to be so, and until a complete and accurate proof has been given no mathematician could possibly accept the result.

But, on the other side, take the case of the scholar; one of the questions he has to settle is the text of his books, the reading in a manuscript; and in this case he has to deal with probable evidence. He has to array side by side the arguments for and against a particular reading, to carefully balance all that can be said on this side and on that, and then to draw his conclusion; probable evidence is to him the breath of life, certainty in the mathematical sense he cannot have.

Now, if we consider for a moment two men specialized in these two lines, we must at once admit that either of them would be quite unfit to enter into the work of the other; that the scholar could hardly be trusted to judge correctly as to what was an adequate proof of a mathematical proposition, or the mathematician to estimate correctly the arguments for and against a particular reading in a manuscript. I do not suggest any invidious comparisons between different branches of study, or imagine that the critical acumen of the scholar gives evidence of more or less brain power than the results obtained by the mathematician. My point is this; one man has mental gifts and endowments in one direction, another in an entirely different direction; they naturally, therefore, pursue different lines of study; nowadays the area to be covered in each subject is so large that they must devote themselves entirely to their particular branch of study and become, as we say, specialists. The consequence is they move farther and farther apart, and may at last even lose the capacity of appreciating each other's work. This may seem to be a very fanciful statement; but it is not so. No one but a man who has been specially trained in exact reasoning and is then brought face to face with the necessity of balancing probable evidence can fully appreciate how great the difficulty is: at first, do what he will, he cannot watch the turn of the scale; if he thinks he sees it, he cannot lose sight of the evidence on the other side, it hangs about his thoughts like a dead weight; he cannot be contented with his conclusion, he can find no satisfaction, no rest in it; he finds it hard to treat it as a conclusion at all. But on the other hand, I have heard men say that they could not understand or appreciate the mathematician's satisfaction with his certain results; they appeared almost to assert that they did not understand what certain evidence meant.

The aim of what has been said is this: each one of us, however great his attainments may be, has made himself complete master of only a small section of human knowledge. There lie, and must lie, outside his work lines of thought, accumulations of facts, methods of reasoning, into which he is not trained to enter. He can look at them from the outside, he may object to them and think he refutes them, or he may contemptuously put them aside; but they lie, as we may say, in a plane parallel to that in which he moves, and, as a matter of fact, he cannot get into contact with them at all. Thus there is a truth in the statement which has been made, that no system of philosophy as a system can be true; for a system of philosophy is, after all, only a view more or less complete of one side of truth. On that side, no doubt, it has much to say for itself; but it is impossible to admit its claim to be the whole of truth. To be such would demand, on the part of its author, complete encyclopædic knowledge both of facts and methods, besides the necessary corollary that all additions to knowledge should at once find their natural place in the teacher's system. Thus when any new theory or system is put before us, we know at once that it cannot be the whole truth. We shall therefore be anxious on the one hand not to lose the truth that is in it, while on the other hand, we cannot, at the imperious demand of this new theory, surrender without a murmur all that up till now we have accepted as truth.

The gospel of evolution is now somewhat loudly clamouring for the complete recognition of its supreme claims on the allegiance of mankind. The facts which are being given us with such marvellous rapidity by the students of nature we accept at once; the relations and inter-dependence between animate and inanimate nature, between plants and animals, between animals and mankind, which they have studied and tabulated, we have no wish to throw doubt upon. We do not reject the laws and sequences in nature which they have verified and formulated. All this is the work of specially trained men, devoted to their own line of study, and the world in general has no claim to review these conclusions. But when the theory, that is the complete generalization of all this work, is set forward as a dogma to be taught to children, as the answer to all our questionings, whence we have come and whither we are going, as containing in itself the sufficient and only explanation of all the complexities of conscious existence, then we are not called upon to give our assent to it. This claim, that is made with so much urgency and insistence, comes from the students of one special side of knowledge. It is the claim that their own special aspect of truth should be acknowledged to be the whole of truth; that its methods should be accepted as of universal application, as giving the solution of all the mysteries of thought and consciousness. If the demand were granted on these terms one thing at least is certain—religious life, as we Christians understand the words, would cease to be; its hopes and fears alike must be remembered only as the dreams and hallucinations of childhood. God, we are told, is no longer a necessary hypothesis in this world of ours, and being unnecessary, we shall take leave to dispense with Him. The history of life is one long chain of cause and effect, each event involving its successor, and involved itself in its predecessor. Throughout all time the magnificent panorama has been unfolding itself; the evolution of life, from its lowest to its highest forms, has rolled on through ages which we cannot count or conceive. The earth, indeed, groans and travails in pain; the cries of anguish come to our ears from the dying, the wail of distress and pain from the living; there is the wild fury of human passion, the deep blackness of human ingratitude and crime and sin. But all these are of no account; there is no voice nor any that answers. The dumb universe moves on its resistless course, and man is bound in chains more tightly than ever in the ages past, since he has bowed down his whole moral and intellectual self to the bondage, and closed round himself the iron grip of a remorseless necessity.

In the midst of so much certainty we hesitatingly ask for some explanation, since the old difficulties still occur to some of us. Where is the first link of this great chain of cause and effect suspended? How did animal life or human thought first appear? But we are told the answer is very simple. Myriads of years ago some inorganic carbon compounds met by chance in a favourable environment beneath the water of the ocean, and their chemical affinities acting under these circumstances produced spontaneously the lowest form of animal life, and from that hour the development has gone forward. It may indeed be that life can be traced back to this primeval form, and thence followed upwards to its infinite varieties in the nineteenth century. We can only bow to the decision of men more qualified to answer such questions than we are. It is indeed very wonderful, and it may be very true; but where did these inorganic carbon compounds come from? How is it they were endowed with these singular capacities of development? Is it possible to attach much meaning to the word chance in this connection? unless, indeed, it is under a different form some recognition of an unknown power, which, as it were, set in motion this mighty machine, and which sustains it from moment to moment. These old questions still live on, as urgent, as relentless as ever, at the bottom of theories which cannot make any attempt to explain them; and every fair mind must acknowledge that materialism has its ultimately insoluble problems as certainly as the creed of the Church of Christ; and that the man who believes in a Divine Ruler of the world at least does no greater outrage to his reason, than one who believes that all this wonderful world of life is the outcome of nothing more than the chance meeting of atoms of carbon and nitrogen "in the infinite azure of the past."

If they could bear this in mind, men would not be so easily persuaded on intellectual grounds to loosen their hold upon their religious beliefs, and so finally altogether to drift beyond the reach of the Christian Creed. Men are too ready to become the slaves of a theory; they feel themselves compelled to accept any and every consequence which appears to be deduced from their premises; their very virtues, their honesty and thoroughness of purpose are arrayed against them; they feel, and rightly so, they must follow truth wherever it may take them; but they forget that this is, as a thoughtful writer tells us,[1] a very different thing from following an argument whithersoever *it* may take them, seeing that the course of an argument is always steadier and more incisive when it does not embarrass itself with the consideration of all that opposes it, or lies beyond its own immediate purpose. As the critical instinct develops, which it must do here in Oxford, men understand what demands are made upon them by the Christian Creed; and the fact of the Resurrection, or the fact of the Ascension seems to pass at once beyond the region of those things which they can acknowledge or believe; and so, some eagerly enough, some with pain and misgiving, they take refuge in theories which appear at first sight to offer an escape from such serious claims on their reason. But they have given up all that makes life hopeful, all that can help them to work on steadily through disappointment and failure and weakness, all that can enable them to show a firm front to the misunderstandings and troubles, that sooner or later life must bring to us all; and instead they have accepted a

[1] Cf. "Human Life and its Conditions," by the Very Rev. R. W. Church, D.C.L., late Dean of St. Paul's, p. 84.

cold and barren theory of existence which, as they must at last find out, makes really the same demand on their faith, and puts an equal strain on their reason; which is ultimately on purely intellectual and logical grounds as incomplete as the faith they have so lightly cast aside; which they discover, often too late, does not only *not* satisfy their intellect, but has no gleam of hope for their heart in the midst of the anxieties of the present, or in presence of the darkness and uncertainty of the future.

This has been the fate of more than one. It need never be ours if we do not carelessly let slip the faith and the hope which have been given us almost as our birthright; let us try to make the collect for Ascension Day fully our own, and pray with all earnestness that we may in heart and mind thither ascend whither our Risen Saviour has gone before, and that we may continually dwell in His presence. The aim of what has been said this morning is to assert that we may do this without losing one iota of our intellectual freedom; indeed it would be truer to say we can only find perfect freedom when we learn to bow down before Him who is Himself the Truth. Here and now we know and can know only in part; the time is coming, God grant it to each of us, when we shall see Him face to face, and shall know even as we are known.

V.

Worship.

"This is none other but the house of God, and this is the gate of Heaven."—GENESIS xxviii. 17.

(TWENTY-FIFTH SUNDAY AFTER TRINITY, NOVEMBER 26, 1882.)

ALTHOUGH we all acknowledge the duty of worship, few, it is to be feared, could give an intelligent answer to the question what its relation to our life really is, what its true function is in the midst of all the varied duties and pleasures, anxieties and amusements, in which the days and months and years go hurrying from us. The reason of this is ready to our hand. We have lost our hold on any clear idea of what worship should be, because we have altogether neglected so much that should have helped to make the unseen world a reality to us. The unseen world—we talk about it—"The things that are not seen and eternal;"[1] yes, we acknowledge their existence; we allow ourselves to say that they are the only reality, the one supreme end of our present life. We say this,

[1] 2 Cor. iv. 18.

but our words seem sometimes only words; they are, indeed, for too many of us what we call a survival—a way of talking about things that has lived on in outward form, when it has lost its inner meaning. And yet this unseen world is close around us, and we are living in it; round about us are the angels of God, those guardian angels who, as they turn from us, look up and "behold the face of the Father which is in heaven."[1] There, too, are the dead, those whom we have lost, and of whom, if we are driven to speak, we say in somewhat uncertain tones that they still live awaiting the day of the Resurrection: but we venture no further than this; we put aside at once as superstitious any thought of real union with them; we forget, or we explain away, the article of the Christian Creed which acknowledges our belief in the Communion of Saints. The mother may pray for her child with her last breath, but when she has passed into the unseen world, we may not think of her as praying still. We stand beside an open grave and say the words which are put into our mouths, for the dead as for ourselves, that we and they alike may, by the mercy of God, attain in His own time the peace of heaven; but as the thought flashes on us, and suggests something of the reality of our union and communion with the Church that have passed within the veil, love is chilled and disappointed, and the hope that made the

[1] St. Matt. xviii. 10.

unseen world for one moment a reality is thrust aside by current phases of thought that seem unable to endure the touch of the supernatural.

We say that we believe in the doctrine of the Incarnation; we acknowledge that at the appointed moment in time, God, in His great love and compassion for His fallen creatures, was born into the world, that the Word was made flesh and dwelt among us, that He lived that wonderful life in Galilee and Judæa, that He died upon the cross, that He rose again the third day from the dead and ascended into Heaven; when ever we say the Creed we assert our steadfast belief in these facts as historical. But even those who heartily accept these articles of the Creed, accept them as belonging rather to the past than to the present. The historical fact of the Incarnation is indeed acknowledged; but it, and all its miraculous surroundings, began with the birth of Jesus Christ, and as far as mankind were concerned, came to an end at His Ascension. It never seems to occur to many people that such events as these, if true at all, must have some immediate and direct relation to men now at this present moment. We indeed recall His own words, "Lo, I am with you alway, even unto the end of the world;"[1] "Yet a little while and the world seeth me no more; but ye see me: because I live, ye shall live also."[2] They come upon our ears, the

[1] St. Matt. xxviii. 20. [2] St. John xiv. 19.

far-off echoes of a promise that at least is clear and simple and direct: but if we question ourselves closely we find we attach only a vague meaning to them; we seek their fulfilment apart from Him, rather than in the certainty of His own promise; for we make their living power depend on the shifting phases of passing emotions, on the rise and fall of religious enthusiasm and excitement.

But we are surely falling short of the faith of the Bible, we are deaf to the teaching of the Christian Church. We do not worship a dead Christ; One, who more than eighteen hundred years ago had something to do with the human race; a Christ who once lived, once suffered, once long ago cared for men; but who, after a few short years, passed away beyond the limits of space and time. The Incarnation is a living present fact now at this hour, as surely as it was during those three years when the disciples looked upon the human form of the Son of Man. He is near us, with us now, closer than our own thoughts, near us in every temptation, near us too—may His great mercy help and pardon us—when we sin wilfully, when in thought or word or deed we clasp the evil close about us; when we trample under foot His cross, and do despite to the Spirit of His grace. For, on each one of us the sacred water has been poured; on our forehead has been set the Sign of the Cross; over each one of us the solemn declaration has been made that we are regenerate and grafted into the Body of Christ, and for this His great mercy to us thanks have been rendered to Almighty God on our behalf. These are not empty formulæ or charitable assumptions; they are simple, straight-forward statements of fact. By Christ's own ordinance we have each of us been grafted into the Body of Christ; we have been made children of God and heirs of the kingdom of Heaven. What we have done with the gift He gave us, whether through indolence or wilful sin we have stifled and done much to destroy that new life then planted in us, are questions we may well ask ourselves; but the fact remains that He gave the gift, and so brought us very near His own Incarnate Life.

And in that other Sacrament, to which Sunday by Sunday we are all bidden to come—to which a few, a very few, habitually do come—we are brought close up to the foot of the Cross. Here throughout all the Christian ages is the visible pledge of the living Presence of the Saviour with His Church. A small piece of bread, a few drops of wine—there is little enough in these as far as man can see; and we cannot explain how in this way God visits and sustains the souls that He has redeemed. But neither can we say how God who made the world could become man, could take upon Him our finite nature. We know, however, that we are called to take our part in no empty commemoration, where all the strength and glow and power springs not from Him, but must be looked for in ourselves. "Except ye eat the Flesh of the Son of Man, and drink His Blood, ye have no life in you;"[1] it was a hard saying; "How can this Man give us His flesh to eat?"[2] and so, in confusion and dismay, many went away and left Him. But when at the Last Supper He said to His apostles, "Take, eat, this is My Body," "Drink ye all of this, this is My Blood," they knew that, so far as was necessary for them, they had the key to His hard saying; and so they taught the Church which Christ committed to their care.

"This is none other but the house of God, this is the gate of Heaven;" and we have not known it. We have used the old words and phrases; they are in our Bibles and Prayer-books, and are often on our lips. There is a glow and warmth about them still; but for only too many it is the glow of a sun that is set, of a faith that is dying and almost dead. For even as men feel its power they make haste to explain that they do not really mean what they seem to say; that they have passed quite beyond the thought of any immanent presence of the supernatural, any superstitious conception that could bring them into immediate contact with the unseen world. There remain indeed some few shreds of the old faith; there, in the long past centuries, is the miraculous life and work of Jesus Christ; far away, too, in the dim background of the long past we get some glimpses of a Father in

[1] St. John vi. 53.   [2] St. John vi. 52.

Heaven, as One who set in motion this wonderful universe around us, which throughout all the ages of time has been moving on through its ceaseless evolution. But when we have read and thought a little more we find that there is one thing more demanded of us, that we are asked to give up even these remaining fragments of the Creed; we are startled at first, but it is not long before some at least are ready to do even this. The life of Christ still remains full of all possible grace and tenderness, raised indeed far and away above any ordinary human standard, still only a human life, and only a human death. It was, however, so remote, so unreal before, that to accept this conclusion does not make any very serious change in thought. And then, last of all, men are told of "a power not ourselves that makes for righteousness;" or where they have until now been accustomed to think of God, they are bidden to think of a vaguely personified nature: and they soon discover that, as they have travelled so far away from the Creed of the Church of Christ, even in admitting this, no great shock is given to their mental conceptions. Whether such hypotheses are better verifiable than the articles of the Creed, or whether they give a more stable resting-place for thought, are questions we cannot consider now; we must be content with tracing a movement with which many of us must be more or less familiar.

Remember, we pray you, what it means to be

members of the Church of Christ; if you allow yourselves to sink down to the level of the meagre conceptions of the Christian Creed which are current in some places—conceptions which are, let it be frankly admitted, sufficient to sustain real faith in very simple lives—you will find, as thinking men, if ever your minds are fully turned upon the questions, that you have no halting place left you within any limits that can be recognized as distinctively Christian. Make then some effort to understand in its fulness the Creed you profess. We may forget or ignore or deny it, but still the word of God stands sure and steadfast; we "are come unto Mount Sion, and unto the city of the Living God, the heavenly Jerusalem, and to an innumerable company of angels, to the general assembly and church of the firstborn, which are written in heaven, and to God the Judge of all, and to the spirits of just men made perfect, and to Jesus the Mediator of the new covenant, and to the blood of sprinkling."[1] This world of God, in all its wonder and glory, is close around us whether we know it or not, and we have our place in it; here is the sphere of our worship, the true home of our prayers. We are citizens of this heavenly kingdom; a kingdom which we cannot see now, but which we shall see hereafter. We kneel and pray at our bedside or here in church, and we kneel in the presence of all the hosts of heaven;

[1] Hebrews xii. 22-24.

we worship with all the faithful dead, who with us are "knit together in one communion and fellowship in the mystical Body of Christ our Lord."[1] We come here to church and kneel and bow down before the Lord at the Holy Table, and we are close to One whom indeed we cannot see, but who is now our all-merciful Saviour, who will one day be our Judge—whom our eyes shall behold—the King in His beauty—and this sight shall be our unspeakable happiness, or a consuming fire.

Must life, then, be one ceaseless round of communions and of prayers? No; we are set here in the world to work as well as to pray; we all of us have our duties, and it is of the last importance to us that we should fulfil them. We are here in the world as workers; be sure of this. But work becomes worship; for prayer takes our work and lifts it to its true level, and presents it, through the merits of Christ, a living sacrifice to the Father in heaven. This is the only true sense in which we can say work is prayer. Men who have lost all hold on the reality of prayer are apt to say to themselves, "I really cannot pray, but at least I can work," and then to act as if the well-known motto, "laborare est orare," justified the conclusion that work was a substitute for prayer. This we know it can never be. And yet it is wholly true that it is good to be a worker in the world, even though we cannot pray.

[1] Collect for All Saints' Day.

One cannot doubt that there are many such lives amongst us, going bravely on, wistfully conscious of a need for which they can find no satisfaction; to them sooner or later the answer will come, and work will be seen for them to have been prayer. But in these busy, restless, faithless days, we have need to remember the other aspect of the question, and to insist that prayer is work. Certainly prayer, as we have been reminded, does not conduct engineering operations on a gigantic scale; it does not level mountains or literally cast them into the sea; but, in virtue of our Saviour's promise and command, we know it has a place and function in the lives of men. We believe that they who can only stand and wait do serve the King of Heaven: we have no gospel of Euthanasia for incurables; we do not look on them as merely unproductive consumers; in their patient endurance of suffering, in their many fervent prayers, they may teach us and they may work for us in ways we cannot know or conceive.

It is indeed difficult, let us at once admit it, to hold firmly and steadily to the assurance of "the life of the world to come." But for this very reason we must never neglect any means through which God gives us help and guidance. We have had before us this morning the ennobling thought of companionship and association, the gifts that are so freely bestowed upon us in our common worship. We are members of the Church of Christ; as such we are united to the countless multitude of the saints who have lived before us; we are also closely linked to all who are now on earth fighting as soldiers of the Cross. Here indeed is a wonderful source of strength. We, too, in this place are members of this ancient House which bears our Saviour's name; here also none of us stands alone; others share with us the contest, and give us all the help that example and patient and faithful leadership can give. We surely must be indeed dull and slow of heart if we cannot respond to such calls as these. Our feet have been set within the house of God, our faces have been turned towards the gate of Heaven; the power of God is round us on every side; may He of His infinite mercy grant that when its open glory shall appear, the sight may not draw from us what must then be a cry of despair, this was indeed the gate of Heaven, but we would not know it.

VI.

The Church and Wealth.

"Son, remember that thou in thy lifetime receivedst thy good things."—St. Luke xvi. 25.

(First Sunday after Trinity, May 27, 1883.)

It is curious to mark how gregarious men are, not only in their habits, but in their opinions. An idea is started in some society or community, among a body of men, larger or smaller as the case may be, who are linked together on some ground, whether political, or religious, or social; it is repeated from mouth to mouth; it takes its place in the current literature, newspaper or other, of the party; and at last it reaches the dignity of an axiom or truism. Henceforward a man will need some audacity if he ventures within the limits of that society to question its truth, or to inquire into the foundation of fact on which so generally received a proposition rests.

In some such way as this the theory has grown up among certain sections of society, that Christianity is a religion that exists in the interests of the rich.

There can, I fear, be no doubt that some of the difficulties that the Church of England has to meet lie in the fact, that many of the poor are persuaded that its teachings and its ultimate purposes are bound up with the well-to-do; that is to say, with those who up to the present time have formed the governing classes of the community. There is an idea that Christianity exists to support the established order of things; that its precepts and catechisms are primarily directed to the maintenance of the present distribution of wealth and social comforts; that its one supreme object is to keep in order what are called "the lower classes," and to teach them, at the peril of their happiness in a future life, "to order themselves lowly and reverently to all their betters," and "to do their duty in that state of life" in which they find themselves placed.

These two precepts of the Church catechism are apt to be quoted as if they formed the special message which the Church of England had to deliver. They contain, it need not be denied, a truth which none of us are the better for having forgotten. The world would certainly be no worse if there were in it, in the upper as well as in the lower classes, a truer perception of the value of order, and of the social happiness that can only be found in the submission to due and reasonable authority. If the Christian ideal of a quiet and contented life were to wholly disappear, the world would be in great danger of becoming the scene of a fierce and wolfish struggle for existence, without pity and without remorse. We may, however, readily admit that the wording of these clauses of the catechism is old-fashioned, and that they belong to a time when social ideas were very different from those current amongst us in the present day. We may admit, too, that these particular words have been at times unduly and unfairly emphasised; and consequently a good deal of excuse may be found for the distrust with which the Church of England is now and then confronted when it comes into contact with the masses of the working people.

Since the fourth century Christianity has been the acknowledged creed of the nations of Europe. Bishops have taken their seats in legislatures on a level with, or even superior to any who sat there; and consequently the Church has been closely linked with the governing classes and has had a very large share in moulding for good and for evil the political development of the world—for good and for evil; its enemies forget the former and lay stress on the latter. It is a mixed history; dark blots are to be found upon it. It is impossible at times to bring the lives of those who were the successors of the Apostles into any relation to the ideals of the New Testament,—ideals which have their roots in self-abnegation and self-surrender; or to recognize in the earthly Prince the fitting representative of the Faith of Him " who had not where to lay His head." In our own day, the wealth and temporal dignity that surround the Church of England are not wholly without their disadvantages; they lend colour at all events to these suggestions of partizanship, which we should do well to keep in mind; for it is our bounden duty, in all we say or do, to be on our guard against any line of action which could give real justification for these thoughts about us.

Historically, then, the connection between the Church and the governing classes is a fact; it has brought, as all things do, both good and evil to men. The Church in our day is paying the penalty for the mistakes of those of her rulers in the past, who, forgetful of their high responsibilities and wonderful opportunities, gave to the few that which was entrusted to them by Almighty God in the interest of the many. The Gospels in no way sanction —it ought to be perfectly unnecessary to say it—this tying up of Christianity with wealth and temporal power. Indeed, the whole drift of the teaching of the New Testament is quite in the opposite direction. Nothing but our long familiarity with the Bible shuts our ears to the perfectly startling character of what we read there. There is sentence after sentence which declares in the most emphatic manner that the possession of riches, in itself and apart from the consideration of the use that is made of them, is a dangerous, almost fatal hindrance to the spiritual life;

that wealth is a positive evil; that to be a wealthy man makes it additionally difficult to reach the kingdom of God. "Woe unto you that are rich! for you have received your consolation."[1] "How hardly shall they that have riches enter into the kingdom of God!"[2]

It is true, we persuade ourselves, that our Lord explained away this, as we think, too severe sentence, when He added the words, "How hard it is for them that trust in riches to enter into the kingdom of God!"[3] But there is really no qualification here; our Saviour merely explains the grounds on which He had made His previous declaration; how hardly shall they enter in! hardly, because, surrounded as they are by wealth and all that wealth gives, they are soon entangled in its meshes and learn to put their trust in their riches. Everything around them calls them to present enjoyment and present gratification; bids them to eat, drink, and be merry, and let their soul rejoice in all the abundance of satisfaction which is immediately within their reach. All this is close at hand, and the thought of God is very far off; death, judgment, eternity, of the haunting shadows of which even thoughtless persons are never quite able to rid themselves, are so doubtful, so uncertain, that we cannot get any hold upon them. The present world we

[1] St. Luke vi. 24.   [2] St. Mark x. 23.
[3] St. Mark x. 24.

understand; here, at least, there is something fairly solid; on every side it calls us to what we know to be pleasant and attractive; and in the end the warning is found to be true in our case, "Where your treasure is, there will your heart be also." [1]

All this of which we have been thinking, is brought before us to-day with wonderful vividness by the Gospel from which the text is taken. In this story the veil that hangs between this world and the next, is for one moment drawn aside, and we are given the history of one who had lived and died; who in this life had enjoyed all the luxuries that great wealth could put within his reach, and who, in consequence, suffered utter ruin and loss when he passed into the unseen world. I say "in consequence" deliberately; for if we attend to the conversation given in the parable, and try to gather from it what it was that brought him to this end, we shall find we are not told of any things that we usually regard as sin; the only suggested ground of his failure is the utterly selfish use he made of his wealth. He "fared sumptuously," and was ";clothed in purple and fine linen;" he lived well, and he dressed well; he was a person of great social consideration, and he filled a great position with magnificence. And then the contrast is set before us in the life of the poor. One man is singled out, who, hungry and diseased, is brought and laid at the gate

[1] St. Luke xii. 34.

of the great house, desiring to be fed with the crumbs which fell from that sumptuous table. Dives, however, could feel no sympathy with the sufferings of the beggar who lay at his gate; he showed no compassion, and he gave no help to a sufferer on whom the very dogs took pity.

"And the rich man died and was buried." He was given a magnificent funeral; men recounted his greatness and his high dignities; funeral orations were delivered; his virtues were extolled; his munificence here, his magnanimity there, duly commemorated. But in the parable, the veil is lifted, and we are told what happened to his real self, which his fellow-men had never known. "And in hell he lifted up his eyes being in torment," to hear the words that told the one ground of his condemnation; "Son, remember thou in thy lifetime receivedst thy good things;" the good things that belonged to thee, that were to thee the whole of good, the one only good for which thou hadst any thought or care. His one purpose in life had been to protect himself from all that was disagreeable or unpleasant; he had lived, in a word, the ideally selfish life of the cultured, educated, and wealthy man. He had forgotten his responsibility to God for the wealth he had received; he had refused to recognize that he was but a steward, that he had duties towards others which he dared not neglect; everything that had in it a touch of self-discipline he had pushed away from him; he had lived simply for himself, and consequently he had already received to the full the reward that he had desired. There is no hint whatever that he was, what we call, an irreligious man; Moses and the prophets were not unknown to him; and there is nothing to suggest that he did not believe what they taught; or again, that he did not attend with regularity on his religious duties. His conversation with Abraham shows us that he had little to learn; the picture of his home is what we should recognize as an outwardly religious home. The fact that the ordinary calls of religion had failed to reach him is indeed the special ground of his plea on behalf of his brothers, that one might be sent from the dead, who should rouse them from their lethargy and compel them to that real repentance without which, as he now knows, they too must come to this place of torment.

"This scripture," says Bishop Andrewes, "hath the name given it in the words 'recordare fili'—son, remember; it is a remembrance, and such a remembrance that it toucheth our estate in everlasting life; that is, the well or evil hearing of this 'recordare' is as much as our eternal life is worth. For we find both in it. Our comfort or torment eternal—comfort in Abraham's bosom, torment in the fire of hell—depend upon it; and, therefore, as much as we regard them, we are to regard it." [1]

[1] "The Works of Bishop Andrewes," vol. ii. p. 78.

Our Lord does not teach us that no rich man can enter heaven; for Abraham himself was a man of great wealth, and thus it is through the lips of a rich man that the warning comes to rich men. The warning is the old one; life must bring us discipline; it is true that none of us can escape the heavy troubles which at times come upon us all; but apart altogether from these there is the daily discipline of life. In the case of the poor this is unavoidable; we, however, can escape it if we choose to do so, although it lies near enough to us. The trivial round, the common task, furnish for all the opportunity of self-denial, point out the road by which we may, if we will, day by day draw nearer to God. The terrible peril of wealthy men is that it is open to them to refuse this daily trial, to avoid the discipline of life, to think only of present pleasure and present gratification. Here is a real danger for all of us in this place; in our better moments we desire sincerely to attain that nobler ideal of life which is set before us in our Bibles; but it can never be ours without effort, without definite and determined push and struggle. It is so hard to nerve ourselves to the contest; it is so natural to avoid it, and to take the immediate pleasures that temptingly invite us. If now, in indolent self-indulgence, we choose the easier road, as years go by the higher ideal will fade away and be lost, and there will remain only the good we have consistently chosen and have made our own, and in receiving which, for a few years, we have received our payment in full for all eternity.

This seems, perhaps, a somewhat sombre view of life to set before young men. No doubt it is pleasant to retain as long as we may the happy carelessness of boyhood; but, after all, we are men and not boys, and we must, therefore, put away childish things. We must let this "recordare" of the gospel come home to us—Son, remember. We must look at life seriously, we must let the shadow of work and duty and earnest strenuous purpose fall across our path; it is positively wrong that we should now be as lighthearted and as thoughtless as we were when we first went to school.

Some of us may, I think, be pardoned if at times we mark with anxiety and regret failures in the University examinations which, too often, are wholly gratuitous and unnecessary; the consequence of careless indifference to the mental training and discipline which are, after all, among the main purposes of the existence of a University. This is, it is true, only a single point, and I do not wish to speak of it as if it were the only thing we had to think about; but tested in this one matter, only too many of us fail to respond. Why should we work? What is the use of it? For us there is much goods laid up for many years, we can surely take our ease. Hunting, rowing, cricketing—these are what we care for, and there is nothing wrong in them. This may be true enough, but still we must not live to hunt or to row. In merciful warning to us against so ruinous a mistake our Saviour has given us this "recordare" in the gospel: beware lest you are receiving now in this life all the good you know and care for; for the time cannot be very far off when your life must be given back to the God who gave it, and what then will be your place in that future world? How can you receive a good you have never learned to desire? How can you find your eternal happiness in the presence of God if, in this life, you have had no thought of loving or of serving Him?

Our Saviour is ready and waiting to help us tread the path He bids us follow; but we must, each for himself, accept the help He offers. There is the deep mystery of our freewill; our freewill to reject, if we choose to do so, the love which created and redeemed us. If, however, we will hear His voice and accept the discipline to which he calls us, He will give us, through that discipline and that service, a freedom and a happiness that a selfish life can never know. When wealth, and all the gratifications that belong to wealth, when power and influence are given to us, whether they come to us by birth or inheritance, or are won directly by our own personal work and effort, we should do well, as we receive them, to kneel down and pray with our whole hearts and souls that we may not receive our reward in full now in this present time; that God would give us here whatever He will, but that we may so receive all which He sends us in this life, that we may be received ourselves hereafter into the kingdom of His Son.

And as our Blessed Lord's merciful "recordare" sounds in our ears, let us plead with Him our own "recordare," that He would remember us in all the work of life, in the hour of death, and in the day of judgment:—

> Recordare, Jesu pie,
> Quod sum causa tuæ viae
> Ne me perdas illâ die!

VII.

Faith and Knowledge.

"Except a man be born again, he cannot see the kingdom of God."—
St. John iii. 3.

(Quinquagesima Sunday, February 24, 1884.)

FAITH and knowledge—how great the contrast is between the ideas called up before us by these two words as we generally understand them. Knowledge seems to be something substantial, solid, positive; it deals with the things we can taste and smell and handle and see and hear; it feeds and clothes and sustains us; it annihilates, at all events on the earth, time and space; it brings the fruits of distant lands into the small island in which we live; it has put close at hand, and within the reach of the vast majority of living men, luxuries that have now become almost necessaries of life, of which even our wealthiest ancestors scarcely dreamed. It is no doubt true that if we penetrate ever so little beneath the surface of things, and ask questions as to first principles, various more or less difficult problems present themselves for solution. But we English are before all things practical men, and even the better educated of us push aside with a certain impatience such discussions as these, regarding them as matters that it is well enough for thinkers and dreamers to spend their time upon; for us it is sufficient, as our everyday experience teaches us, that knowledge practically applied is the means of attaining wealth and comfort and prosperity.

But the conception of faith is so very different to this. Faith deals with things that are shadowy, vague, impalpable; we can bring its subject matter to no such tests as those we have applied with brilliant success to what is called positive knowledge. Faith will not correspond with our favourite methods of investigation, it declines to submit to our verifications. The ages of faith appear to us, as we look back on them, the ages of gross superstition; and, consequently, to men overwhelmed with the urgent work of this hurrying life, faith seems to be little different from credulity, to be the child and the offspring of ignorance.

But there are others who, although they accept absolutely the principle that the subject-matter of knowledge can be only that which appeals to the senses and to the experience of the senses, yet recognize that it is not possible to leave things exactly at the point they reach in our laboratories or our workshops. There open out before them the questions suggested by mental and physical pain, the problems of decay and death—I say nothing of sin, as this is a specially theological conception—the tragedy of human life pleads with them, and they cannot escape its importunity. They must make some effort to find out how men may be made better and happier; how pain, distress, and sorrow may at least be lessened, if they cannot be destroyed; and how death, although it is the inevitable lot of all men, may yet, perchance, be robbed of its agony and its terror, and become the peaceful sleep, in which a life that has known happiness and steady growth and progress may at last lose itself without regret and without apprehension; and in this attempt really to look before and after, really to answer those questions whence and whither, men necessarily rise to some higher level of serious purpose than those who live only for the passing moment. In the effort to learn from the past, or to provide for the future, men are lifted into those wider spheres of thought and emotion, where they can form great purposes, and shape for themselves great ideals; and then, braced and steadied, they return to everyday life to do and sometimes to suffer, and if they can, to persuade others to do and suffer too, not for anything they can see with their eyes, or handle with their hands, but for something they hope for—they work, in a word, in faith.

This is the faith that has nerved all great human teachers as such—the statesman, the politician, the poet, the thinker—and faith looked at in this way has, no doubt, much in common with poetic instinct and poetic enthusiasm. Reason—using the word, as Christians would say, in a somewhat restricted sense—can, it is certain, teach us that life is wrapped round on every side in mystery; reason vainly seeks to fathom or to understand it; it can only reach such satisfaction as is to be found in calling the mystery unknowable. Behind the veil we cannot penetrate, there may be or there may not be a God; but this much at least is certain, that if there is a God we can know nothing about Him. This, indeed, is no new discovery. "Canst thou by searching find out God? Canst thou find out the Almighty to perfection? It is as high as heaven; what canst thou do? deeper than hell; what canst thou know?"[1] So we read in the Book of Job. And St. Paul, speaking at Athens, tells his hearers how vainly the heathen world groped after God; and again in the First Epistle to the Corinthians he writes, "The natural man receiveth not the things of the Spirit of God: for they are foolishness unto him: neither can he know them, because they are spiritually discerned."[2] And then, in the words of the text, our Blessed Lord declares the impossibility that a man can reach any true conception of the kingdom of God unless he be born again—unless, that is, new powers are given

---

[1] Job xi. 7, 8.   [2] 1 Cor. ii. 14.

him; unless channels of communication are opened up between him and the life that is unseen and eternal, as real as those physical powers which became his at his physical birth, and connected him with the material universe.

The blindness of the blind is no argument to any one who can see against the truth of his sight. Imagine the most ingenious and powerful arguments supported by the subtlest intellectual ingenuity of a number of blind men, which tried to prove that all we had to tell of the glories of the visible world, revealed to us through our eyesight, was but the product of a fervid and poetical imagination playing round the sensations which reach us through touch or taste or hearing, and that it was clearly impossible, for this, that, and the other reason, all of quite irresistible cogency to the blind, that an independent faculty such as sight could belong to men. Would this move us for one moment? Why, then, should we allow ourselves to be made anxious because men who have no idea of what is meant by faith, prove to us with elaborate care and completeness that we have no right, if we are honest and sincere men, to have any faith ourselves?

Faith, no doubt, has, in one sense, kinship with poetic enthusiasm, and the noble ideals of unselfish men; but it is infinitely more, infinitely greater than this. To the Christian Church faith is not a dream or an illusion, however beautiful, however graceful, but "the substance of things hoped for, the evidence of things not seen." It is, in short, the sum of all those powers of the soul in which, and by which, God is known and understood, as surely as the eye takes in the light, or the ear hears the voice of the friend. If we have once really known, however dimly, that God is; if He has once spoken to our hearts and consciences; if the veil that hangs between us and the unseen world has been withdrawn for us but for a moment; then we know that there is a region of true knowledge open to us which is not reached directly through the bodily senses, which is not included under what we generally mean by the knowable, but which belongs to the mystery that is round about our life: human philosophy can recognize but cannot fathom it: it is revealed by the Spirit of God to those who in humility and patience wait and work and pray.

And we Christians believe that this knowledge is the gift of God, in and through the Incarnation of our Lord and Saviour Jesus Christ. We believe that the germ of this spiritual life was given each one of us in our infancy when we were baptized into the Name of the Father and of the Son and of the Holy Ghost; and since that moment we have been gaining an ever-deepening knowledge of God, or have been doing what in us lies to quench His Spirit which then was given us. In our early days Christian influences were round us; we were taught to read our Bibles and to say our prayers: but how slight the impression is that many of us now have of that early teaching. We do not, it is true, feel the day has begun quite rightly if we have not said our prayers; but a few hurried sentences, one or two collects not very carefully or thoughtfully repeated, easily satisfy the demand our consciences make on us; and if this is so, a few more months or years, and it will cease to trouble us at all that we regularly enter on the duties of each new day, and go out to meet its temptations without one thought of God.

Men often speak of a judgment to come, and they speak rightly and truly; but even now the judgment has begun. We should do well to lay to heart the lesson God teaches us, by His working in the visible world, as to the laws by which He governs the spiritual and unseen world. Take one instance: the mole has chosen to burrow and live beneath the surface of the ground out of the reach of the light of day, and Nature has done what she always does in such cases, and has taken away a gift of which no use is ever made; the mole, living continually in darkness, clearly has no need of the power of sight, and so it has been taken away. Just so, if we forsake the Light of God's Presence, the spiritual sense through which alone He can be seen will lose its power; and if we choose to burrow down among the things of this lower world, we must lose the sight of the soul as certainly as the mole has lost its physical sight. And in the realm of external nature nothing is done in a hurry, or by leaps and bounds; slowly and step by step the disused organ decays and loses its capacity for usefulness: for a long time recovery is still possible if only the right means be used; but at last the sense is completely lost, and only a miracle can restore that which has been wholly destroyed.

The same law rules in the spiritual world: and equilibrium is an impossibility; backwards or forwards, evolution or degradation, gaining a deeper knowledge, or losing the feeble light we still have,—one or other of these is happening to us all. Day by day, hour by hour, the judgment is going on; to-day is judged by yesterday, to-morrow by to-day, this Term by last Term, the next by this. Of what infinite importance is all this to us here in Oxford, when life is just opening out before us; when all the wealth of associations and memories that belong to this place, all the varied influences of its intellectual activities are moulding and shaping our lives; when, perhaps for the first time in our experience, we are reading books, and are brought into contact with brilliant intellects in whose scheme of things in general no place can be found for all that we have been taught to believe; when at times we find ourselves travelling along lines of thought and speculation which are insensibly undermining much that is essential in the foundations of our faith. We are no longer children; we are fairly afloat on the sea of life, and we need all our spiritual strength and all our readiness. If in the past we have done little or nothing to utilize the gifts and powers that belong to our spiritual nature, we shall find ourselves in serious jeopardy of shipwreck: we have need to work hard and watch and pray lest the last and most terrible judgment of all be passed upon us,—that the light that is in us has become darkness.

Lent is once more close upon us with its overmastering sense of sin—of sin not as a figment of theologians, but as a real power and potency, crushing the life of the soul, separating us from God our Father, and hiding His mercy from us. None can venture to say he has not sinned—sinned in thought and word and deed; sinned, too, in omission, in neglecting to fulfil the duties which God had given him to do; sinned, too, with his intellect, those sins which we so rarely recognize or acknowledge, but which, perhaps, set the most impassable barrier between the soul and God. "If we say that we have no sin, we deceive ourselves;" Lent bids us remember this, and bids us come to prayer. If we could once say, "Our Father, which art in Heaven, hallowed be Thy name, forgive us as we forgive;" if we could once say these words as our Saviour would have us say them; if we could once know what communion with God really is,—then God, the soul, eternal life, would no longer be only words; we should understand what spiritual communion means; and the knowledge of God would be so sure and certain that no one could ever take it away from us.

How differently we live from all that is implied in this. We can find our complete satisfaction for our spiritual needs in a single service on Sunday, in coming to listen to the anthem on Sunday afternoon; instead of coming to this church as often as we may with all our powers of body, soul, and spirit, with all our intellectual enthusiasms and mental activities, with our sorrow and our penitence, and kneeling down in His presence, and being still and learning to know that He is God. Out of some two hundred baptized and confirmed members of the Church of Christ, only ten or twelve come here Sunday by Sunday to fulfil His last command and to show forth His death. How can our spiritual life be vigorous and strong, if we take no thought or care for it? if we use none of the help God has put into our hands? if we neglect prayer, communion, almsgiving, self-discipline, and so leave it to grow as it may, or to perish if it must? We implore you, by the mercies of God, that you would not neglect the grace of God that is in you; that you would present yourselves with all your powers of body and of intellect a living sacrifice to Him who has done so great things for you. Come with us this

Lent, we beg you, and kneel down here and think and pray; we must all seek forgiveness, that we have misused and neglected the grace and mercy that have been round us since first we were gathered into the fold of Christ: and may He in His great mercy hear us and bring us at the last to His eternal kingdom, where Faith will be lost in sight; where knowledge as we now understand it will vanish away; but where a new and an enduring knowledge of all the infinite depths of the wisdom and the love of God will, through all the ages of eternity, for ever grow from more to more.

VIII.

The Church the Body of Christ.

"The Church which is His Body."—Eph. i. 23.

(Twentieth Sunday after Trinity, Oct. 26, 1884.)

We may well wonder how it comes to pass that some parts of the teaching of the Bible are so readily accepted by many Christian people, while other parts of its teaching, equally clear and definite as they appear to us to be, and after all little more than necessary complements of that which is generally believed, are often ignored and sometimes denied; while those who press home upon men the duty of the acceptance of the complete Creed are declared to be enemies of the Cross of Jesus Christ.

All Christians who are worthy of the Name they bear teach the doctrine of the Incarnation, and the truth of the redemption of mankind by the one sacrifice once offered upon the cross; but many pass by, without any serious consideration, the truth of our Blessed Lord's perpetual intercession and the fact of His present mediation on behalf of His Church. "Lo, I am with you alway, even unto the end of the world;"[1] these were among the last words our Lord spoke to His Apostles before the ascension. He then, the God-Man, perfect God and perfect Man, though henceforward no longer seen with the outward eye, would yet be with them till the end of time; with them, that is, in the reality of His Human Nature. But since His Human Nature is a fact, it is against the truth of that nature, that It should be anywhere else than where we are told It is since the ascension, that is, at the right hand of God. His Humanity can therefore only be present with us after a spiritual manner, in the power, that is, of His Divine Nature; and it is the special office of the Third Person in the Blessed Trinity, God the Holy Spirit, to be the agent through whom this spiritual Presence of the One Mediator is given to the Church. "I will not leave you comfortless: I will come to you."[2] "If I go not away, the Comforter will not come to you; but if I depart, I will send Him unto you."[3] "He shall glorify Me: for He shall receive of Mine, and shall show it unto you."[4]

Therefore it was on the day of Pentecost that our Lord's words, "I will come again, and receive you unto Myself,"[5] had their fulfilment; for it was to His Church only that this Presence was to be given. "A little while, and the world seeth Me no more; but ye

---

[1] St. Matt. xxviii. 20. [2] St. John xiv. 18.
[3] St. John xvi. 7. [4] St. John xvi. 14. [5] St. John xiv. 3.

see Me: because I live, ye shall live also."[1] These words cannot be taken as if they were fulfilled at His second coming to judge the world; for then every eye shall see Him: they can only refer to the Presence with His people, and to the divine life given them with that Presence, which was bestowed upon the Church on the day of Pentecost. Obviously the words are not explained by the supposition that our Lord uses them of Himself as God, since as God He must be present everywhere. Moreover, this Presence with us as God is not that which we sinners ask may be given us; from that Presence we seek to hide ourselves as our first parents did in the garden of Eden; it is the Presence with us of our Mediator we so sorely need; that Presence through which alone we can dare approach God as God, through which alone our sins can be blotted out, through which alone we can receive strength to live the divine life which was implanted in us at our Baptism. "We will come unto him and make Our abode with him,"[2] are our Lord's words. "Where two or three are gathered together in My Name, there am I—I, that is, in the power of My glorified Humanity—in the midst of them."[3] As God we cannot escape from Him; if we climb up into heaven, He is there: if we go down to hell, He is there also.[4] From the Presence of God we cannot

[1] St. John xiv. 19.   [2] St. John xiv. 23.
[3] St. Matt. xviii. 20.   [4] Ps. cxxxix. 8.

escape; from the Presence of the Saviour—the Mediator—we can, and may God help us, we do again and again cut ourselves off by wilful sin.

This spiritual Presence is then a reality. How is it given us? Clearly a moment's thought will tell us there are two sides to this question; since we are free-agents, and God wills that we should be so, there is something required on the one hand from us; and on the other hand, since our Blessed Lord's Intercession and the fact of the Presence of His man's nature in the world are truths entirely independent of any one of us, there is, if we may put it so, something to be done on behalf of Almighty God. For the moment we will think only of the latter aspect of the question. On this side when we are asked how this spiritual Presence of our Lord is given to us, we can only reply, that it is given us through the Church which is, as St. Paul teaches us, the Body of Christ. We are bound to the Church through the Sacraments, and they derive all their power and efficacy from the truth of the Incarnation; and hence, to quote the words of Archdeacon Wilberforce, "It is impossible to answer the question whether men are joined to Christ by being joined to His Church, or joined to His Church by being joined to Him. It would be a parallel question to ask, whether we were sharers in Adam's nature because we were men, or men because we were sharers in Adam's nature. The two relations hang inseparably together.

By the mystical Body of Christ is meant the whole family of those who by the Holy Ghost are united in Church ordinances to His man's nature. Our real union with each is what gives us a part in the other."[1]

But it may be said, you are really taking as a serious statement what is intended only for a metaphor. Yet, after all, a metaphor must mean something. When our Lord speaks of Himself as the Good Shepherd, as the Door of the Sheepfold; when He compares the relation between Himself and His followers to the union between the Vine and its Branches, we understand at once what He means. You may speak of the members of a society as a body, or you may speak of the citizens of a country as a body, but would there be much meaning in calling the inhabitants of a country the body of their king or their president?[2] Now St. Paul over and over again speaks of the Church as the Body of Christ; words could not be stronger or more definite than those he uses, "We are members of His Body, of His Flesh, and of His Bones;"[3] and thus (I again quote Archdeacon Wilberforce) "It seems unquestionable that some real relation must bind together the natural body which He took at the Incarnation, and His Mystical Body the Church, so that our union with the one must be a ground of union with the other."[4]

---

[1] "The Doctrine of the Incarnation," by Archdeacon Wilberforce, 2nd Edition, 1849, p. 312.
[2] Cf. Wilberforce, p. 313. [3] Ephes. v. 30. [4] Wilberforce, p. 315.

But it will be said, this is to limit the grace of God; the way is open and clear, and "spirit with spirit can meet;"[1] we can go to God freely and simply; you are setting purely imaginary obstacles before us— human inventions they are often called. There might have been something to be said for such a position as this if we had not been fallen creatures. If sin had never come between God and man and destroyed the right of access which man, as he came from his Creator's hands, undoubtedly had to his Creator, then, no doubt, to have been a child of Adam would have given the right to have come into the Presence of God. But the very ground of the necessity of the Incarnation lay in the fact that we men could no longer approach the Presence of God; that a new way must be opened for us; and this new and living way is "through the veil, that is to say, His Flesh."[2] How many there are who stand up with all their sins upon them, and in proud contempt ask with Naaman, "Are not Abana and Pharpar, rivers of Damascus, better than all the waters of Israel? may I not wash in them, and be clean?"[3] Think, they say, of the greatness of the human intellect; remember the heights of inspiration to which the poet can rise; call to mind that spiritual insight and glow which we find in page after page of writers who do not admit for one moment the truth

---

[1] Tennyson's "Higher Pantheism."
[2] Heb. x. 20.　　　　　　[3] 2 Kings v. 12.

of the Christian Creed. Such writers and thinkers lift us above the present; in their enthusiasm we find our freedom; we lose sight of misery and death; we are lifted into a new world, we breathe a new air. Are not these better than the narrow path of Christian doctrine? than the weary round of penitence, self-discipline, and prayer, which may only make men morbid, self-analytical, and nerveless? We rise above all that is base, above much that you call sin; you would have us remember past sin, you preach contrition and amendment; we move in the free atmosphere of great thoughts and ideals, you tell us we must travel along a steep and difficult road of doctrine and discipline, and would forbid us to turn from it to the right hand or the left. The picture is an exaggerated one; still it has its side of truth. All we need say is, the way of penitence is God's way, and is the only way of salvation. We are sure of this; and men who have travelled along it only a little distance know that it is a path that leads to the only possible freedom, the freedom that is of a perfect and willing service. Such men know that penitence lifts them into a serener air than this world can know; that through it God grants them a peace that passes the understanding of men, a hope that cannot fade away, a light that will shine brighter and brighter till the day of Christ. We say nothing of those to whom the gospel of the grace of God has never come, to God alone they stand or fall; but for us "who were once enlightened, and have tasted of the heavenly gift, and were made partakers of the Holy Ghost, and have tasted the good Word of God, and the powers of the world to come,"[1] to cut ourselves off from His Church is to cut ourselves off from Him; to refuse or to slight the spiritual food which He gives us in the Holy Sacrament for the nourishment and sustenance of the life He has bestowed upon us, is, in one word, to reject Jesus Christ. To go back is to reject the revealed mediation of our Lord and to assert, directly or indirectly, that man has in himself and of himself the right to approach Almighty God; that is, to deny that we are sinners and have fallen away from Him, and thus tacitly to deny altogether the doctrine of the Atonement.

All of you have at your Baptism been made members of Christ, sharers in the divine humanity, members of His Mystical Body. You have the right of access to the throne of God by the one and only mediation of Christ our Lord. You share in the continual cry of the Church, "Agnus Dei qui tollis peccata mundi, dona nobis pacem, miserere nobis;" "Thou that takest away;" now as we kneel before God, the sins which otherwise would shut us out from His presence are taken away from us through the power of our Lord's ever present intercession and mediation. Thus only are we able to pray at all; and God becomes,

[1] Heb. vi. 4, 5.

not one against whom we have most grievously sinned, a just and awful Judge, but "Our Father, which is in Heaven." And this right and gift is ours as members of the Mystical Body of Christ, and therefore united to His human nature.

And further, it is only in virtue of the same union that we have the right to come before Almighty God with our private prayers; it is this that makes each one of us in his own order and degree a "priest unto God."[1] Do not be afraid of the truths that belong to the Faith; understand what it teaches you, and when you understand it believe it fearlessly, confess it boldly, and pray God to bless your endeavours to act it out in your life. The faith of Christ, fully grasped and heartily accepted, places beneath your feet a firm solid rock which no waves of human passion or human ingenuity can undermine or wear away. Instead of groping your way uncertainly, hesitating as to how this or that thought you meet with will affect your beliefs and hopes, doubtful as to what place you must give to this or that theory, to this or that new bit of knowledge, you will go through life with courage and confidence, since you serve the Lord of Truth.

[1] Rev. i. 6.

IX.

Penitence.

"My sin is ever before me."—PSALM li. 3.

(SEXAGESIMA SUNDAY, FEBRUARY 8, 1885.)

THE mystery of the Fall of man is set before us with wonderful vividness in the first lesson for this morning's service. Last Sunday we read of the Creation; the marvellous work moved on through its ceaseless evolution under the sustaining life-giving hand of the Lord God, and when each period reached its close, when the evening and the morning had come and gone, He beheld all the work that He had made, and saw it was very good. And as the scene unfolded itself at last the crown and climax of visible created life was reached, and man came from his Maker's hands, marred by no defect, stained by no sin; and God saw that he, too, was very good.

To-day all this is changed. Almighty God, in His wisdom, had given His creature a perilous gift; in the mystery of his free will he was at liberty to choose whether he would serve God or no; he had the power, if he chose, to take the gifts God had given him, and turn them against the Giver: and the time came when he did this: he asserted his freedom, his independence, and in the very act of the assertion of his freedom he lost it, and became, save for the mercy of God, for evermore a slave. In this disaster all his descendants were overwhelmed: it could not be otherwise; his nature crushed, maimed, torn, and tangled was not as it had been before he fell; he could not transmit to others what he himself had lost; and so sin passed upon all, and in Adam all died.

It is sometimes said, and we are conscious of an inclination to assent to the doctrine, that it is inconsistent with the idea of the justice of God to allow the innocent to suffer with the guilty. When men stand, as all must hereafter, before the judgment seat of our Lord and Saviour, to answer for all that they have done and all that they have left undone in life, we at all events shall not be able to make this defence for ourselves. It is true that we inherit the consequences of the Fall, but we have also received a gift greater than any Adam had; God's presence and His very self, given to us in the Incarnation of our Blessed Lord; in our Baptism we were made partakers of His Divine humanity, and received graces and gifts in the strength of which we could beat down and hold in check the power of evil. No one of us is sinless; this is true, but can we stop there? Can any of us venture to say that he has not knowingly and even wilfully sinned against the grace of God? fallen, too, not into slight or venial sin, if we can venture to speak of any sin as venial, but into sin which has opened a great gulf between the soul and God? There have been those who have thought so seriously of sin committed against the grace of God, that they have taught that post-baptismal sin cannot be forgiven. The Christian Church has always held such teaching to be erroneous; but it is the exaggeration of a truth which we should do well never to forget: it is, indeed, a far truer estimate of the disastrous results of sin wilfully committed against the grace of God, than the easy-going theories which only too many who have been baptized into the name of Christ, hold concerning sin committed by Christian men and women. But we know that even here there is a way of restoration open to us; it is not an easy or smooth path, but rather rugged, and steep, and toilsome; the way, the one and only way open to us, is the way of penitence.

Penitence;—it is a word we often use; how many of us, I wonder, have any conception of all that it connotes? There are two things which are often mistaken for it, but which most emphatically it is not. In the first place it is not that ready glib admission that we are sinners which is sometimes made without any serious thought or recollection, a sort of formula repeated as a matter of course. Sinners? Yes, no doubt we are sinners. Do wrong? Yes, certainly we do wrong; we quite see we are not what we should be; we know we are not all we would be. But all the time men say this, there is in the background of their thoughts a kind of reserve, that really they are not so very bad— that they are much better than the ordinary run of people. So far as they think thus, they can have no real conception of what sin is; and those who do not know what sin is, cannot know much about penitence.

And, secondly, penitence is not merely emotionalism, or a facility for passionate regrets. We vary very much on our emotional side, just as we do on other sides of our wonderfully mysterious nature; some are easily moved, others are constitutionally phlegmatic. We should do well to remember that easily roused feelings are not in themselves certain evidence of the work of the Spirit of God: there is a luxury in excited emotions which is a most serious danger to the spiritual life; a kind of spiritual intoxication which is only too easily mistaken for deep earnestness and true devotion. The power of evil is never so dangerous as when it comes to us dressed in all the glory of an angel of light, and nowhere and at no time does this happen more effectively than when undisciplined emotions are being played upon in a way that suggests the presence of the grace of God in the soul.

What, then, is penitence? It is indeed no vague, indefinite regret, no general feeling of dissatisfaction with self, such as depends to a very large extent on the state of our bodily health; it knows nothing of, and is altogether untouched by any of the external or social discomfort and disquietude which are at times the accompaniments of the sins of men. Penitence is rather in the profound emotion which once for all takes possession of a man who has stood face to face with his own sin; who has learnt to know its hideous deformity; to measure in some degree its base ingratitude, its overwhelming shame. Once awakened in this way, he cannot be content with uncertainty or indefiniteness, he cannot rest in vague generalized acknowledgment of sin; the whole past life must be taken and looked at through and through. With prayer that cannot shape itself in definite words, he looks up to the God he fain would reach, that he may be able to do the work effectively, that nothing may be forgotten or lost sight of. Sin indeed haunts the soul as a nightmare: look where the man will he sees, he can see, only the one picture. Hitherto, it may be for years past, he has been able to avoid this; but escape is now, by God's mercy, no longer a possibility, and he is compelled to realize to the full that he has sinned against the grace of his baptism, that he has trampled under foot the Cross of the Lord, and by his faithlessness put Him to shame before an unbelieving world.

Very morbid and very unwise all this, some people will say; but sin wilfully forgotten and wilfully ignored is unforgiven sin; we may be sure of this. There is nothing the enemy of your souls would like better than that you should forget your sins. There is something very specious about this kind of advice, and very much that is wise and influential in the world combines to offer it to us, and we are easily enough persuaded to follow it. Surely, men say, the best thing that you can do with the past is to forget it, and put it out of the way. It is the future you have to think about, and all your endeavours should be directed to doing better in the remaining years of life. Certainly this has to be done; but you may not on that account leave the other undone. You may no doubt ignore the past if you like, but you will not get quit of it in that way. Your life is one complete whole. You cannot disintegrate it or snap it asunder by any effort you can make. Your past for evil as well as for good makes and shapes your present; so be quite sure of this, that the right course is not to ignore it, but to learn from it. The true line of action is, after all, the brave and manly one; if, therefore, you know you have never been really clear and straightforward with yourself, face boldly the disheartening task that you have before you, and then bring your past life—acknowledging everything, all that you recall, and all, too, that you cannot now recall—and lay it down at the foot of your Saviour's Cross, plead His death and passion, and hear, as you may, His voice absolving you from all your sin, since He has left in His Church power to forgive the sins of those who truly repent and believe in Him.

But penitence is the work of a lifetime, and not of an hour or a week. The soul never knows the full horror of sin till it sees it in the light of the Cross of the Lord and Saviour. Forgiveness does not lessen, but, on the contrary, increases the pain which is the consequence of sin—the pain which every soul must go through, when it really knows what sin is, and who He is against whom the sin has been committed. "The Lord turned, and looked upon Peter,"[1] and that look St. Peter never forgot. God in His mercy grant to us, that we may know something of what it is to feel that same glance bent upon ourselves; if so, it will pierce us through as nothing we have ever felt before. Pain, mental or physical, most of us know what this may mean; but pain, sorrow for sin burning into us, a consuming, cleansing, purifying fire—this is what God will give us. And it brings with it a happiness all its own, for it is the pledge of the grace of God, cleansing and renewing all that has been defiled and broken and ruined by the wilful misdeeds of life.

And this contrition shall by God's blessing remain with us until the battle of life is over, never losing anything of its power, but rather growing in vividness

[1] St. Luke xxii. 61.

as the spiritual life deepens and strengthens. It may be, as the years go on, that He will grant days of the peace and rest and quiet which they only can know who strive to live in the presence of their Saviour. Such days, however, cannot last; life under its normal aspect must be stern conflict and persistent discipline up to the end. It is true we are not called upon to use physical violence to ourselves; but it is also true that we are bidden to put ourselves under the discipline the Christian year brings to us. We may at least restrain the unnecessary luxuriousness of our food; we may use it to sustain life, and not to minister to mere sensual enjoyment; we can deny ourselves, that we may be able to give more liberally to God's poor. We may well be reminded of this now when Lent is close upon us, bidding us once more remember all that our Blessed Lord endured for us men and for our salvation. And as we, mindful of that life and death, look back upon our past lives, with all their ingratitude and carelessness and sin, we can only ask that God would give us true contrition for wrong done, for duties so often sadly neglected, and try in solemn earnestness to make our own Bishop Andrewes' penitential prayer,—

> Domine, pœnitet, pœnitet, Domine,
> Adjuva impœnitentiam meam,
> Et magis adhuc magisque
> Compunge, scinde, contere
> Cor meum.

X.

The Holy Trinity.

"Blessed are the pure in heart: for they shall see God."—
ST. MATT. v. 8.

(TRINITY SUNDAY, MAY 31, 1885.)

THERE are, if I may put it so, two aspects under which the thought of Almighty God may present itself to us. We can, on the one hand, think of Him as the God who created, and redeemed, and sanctified us, as upholding and sustaining us and the world around us by His presence and His power; we can think of Him, that is, in His relation to ourselves, in what He has done, and is doing at the present moment for us. Again, we may, on the other hand, think of Him as He is in Himself, apart from and without any created thing, as He was before the worlds were made, in the boundless changeless glory of His Eternal Being; and it is this latter conception that belongs especially to the festival of Trinity Sunday.

As we try to give some outline and form to our thoughts, we are of necessity brought face to face with dogmatic definitions and formulæ, that is, with the Creeds of the Church of Christ; and we draw back puzzled, with a sense of difficulty about us; difficulty, too, rather needlessly created, we are inclined to say; and perhaps we are even seriously offended. If we think for a moment, we shall discover that these difficulties, at all events for Christian people, spring up from two very different sources. They may arise from our recognition of the truth of God's greatness and our own absolute nothingness; from our knowledge of what God must be, and our knowledge of what we ourselves are; so far, even if mistaken, they are the expression of true reverence. But, if we are only perfectly honest and sincere with ourselves, we are compelled to acknowledge that they may also have their origin in the secret power and strength of sin within us.

We may, it is true, shrink from definition because we feel how utterly impossible it is for us, with our finite words and thoughts, to attempt, as it were, to set limits to the truth of Almighty God. And, so far, we are not very wrong. Yet we are mistaking the purpose and object of such definitions as those of the Creeds. Faith alone can enable us to know God; faith alone can give us the capacity to understand Him, to see Him, to love Him; but, given the belief that is the outcome of this faith, from the very constitution of our complex nature, our reason must take cognizance of, and bring itself into relation with our beliefs; and it is at this point that the Creeds become necessary. As a matter of fact, definition has invariably been forced on the Church from the outside, and consequently her definitions are, in the first instance, warnings—warnings that, if we accept particular presuppositions or surrender ourselves to particular lines of thought, we do so with the certainty of arriving, sooner or later, at conclusions for which no place can be found within the four corners of the Creed we still profess to hold. Once started on these lines, we must surely reach at last the dilemma, that we must either follow boldly along the line in which our reason, following out the particular presuppositions we have accepted, is leading us, and, as a consequence of this, surrender our hold upon the truth of the Creed; or that we must have the courage to retrace our steps, and modify or set aside altogether the intellectual conceptions from which we started, and which are the actual cause of our present anxiety. It is, no doubt, a fact that there are many men who are true and sincere Christians, but who have accepted intellectual premisses which, if they were worked out to their logical conclusions, would render it impossible for those who held them to acknowledge the truth of even the most elementary doctrines of the Creed,—of those simple truths, as they are often called, which are still accepted by the great majority, at least in this country, of those who call themselves by the name of Christ. Individual men, it is certain—perhaps it is especially true of us slower Northern nations—can and do rest with complete satisfaction to themselves on the middle of what one must speak of as a logical slide. Men can do this for themselves—you or I may do it; but be sure of this, the Church cannot do it, and generations of men cannot do it.

Surely and certainly, although it may be very slowly these things work themselves out; and, if men of one generation are not logical, their children or their grandchildren will be so; they will carry to its natural conclusion their fathers' teaching, unhampered, it is to be feared, by their fathers' faith. I can imagine no more painful reflection that could occur to any one when he comes to die, or when with fuller knowledge he sees things more nearly as they really are, than to have to say to himself,—yes, I thought I was living as a Christian should; but I forgot that the intellectual, not less than the moral side of my nature needed discipline; and so, neglecting the gifts which God had put within my reach, I allowed myself to think and to speak as though my intellect had been untouched by sin; I never watched myself or hesitated to accept or teach any theory that at the moment commended itself to me. I never accepted any responsibility for consequences, I was quick and superficial. I made no attempt to work things out or to see what they really involved; but those, whom I have influenced—and, after all, few of us have no influence—will do this. And, therefore, in my day I have done what I could to add to the difficulties of those who are striving to be true servants of Jesus Christ.

Now the Creeds will save us from this danger, if we will let them do so. The Church is not the witness for her Master only to us; we are but one tiny link in the vast chain of immortal beings for whom she has to care. She has the care of all the ages; and so she warns men with no uncertain or hesitating voice, that this and that thought about God is false; that to hold it, to give ourselves up to it, is implicitly to deny the fact of the Incarnation, the truth of the Atonement, the life in the world to come; that, however it may at first sight catch our fancy, or appear to meet our wants, it is, in its essence, entirely contrary to the highest truth, and must surely, if accepted and made the groundwork of our thoughts about the unseen world, undermine our faith, and leave us without God and without hope. Thus the Church warns us of pitfalls and morasses in the sphere of intellectual activity in which faith has been swallowed up in the past, in which ours, too, will be lost if we venture lightly upon them. The Creeds are in one sense summarized experience; they do not set bounds to Almighty God, or shut up His Glory within the limits of verbal definitions: they tell us how Christian men and Christian thinkers have learned to think and speak of Him, "Quem nosse est vivere, Cui servire regnare est." Quem nosse est vivere,—yes, little as we think it, we only live, live in the full sense of all that the word means, for intellect no less than heart and will, when we surrender ourselves to the willing service of Almighty God, when our one desire is that we may know His will, and our one purpose that we may, by His grace, fulfil it.

But there is a second and more serious reason why we are distressed at the definitions of the Creeds. Assertions such as these—so direct, so immediate—are not made about a God who is far off, who may be, but of One who is a present and most solemn reality; not indistinct, remote, uncertain, but close to us and with us in all we think and do. The hazy Christianity, or rather Christian sentiment, which satisfies very many people, is so different from this; it is content with the vague recognition of a God, for whose existence there is some slight probability. Under such a conception men find themselves able to admit, in a sense, the existence of sin. They are educated persons, and so can appreciate the beauty of Christian ethics and Christian ideals. Their natural refinement revolts against sin, at all events in its grosser forms,—revolts even as they yield to those temptations to which their position in life and their natural tendencies especially expose them. But all this is changed when men intelligently recite the Creed. It is just the definiteness of it which produces the sense of irritation and dismay; for in presence of these clear assertions sin and evil, however lightly we may have regarded them before, appear in darker and more serious colours. After all—as far as verbal statement can do it for us—we are brought face to face with the reality of the existence of Almighty God; and the question we have to ask ourselves is, how we can dare to stand before His presence. And so, perhaps, in our desire to get rid of a serious difficulty in the easiest way, we take refuge in some such objection as that of which I have already spoken,—the objection that to attempt to define the nature of Almighty God is to introduce an unworthy conception of Him; when, if we were quite honest with ourselves, we should see that our real motive was not zeal for God's glory, but rather a desire to silence an inconvenient thought that pressed very urgently upon us, one that demanded from us a sincerer purpose and a clearer recognition of the heavy responsibilities in which the gift of life has of necessity involved us.

We do, all of us I hope, at times call to mind what we are, and what we know, from His revelation of Himself, God intended that we should be. What we are—nothing and less than nothing, we are apt to say; and yet how untrue this is. The doctrine of the Incarnation is the measure of the dignity and greatness of human life. The love of God manifested then, was not manifested on behalf of some vast stupendous creation, but for men, women, and children; for the human race, indeed, as a whole, but still for the race as made up of separate personalities, and therefore for each one in his separate existence. Yes, never forget that for each one of us, as if we alone had sinned, our Saviour died; for each the rest and peace of heaven is prepared, that mansion in the Father's house which shall be one day ours, unless, which God forbid! we forfeit it now by sin and selfishness. We cannot think little of human life who believe these truths. We cannot contemn even our own selves, sin-stained as we know ourselves to be. He made us, He redeemed us, He wills that we should be His children. But only the pure in heart shall see God; and never forget that, if we do not learn to see Him now in this present life, we shall never see Him in that which is to come. Thus it comes about that the cry of the heart for purity, the sense of the deadly power of sin, is even more urgent on Trinity Sunday than in the penitential season of the Church's year. Those who have made the effort, with whatever of weakness and hesitation, to live only to God, to have no thought, no purpose, save only His Glory, no desire but what He commands, no will but what He wills,—they know how past sin parts the soul from Him whom they long, with the whole purpose of their heart, to know and to obey.

My brothers, I pray you in God's name not to

imagine for one moment that a little more carelessness, a little more self-indulgence, a little more sowing of wild oats, as people euphemistically speak of things which otherwise they would not venture to talk about, will make no difference in the end—no difference because we mean to repent before we die; and God, in His mercy, will pardon even the greatest sinner. If we can think such thoughts as these, the light that is in us has already become utter darkness. Believe me, it is most terribly true, even forgiven sin stands between the soul and God. The vain, the frivolous, the self-indulgent, the impure, will not—simply because they have found out the sinfulness of sin, and have by God's grace begun to forsake the evil—at once and easily learn to see the face of God. Their upward path must be steeper, their discipline severer, before their eyes can look upon the King in His beauty, than it would have been had they never lost their baptismal purity. For those who are really honest with themselves, who under whatever difficulties in the present, out of whatever slough of sin in the past, are steadily set to live to God, this knowledge will have no terror; rather the certainty of the trial will only nerve them to be patient and faithful, and to "bear the dimness for His sake;" for they know that in the end, through the discipline and training of life, He will give them the purity of heart they long for, and show them His glory; and that hereafter they will learn to know

Him more and more fully, when the work of purification is accomplished and they take their part in the ceaseless worship of the courts of heaven, where angels and archangels, and all the hosts of God, and all the multitude of redeemed rest not day and night, saying, " Holy, Holy, Holy, Lord God Almighty, which was, and which is, and which is to come."

XI.

Christian Self-assertion.

"I can do all things through Christ which strengtheneth me."—
Phil. iv. 13.

(Twenty-fifth Sunday after Trinity.—November 22, 1885.)

Life is of necessity self-assertion; every action and almost every word and movement is the intrusion of ourselves upon others. Welcome or unwelcome we are there, making ourselves felt, and the lift and enthusiasm we are conscious of come to us through this activity.

Watch a child at play. It rides its mimic horses; it fights its mimic battles; it creates round itself a fancy world in which it moves with unfettered freedom. There is no sense of opposition, no check, or restraint, or doubt; it reigns the unchallenged monarch of all the worlds, and in this freedom it finds full enjoyment and complete happiness. If we can only learn, ever so little, to know the radiant gladness that fills the world of God's love around us, we may receive for ourselves something of the same sense of power and freedom which the child has; we may become, with deeper truth than we usually find in the words, "as little children." For self-assertion is our true life, if we only use the word in a right sense. Christianity must necessarily, as a consequence of all its teaching, lay stress on this; the doctrine of the Incarnation, rightly understood, is the measure of the value we are to set on the lives God Himself became man to redeem. This truth dignifies and raises every conception of work and duty; it lifts men up, as they learn its meaning, into the unseen world of God, where they see His glory, and know that they are the children of an infinite hope. To the child everything is possible; the imagination moves easily from point to point; it knows nothing of any let or hindrance. Existence seems to be summed up in one boundless "I can";—"I can," the cry of life and of hope, as "I cannot," is the wail of despair and death.

When we grow to manhood, when the hours of inspiration of childhood and youth have passed from us, and all the glory that filled the horizon has faded down into the light of common day, the thing of all others that most chills and disappoints us is the discovery of the effort which every task demands from us. Life, instead of being free, as we fancied, appears to be restrained and fettered in countless ways. The chains irk and irritate us; and the result is, men only too often develop into what we ordinarily mean by selfish and self-asserting persons. These may be classed for all practical purposes in two main divisions, who may be said to take for their mottoes the words "I can" and "I cannot."

The former, by sheer force of character, as we so often say, defy the difficulties they meet with; they steadily and persistently assert their power to rise above and to conquer the untoward circumstances of their lives; they are men who are by nature persons of determined character, over whose headstrong wills the teaching of Jesus Christ has had little or no restraining influence. Standing alone, consciously or unconsciously without any knowledge of God, uninfluenced by any thought of a future life, without any intelligent conception of the responsibility we all have for those among whom we live, such a man becomes to himself the centre of thought, almost of worship; his wishes, his wants, his success,—these are the sole motive forces within him; and in the full strong belief in his own capacity to push his way—not sensitive enough, or finely strung enough to contemplate the possibility of mistake or failure in himself—he goes forward, regardless of what may happen to any with whom he comes in contact, utterly indifferent as to who may fall or who may suffer, provided only he may succeed. And so, step by step, the strong pushing man grows into the hard selfish man of the world, who, making great boast of his own capacities and powers, forces his way right on to the prize he means to grasp. Of course, the refinements of cultured life do something to conceal such a character under a decent varnish of consideration for others; good taste and the laws of society require certain courtesies from us in dealing with each other, and he is too shrewd and too alive to his own interests not to comply with these demands.

But selfish as all this is, it is very doubtful whether such a character is really worse than the man who is always depreciating himself. The latter broods over and exaggerates the anxieties of life as they come upon him. He, too, has no sustaining belief in God's goodness, no sense that His Hand is guiding and upholding the course of the world's movements, he takes for his motto the gloomy "I cannot," and refuses even to attempt to make any real effort, but just exists in hopeless listlessness; at times, perhaps, he rouses himself enough to point an epigram or give vent to a sneer at others who are not quite faithless, and are brave enough to be in earnest. This man is just as selfish as the other, quite as intolerable and wicked, and utterly weak, too, into the bargain. Only a miracle could change a character that has developed into any of the worst forms of this indolent selfishness; for here even the feeblest elements of faith are wanting. He that comes to God must at least have some belief that He exists, and that He can in some way give an answer to those who seek Him. The former class had at all events the merit of being alive; this man is dead while he lives. There are, it is to be feared, only too many who have hidden sympathies with such a character; all moody, ill-tempered, grumbling people really belong to this category; they are as selfish as the most pushing self-asserting man could be, and, moreover, they glory in it; they commend themselves for their far-sightedness and good sense in seeing that this world is really very badly put together, and in refusing to show the least contentment amid so very ill-arranged surroundings.

Now both these attitudes of mind are wholly wrong and wicked. They both imply an entire refusal to submit to or to acknowledge the will of God as revealed in the course of the world. They are, in their extreme forms, in reality deadly sin. None of us, we may trust, are as yet entirely given over to such evils as these; and yet we may, many of us, be only too sadly conscious that we are by nature liable to the temptations either of arrogance on the one hand, or of indolent despair on the other; and therefore we need to be carefully on our guard. We must never forget that the bright enthusiasm and eager hope, untouched by personal self-assertion and personal pride, of the simple child-life, the sense of power to do and to be, which is really our birthright, can only be given to men, through the grace of God, as they kneel at the Cross of Jesus Christ. But, it may be said, surely submission to the faith of Christ is the very reverse of self-assertion. True; and yet not the whole truth. You lose your life indeed, but only that you may find it; you lay it down, but only that you may receive it back again; you put yourself under discipline, you struggle against sin and selfishness, and, by God's blessing, gain some mastery over them, but it is only that you may obtain your freedom. You cannot, however much you resent it, get away from the restraints that hedge your life about. It is useless to say, I will be free, I will be independent; after all, try as you may, you cannot be so: servant, ay, slave, you are and you must be; God or the world must be your master. You have, it is true, a power of choice, but however you choose, you remain a servant. People often talk as if the Christian's life must be harder than other men's, because he has to deny himself this and that which otherwise he would allow himself. But, after all, there is no servitude more galling than the hopeless servitude which is the result of the want of all restraint. Ask any one who has, in popular phrase, been living as his own master, recognizing no check on thought or on action, and who then has by God's blessing pulled himself together, and controlled the evil habits and wayward passions, in the full liberty of which he had hitherto been living, he will tell you how hardly he has won his freedom from what, even in those days of boasted liberty, was a detested slavery.

But pass under the yoke of Jesus Christ, accept the teaching of His Church, surrender yourself fully and for ever to His service, and at once all the fetters and chains begin to fall away from your life. Anxiety and worry and pain and sorrow and death—the servant of Christ can go out to meet all these in quietness and confidence. The hope that dominates his life is far away out of their reach; "none of these things move"[1] him. He has but to seek to know the will of God, and then to bend all his energies, come what may, at any and every cost, to fulfil it. He will make mistakes, ay, and what are for the moment even bitter mistakes; but in the mercy of God he knows he can through these mistakes reach the goal towards which his face is steadily set. He knows, too, that, however he may fail, the truth stands for ever unchangeable, and knowing this, he can work and hope under conditions that otherwise would seem the completest failure. For life has been given back to him by his Lord and Master, endowed with the strength of an unfading hope. His trials are the pledges of his redemption; the chains that bind him are the means whereby he works out his freedom. The sense of capacity and power, always stunted and distorted when it turned only to himself, now knows

[1] Acts xx. 24.

neither limit nor restraint. As his faith grows clearer, he moves onward till he reaches the magnificent self-assertion of St. Paul, "I can do all things;" but he adds, "through Christ which strengtheneth me."

Let no one, however, imagine that because he can rise for a time to the height of a true sympathy with these enkindling Christian ideals, he has therefore a right to call this hope his own. All this which has been spoken about is the end, not the beginning, the goal and not the starting-point, of the Christian life. If we desire to have a real share in this hope, then we must endure the hardness of the contest through which it can be won—a contest not so much of words as of acts—a moral as well as an intellectual struggle. If we will not do the will of God manifested to us in our consciences, which says to us imperatively "Do this" or "Avoid that," then it is to little purpose that we spend our days or our nights in discussion as to the being of God, or of our relation to Him, in words and word-fencing, in which the dominant thought is only too often our own cleverness, the last thought the wonders of the goodness and the love of Him whose Name is so readily upon our lips. "If any man willeth to do the will of God"—$\dot{\epsilon}\alpha\nu$ $\tau\iota\varsigma$ $\theta\dot{\epsilon}\lambda\eta$ $\tau\dot{o}$ $\theta\dot{\epsilon}\lambda\eta\mu\alpha$ $\alpha\dot{\upsilon}\tau o\hat{\upsilon}$ $\pi o\iota\hat{\epsilon}\iota\nu$—"he shall know of the doctrine."[1] The question is, Do we, with all the energy of a determined purpose, will to

---

[1] St. John vii. 17.

do the will of God as He has revealed it to us? If so, then in the present knowledge of conquered sin, in the growing self-confidence which has its root in self-discipline and self-dedication, we do, even in the earliest years of our life with God, receive some foretaste of that sense of freedom and strength and power which shall be ours when at the last, through whatever of pain and effort He, in His mercy, may appoint for us, we attain to the glad and willing service of perfect love. When that day comes we shall be able to take as our own these wonderful words of St. Paul, "I can do all things through Christ which strengtheneth me"—Πάντα ἰσχύω, ἐν τῷ ἐνδυναμοῦντί με Χριστῷ.

XII.

Self-purification.

"We know that, when He shall appear, we shall be like Him; for we shall see Him as He is. And every man that hath this hope in him purifieth himself, even as He is pure."—1 St. John iii. 2, 3.

(Sixth Sunday after Epiphany, February 14, 1886.)

The Collect, Epistle, and Gospel for the Sixth Sunday after Epiphany seem at first sight to belong to the season of Advent; a little reflection, however, soon tells us that there is a very great difference between the attitude of the Church to-day and that which she takes on the Sundays that precede the Christmas Festival. There are two great motive powers that draw men to God—love and fear; in Advent the Church appeals, with all the incisiveness she can command, to the second of these motives—fear; and in her Master's name endeavours to rouse souls that are numbed and dead, held in the bondage of sloth and sin, by the vivid announcement of the judgment to come, of the account men must one day give of all that they have done and all that they have left undone in their life here on earth. This morning the second coming of our Lord is put before us as the climax of the great series of manifestations of Himself for us men and for our salvation; we are not bidden to think of a fallen world in the presence of its Judge, but we are pointed onwards to the fulfilment, in the return to her of her Lord, of the supreme hope, in the strength of which the Christian Church has done its work in the world from the first day till now. This hope, "that He will come again, and receive us unto Himself,"[1] is set clear before us, as that, in which we should find the stimulus and the quickening energy necessary for the work of self-purification, which is laid upon each one of us by Almighty God. "We know that, when He shall appear, we shall be like Him;" and he "that hath this hope purifieth himself."

What have we to say to this claim upon us? What is our personal share in this hope? If we are seriously anxious to prove ourselves in this respect, there is, I think, one simple and direct test which we may apply to our lives. What would be the effect upon us, if—to make an assumption, which merely as an assumption seems to be little short of impious— it could be proved to us, by an irresistible demonstration, that the faith of the Church of Christ was an utter and complete illusion? Would this make any

[1] St. John xiv. 3.

serious difference in our mode of life? Should we then do things which now we do not do, or leave undone what now we do? It is not enough to say, that we should think a great loss had been inflicted upon us; that great and wonderful possibilities that up till now we had vaguely felt to be behind our lives, would be there no longer; this no doubt, in the province of thought and imagination, may be very generally true; but beyond and above this, should we otherwise continue to live very much as we do at this moment? or should we know that life had lost its meaning and its purpose? that the very gladness had gone out of the sunshine? that strength and dignity had passed away from human friendship? that grace and tenderness had perished for ever out of human love? In a word, is the centre of gravity of our lives here in the things we see and touch and know through the bodily senses, or there where Jesus our Lord sits at the right hand of God?

But let me assume, as I fain would this morning, that all of us would accept this test for ourselves, that we all claim our part in this hope; feeble, perhaps, our share in it may be, far, very far, short of the vivid realization of its truth that belongs to the strong Christian life; but in the mercy of God it is true that the hope is ours, and, in faith in Him, it is a sure hope, and we know that we can trust it; and so, having this hope, we purify ourselves.

Purify ourselves—is this possible? Surely not; surely we cannot of ourselves do any good thing. We have no power of ourselves to help ourselves. This is the answer that rises at once to our lips. But we must distinguish two parts in the work of purification—the first regeneration or conversion, which is wholly God's work, and the second sanctification, which is partly our own. In the first we are purely passive, and God in His great goodness gives us of His gifts; but in the second we are called to make use of the grace which He has bestowed upon us. He has given us a talent, and we are bidden to use it. This is the simple truth; although it is no doubt also true that we could not of ourselves do even this, were it not that His grace, to uphold and to sustain us, is continually given us in answer to our prayers. Thus it is true to say that God made us without ourselves; that He renewed and redeemed us without ourselves; but that in the mystery of His love He will not save us without ourselves, and against our will; and therefore it is right to say that they that have this hope purify themselves.

When we first understand that God has really called us to newness of life, when we first of set purpose try to be good, there is, only too often, definite and positive sin in our lives, which we have to meet and to conquer. While our attention is thus of necessity taken up with what I may call external aspects of sin, we are apt to neglect the source and spring of sin in the heart, in the affections and the secret impulses of the will. But we soon learn that it is the little sins, more even than the great sins, that determine the life— or, rather, that great sins are only the outcome, the almost certain outcome, of these sins which we call little. "Nemo repente fuit turpissimus;" even the heathen moralist could teach us this. How many there are who, in earlier days of life, have turned away from words of warning or of counsel with the angry exclamation, "Is thy servant a dog that he should do this great thing?"[1] And then, a few years later, these same men, grown accustomed gradually and secretly to the atmosphere of evil, have set themselves, without shame or remorse, to do the very thing against which they had cried out so vehemently; yes, and perhaps even worse things than this.

In money matters we know that the man who takes care of small expenses is the person least likely to run into debt. Who is there who in social or business concerns would entrust with great responsibilities one who in small things had uniformly failed? It is just the same in the spiritual life; these little sins, as we think them, each small and, in one sense, insignificant as it stands alone—the thoughtless jest at goodness, the words that wound and embitter others, the ill-temper that jars on those about us, the unwillingness to put ourselves even a little out of the way for another's convenience,

[1] 2 Kings viii. 13.

the idle story we told, the innuendo of evil in what we said that poisoned our own thoughts, and sent its destroying venom into another's soul, one younger than ourselves, one, perhaps, whom God had committed to our charge—these little sins, as we think them, choke and poison the springs of life, and so make possible those more terrible outbursts of evil at which sometimes the whole world seems to stand appalled. Each snowflake is as nothing, yet the piled-up flakes soon bury the earth out of our sight; each grain of sand is unregarded, but the heaped-up grains may form the graves of cities. So in the spiritual life, the passing touches of impurity and passion, the hasty words of unkindness, the single acts of ill-temper and self-indulgence, the idle words and tales,—these, and such as these, each but little in themselves, are gathering one by one around the souls of men, and burying them beneath a load of sin; of sin, the end of which may sometimes be—God only knows how often—spiritual death. We who have lived but to middle life, know something of broken and wasted lives, that lie, as it were, cast aside along the highway of the world by which we ourselves have come; not always hopeless, thank God for that, despite the outward failure and ruin and disaster; but we have seen the pain and the loss and the suffering, even where there is not the utter darkness of spiritual death, and, knowing this, we would plead with men, and, if God wills, persuade them.

I allowed myself just now to say that there were such things as little sins; I spoke as a man; bring the slightest breath of evil, the least word of unkindness, the least touch of wrong, and set it in thought in the sight of the eternal purity, the boundless love, the infinite holiness of Almighty God, and try to see it but once as He sees it, and you will never speak of a little sin again.

If we would keep this hope, which God has given us, bright and strong, if we would have it grow with our growth and strengthen with our strength, then we must do all we can, to bring every thought and intent of our hearts into obedience to His Divine will. God asks of us a hard thing; yes, that is true, as men think and speak. But He asks no more than we—through faith and hope and love—can learn to do, and in doing win our only true happiness. Let us, then, thank Him with our whole heart and soul for the mercy which has given us this task of self-purification through which we may prove and test the reality of the hope that is in us.

XIII.

The Work of Life.

"Their eyes were holden that they should not know Him."—
ST. LUKE xxiv. 16.

(FIFTH SUNDAY AFTER EASTER, MAY 30, 1886.)

IN the course of the first Easter Day two men left Jerusalem to go to the village of Emmaus, some seven or eight miles distant, where one and possibly both of them lived. The name of one, Cleopas, is given us—he must not be confused, however, with the better known Clopas or Alphæus of the gospel history—the name of the second is unknown, except in a late and entirely untrustworthy tradition. They did not belong to the inner circle of the apostles; they were only ordinary members of that small body of followers of Jesus Christ, who had built their hopes high on the temporal deliverance He would work for Israel; and now that they had witnessed what they thought to be the complete wrecking of these hopes, they were going back to their village life, taking with them the memory of a great enthusiasm which had once possessed them, but which now had entirely vanished away. They walked along oppressed with that sense of desolation, of utter dulness and deadness, that comes over men when all that filled up the expectations of the future, all that gave body and shape to the coming years, has crumbled away into nothingness. At such crises of their lives men must endeavour, if they have character and courage, to construct some new plan of life, something that shall supply anew the motive power to action; if they cannot do this, if they are weak men, they live on as best they can, cheating their fancies with dreams of what might have been, with the memory of what they have lost; they live, as we say, "in the past," the dreariest verdict surely that can be given on any life.

But for the moment, however stable the strength and purpose may be that are in the man, he can only wander in thought along the road he has just travelled; he can only discuss and re-discuss all that he has passed through, if perchance he may discover in what he made his mistake. And so these two disciples were talking together of the things that had happened to them, and trying to see how it was they had altogether misinterpreted the character of their master. And as they talked they were joined by a third Person. How He came we are not told; but He came, St. Mark tells us, "in another form"— with a figure and an appearance different from that they had known—which is but the physical explanation of St. Luke's words, that "their eyes were holden." After a time He joins in their conversation, and asks the reason of their sadness, and the subject of their earnest debate. They, naturally enough, take Him to be one of the many strangers who came to Jerusalem for the Passover festival, and are astonished that He could have been there during the preceding week without knowing something of what had happened. "Knowest Thou not the things that have come to pass?" His reply, without answering their question, leads them to make a fuller explanation. He said to them, "What things?" And they answered, "Concerning Jesus of Nazareth, whom the chief priests and our rulers delivered to be condemned to death and to be crucified. But we trusted that it had been He that should have redeemed Israel. Yea, and certain women of our company who were early at the sepulchre found not His Body, and came, saying that they had seen a vision of angels, who said that He was alive; and certain of them that were with us went to the sepulchre, and found it even so as the women had said; but Him they saw not." "We trusted it had been He that should have redeemed Israel;" "but Him they saw not:" these two sentences sum up the matter. The first tells us of the complete loss of any hope they had: the women's story they put down to mere excitement;

the men of their company went to the sepulchre, and it turned out as they knew it must—"Him they saw not." And then, in answer to their words, our Blessed Lord takes them back through all the history of the Jewish Scriptures, and passing from point to point, explains how there was a divine necessity for this, that Christ should suffer these things, and so should enter into His glory. It is hard for us now to understand how it was they did not know Him; but, blind as they were, they at least perceived that He was no ordinary person. When they reached their journey's end, and He would have gone further, they entreated Him to stay with them. Already He had given them new thoughts and new hopes; He could surely teach them much more, and, it may be, in the end answer those questions they had so earnestly debated when they started from Jerusalem. And then, in the house at Emmaus, He, with no questioning on their part, appears naturally to take the head of the table at their evening meal, and He blesses the bread and the wine, and gives them the Eucharistic Food, and in that act they know Him and He passes out of their sight.

Here we read, as in a parable, the secret of our own life's history: for we all are travellers, journeying forward on our way through the world, sometimes glad and lighthearted, sometimes earnestly questioning and debating, perplexed and confused by the difficulties about us; and with us, close beside us, is One whom we do not know, for our eyes are holden.

"Our eyes are holden." We all admit that we are here to serve God, and to do the work which He has given us to do; but very few of us realize all that is involved in this admission. It means, in truth, a great deal more, and also a great deal less than we commonly suppose. God, indeed, gives us a place and a share in His work; but, if I may put it so without being misunderstood, it is for our own sake, rather than for His. Still it remains true that Almighty God does stoop down to us and consent to need us, His creatures though we are. We each have something to do for Him; perhaps no great thing—here indeed may be the point of our trial—but yet something which He asks of us, and which we can do. We may not understand it, or see clearly what it is—for "our eyes are holden." Think for one moment what it would have meant to have been the author of the thirty-first Psalm, and so to have written the words that would come from the lips of our Blessed Lord at the moment of His death. Is it a great exaggeration to think that the author of this psalm might, in writing it, have done, though quite unwittingly, his special work? But, however we may think of this, depend upon it we have each our task to fulfil: and although we may not know where or when it comes to us, all our life and education is a preparation for it; and the opportunity—it may be but a moment, the supreme moment of all our lives—comes and goes, and we do not know what we have done or what we have left undone. In the clear light of the future, when we stand face to face with our Lord, then we shall hear His gracious "Well done," or shall know that we have failed. "Our eyes are holden" now. The things we think so important, and of which we are inclined to say, "Well, in this or in that I think I have a right to feel I can do something," these are again and again really so unimportant; but some little duty, some effort, some task that now appears beneath our notice, just a cup of cold water given in the Lord's name, we shall, perhaps, one day know to have been the turning-point of life.

But if we think too little of our work in one way, in another we are given to think too much of it. We look round upon the movements and activities of the world; at best we see but the surface of things, and even what we see we misunderstand and misinterpret. When, for example, we think of the many difficulties that beset the Church of Christ within and without, we are apt to attach an undue importance to those who are, as we think, taking the right side; we are apt sometimes to take an exaggerated view of our own personal importance, of our own necessity to God's work. We are by no means so necessary as we sometimes think we are; our exertions, our influence, our undertakings on God's behalf are not, after all, the main life and strength of the Faith. "My Father worketh hitherto, and I work."[1] Here is the true key to the problem: hidden from the gaze of men, beyond their ken and their prying, God works His work in the world; and men shall do to His Church, that which He allows them to do. There will be days of seeming growth and success, of what men regard as prosperity; there will be times of flagging and disappointment, of what men regard as failure and decay; parties will rise and fall; faction and heresy, misbelief and unbelief shall do their utmost even within His sacred fold; but under all and through all He alone works, He alone sustains and guides, and His work cannot fail, the gates of hell shall not prevail against His Church.

Let no one imagine that to think thus robs life of its fulness and intensity; after all it is only saying in other words that we live by faith alone. This knowledge sobers and steadies us; but it does not impoverish, on the contrary it enriches our life. Nothing can be unimportant when such great issues are at stake; not the smallest duty, not the most insignificant act or thought. We do not know where God will meet us, where He will need us; whether in what the world regards as our more important

[1] St. John v. 17.

duties and responsibilities, or in the unnoticed and unrecognized byways of our lives. And so all our work, in the least matters as well as in the greatest, must be done for Him alone. Thus life takes a steadier, stronger tone: "our eyes are holden" it is true, but still we cannot, if we are really faithful, fail in the end. Whatever our weakness, the truth is what it is, and we are servants of the Lord of Truth. We work and are glad; now we are full of excitement and hope, now we are crushed beneath a load of despair; we go eagerly forward on our way, or life drags on with dull and weary effort; but through all our varying moods, under all the changing circumstances of the hurrying days, God our Father works out His merciful purpose for the world, and we are called on to do our part in His service, undazzled by success, unmoved by failure, undismayed by weakness.

Life moves quickly by us: to say so to the young and vigorous is to speak to deaf ears. Some of us, however, look back on many years that have passed away, since first we came to Oxford: twenty or thirty years sounds a long time, and a great deal may happen in them; but they are as nothing to look back upon; and yet they account for all the difference that there is between a schoolboy and a man in middle life. When we remember this and think of the eternal issues for good and for ill that hang upon the use we make of the years that pass so swiftly from us, we may well feel that we would give all we have if only we could bring right home to the hearts and consciences of one single generation of men in this place all that it means to call ourselves Christians; all that the Creed has to teach us as to the end for which we were born, as to the goal towards which our days are hastening on.

All through the journey of your life, though your eyes are holden and you see Him not, Christ is there beside you. He is calling you, teaching you, now drawing you to Himself by love, now compelling you by discipline; He pleads with you in every hour of your happiness, He constrains you by every claim of your work and duty. And you, how often do you think of Him, remember His Presence, or try to understand His words and to learn His lessons?

And in the end, when the evening of life is at hand, there will await you very little of the rest or hope that belong to the peaceful close of a laborious day, unless your heart has burned within you as, unknown it may be and unrecognized, He has taught you in the past His lessons of patience and endurance, of faith and hope—unless now, in the full vigour of your life and powers, you are day by day learning to hear His voice, and to obey His teaching, and to understand something of your pressing need of His abiding Presence. But if you only begin to learn this, you will have the secret, that shall teach you to put on Him then that constraint to which He will so gladly yield, and to plead with Him with an earnestness that will not be denied, "Abide with me, for it is toward evening and the day is far spent." And so, when the work of life is done, when the light of this world is fading from our sight, we shall learn at last there, within the veil, Who it is who has been with us through all these years on earth, and know Him to be—may His mercy grant it to us all—our Saviour and our God.

XIV.

Truthfulness.

"Speak every man truth with his neighbour: for we are members one of another."—EPH. iv. 25.

(NINETEENTH SUNDAY AFTER TRINITY, OCTOBER 31, 1886.)

IT would, I think, scarcely have occurred to any of us, if we had been explaining the ground of moral action, to have laid down that given in the text by St. Paul as the basis of the virtue of truthfulness; speak the truth, he says, for we are members one of another. The apostle lifts the question right away from those passing motives, which belong to the particular time of life, or to the age in which we live, or to the peculiar circumstances in which we are placed, up to the height of a great ruling principle, given to the world directly by Christ Himself through His Church. He tells us that the principle which should govern men's actions in this, as in all their dealings with each other, lies in the fact of the union of each member of the Church with its head, our Lord and Saviour, and so through Him with all for whom He died. We, members of His Church, are one body in Him—linked each to each by bonds which transcend the limits of space and time—and the firm and sure basis for all our duty to God or to man is found in the complete acceptance of this fundamental truth, "we are members one of another."

We are one body in Christ our Lord. The hand is instinctively true to the eye, and wards off the blow which otherwise might maim or destroy the sight; the eye guides the foot away from the pitfalls that lie about its path; if the eye be darkened or the hand paralyzed the whole body suffers loss—the safety and well-being of the whole man is dependent on the entire trustworthiness, the perfect truthfulness of the communications made by every sense to the brain. And, St. Paul says, the same is true of the Christian body; one Christian should no more deal untruly or insincerely with another—to say nothing of direct falsehood and lying—than the hand should fail the eye in warding off a blow, or the eye allow the feet to stray into a trap or a snare.

We Englishmen are apt to pride ourselves on being a truth-speaking and truth-loving nation. It is only too much open to doubt whether our character in this respect will bear a very serious or very thorough investigation; but truth-speaking is, it is fair to say, a public-school virtue. The old theory that the masters and boys were natural enemies, that the relation between them was at best a sort of veiled warfare, and that consequently many things which would otherwise have been wrong—and among them a considerable laxity in the matter of truthfulness—were quite pardonable, and almost commendable, is now a thing of the past; its day was nearly done some fifty years ago, when the boys at Rugby began to say to each other that it was a shame to tell Arnold a lie, because he always believed what was said. The appeal has been made in our schools to all that was chivalrous and generous in the young, and we can say that the appeal has not been made altogether in vain.

But when we pass on into middle and later life, it is much to be doubted whether we find the same high tone of feeling in regard to this question of truth. No doubt the difficulty and the complexity of the questions we have to answer is then more obvious to us; and this in itself somewhat confuses and perplexes us. But, making all allowance we need for this, it would, I fear, require a great deal of courage to maintain that English life in its social, political, and commercial aspects, was wholly sincere or honest or true.

The early dawn of a summer's day is wonderful. Words fail us if we try to tell of its beauty or speak of the newly-awaking life, as the world, fresh and bright and glad, comes, as it were, recreated from its Maker's hands, without a shadow of weariness or pain or disappointment. The hours pass on, the day wearies and grows old, and then, under the burning heat of the midday sun, the world seems tired and worn; the glory of its early promise has been taken from it; in the glare of the noonday all the graces and mysteries of its shadows and lights and shades are wholly lost. In this we see a symbol of our own lives; they open before us full of the boundless possibilities of an unknown and untried future; but the years gather upon us, and the buoyancy and the eagerness of our younger days are very quickly lost, as the stress and strain of our work begin to tell upon us, as we pass under the burden and the heat of the day of life.

It is this that makes the infinite pathos of work here in Christ Church; to look round us each October on the new group of faces, each year younger and more boylike as they seem to us, who are growing older, and so, in point of age, moving farther away from them; to look round and wonder what may be gathering here for the coming years—these faces often so frank, so generously self-confident, so unconscious that to live can ever seriously mean to be unhappy. Again and again the very faults and weaknesses of a character do much to make it only more winning and more attractive: and unconsciously, beneath all the quick and subtle movements and changes that pass hither and thither like flashes of light, there is in each case a future working itself out

—a future of real usefulness, real goodness, real solid work, so that those who know the man shall be glad because he has lived; or a future, dark with self-seeking and perhaps vice and sin, that his friends shall hereafter wish he had died in his schooldays. Yes, this is the point, is there in us that which will last? Have we any real staying power? Anything, for example—to return to my special subject—that will hold us closely and steadily to that high standard of truthfulness which has hitherto been ours? Or will the generous straightforwardness of youth pass into the sordid selfishness of age? Will truthfulness give place to expediency, till, by tampering with sincerity, life has become hollow and false and untrue to its very core?

The morning of life must pass; the burden and the heat of the day must come upon each one of us; the readiness, the ease of movement, the lift we are conscious of, and imagine will always be at our command—these will one day be lost; we shall become conscious of effort, we shall learn the meaning of failure. All that moved about so lightly and so easily, "in worlds as yet not realized," must gather shape and outline and substance, and in doing so harden and stiffen. We must form definite opinions; the questions put by life must be answered; the mists and clouds of the morning that veil the hilltops, or wrap from our sight the depths of the valley or the level sweep of the meadow, must be dispersed by the growing heat of the sun; till at last everything stands before us clear and distinct in the fierce blaze of midday light. Life is not easier for us as it takes this clearer form; on the contrary, it is harder, it makes greater demands upon us, it takes more out of us. We must still make our ventures of faith which we once made without question, almost without thought. Now we have the measure of things, we make our ventures knowingly—knowing that they are ventures; we have passed under the burden and heat of the work of life; have we staying power? Can we set our teeth, face the stress and strain of things, endure the disappointment of finding that much we hoped for can never be ours, that much we thought we could do is beyond our power? We used to think, perhaps, that we could move mountains; now we know we would thank Almighty God to be allowed to place one single tiny stone in His eternal temple; our one doubt, it may be, was only how we could find time to do all that we had it in us to do; now we work in the faith and the hope, that although we can do so little, so very little, yet no true effort, however weak and halting in itself, ever has been or ever shall be wholly lost. We have a truer measure of our powers; we no longer look for or expect results; we only pray for strength that we may not fail or falter in our duty, or hesitate to do with our might what God has put into our hands to do. We have learned that all things come to an end; but we are, it may be, also beginning to know that His commandment is exceeding broad.[1]

Do not misunderstand me. To throw a slur on the ardour and enthusiasm of the young would be little short of sin: thank God for such gifts as these, and count them as the greatest He could give you; but while you rejoice in your youth, remember that for all these things God will bring you to judgment. This judgment, too, is no thing of the future, but is passed each day, each hour as the years of life go by, as the clouds and the mists of the morning roll aside, and the character stands declared and definite in the sight of men. The quick throb of life, the quiver of excitement that is about you now, the bounding health, the generous rivalries and ambitions, these must pass, and then what will be left? That high tone of feeling that makes schoolboys truthful will not last on, just as it is, to make them truthful in middle and later life; in itself it will pass, and then the question is, what will be left? If you could come safely through the ordeal of life, if you would stand firm and unmoved in the day of your difficulty, then be true as steel now to all you have learnt to know of the will of God; let nothing ever tempt you in the least matter to swerve from that high standard of truthfulness and sincerity which is yours, given you

[1] Ps. cxix. 96.

in your homes and in your school life. Never parley for one moment with impurity, in thought or word or deed; and help others when you may, by making your protest as Christian gentlemen, against loose and idle talk; you cannot listen to this, much less applaud it, without sullying and staining your own souls. Practise that true temperance which is the crown of a manly life in every detail of your bodily wants, and, above all, in the more dangerous question of the use of wine; and if it is in your power, do what you can to save others, who may be weaker than yourselves, from temptation to self-indulgence in any and every form.

And that you may do these things rightly, that your own spiritual growth may be a right and noble development, that you may win the kindliness and courtesy and sympathy which cannot offend, even when it has to show disapproval, remember, I entreat you, in God's name, the duty of prayer. It is not a great deal of time that is asked for; only begin each day by receiving it as God's gift from His Hands, praying Him to guide and keep you that you may not fall into sin; and then end it with confession of the failure, where the failure has been, and with prayer that you may, in the days yet to come, "live more nearly as you pray." And then, as the years pass by, and the hopes and enthusiasms that have ruled you are somewhat spent and dulled, there will have grown and shaped a clear understanding of that which alone can keep men steady under the pressure of the serious work of life—a knowledge of what we mean when we speak of the Incarnation, of what it is to be members of the Body of Christ, and in Him members one of another. This knowledge is the gift of God, given by Him to all who, in prayer and quiet devotion to work and duty, have striven to know the will of God and to do it. And if, through the sin into which we have fallen, its fulness must be at present hidden from us, yet we shall, at least, know whom we have believed and be content to wait, if it be His will, till at last the full knowledge of the love of God in Christ is given us in the life of the world to come.

XV.

Love towards God.

"Charity never faileth."—1 Cor. xiii. 8.

(QUINQUAGESIMA SUNDAY, FEBRUARY 20, 1887.)

AMONG the indications that point towards the doctrine of the fall of man, one may perhaps be found in what we may briefly call the "corruptio optimi." I mean this, that our good is so near evil; that our best lies so very close to our worst; that the higher we rise in our moral life the deeper and more disastrous may be our fall; that the very gifts and graces of our character may become, if we are not careful, the cause of our failure. Our highest virtues are virtues, not as the consequence of their external visible forms, but in consequence of the motives which form the unseen principles of their life; and in subtle unperceived hidden ways these motives may wholly change their character, and our good things become shams and falsehoods, and as such more destructive of true spiritual life than things which men count positive sin. We need not travel far to find examples. There is an unselfishness, as it would be reckoned, which is only the outcome of the addition of a cultured hypocrisy to a subtle self-seeking. Refinement, good manners, good taste, make it obvious enough that selfishness is unlovely, or rather positively revolting; and so, for very self's sake, people find it well to assume the outward semblance of unselfishness. Consequently, as soon as we insist on some duty, or press home the practice of some virtue, we find ourselves at once compelled to guard against the special danger which lies very close to the good which God has made possible for us. As He gives it, it is wholly good; we in our wilfulness are able to corrupt it into what is almost wholly bad.

If we had not been all our lives accustomed to the words, to-day's Epistle would startle us by the emphasis it lays on such thoughts as these. We acknowledge the duty of almsgiving: we have no quiver of doubt as to the directness of the claim upon us; and yet we are told we may give all our goods to feed the poor, and it may profit us nothing. Our almsgiving may be ostentatious and self-centred, and so erect an impassable barrier between our souls and God. We urge the duty of self-devotion: we know that we ought to be ready, if the will of God were so, to give up even life itself for His sake: we call to mind the long roll of Christian martyrs: it may be we can look back upon some one whom we have known, who has given his life in the cause of Christ: and we do well to pray that, if the same call came to us, we in our turn may be ready to obey it. And yet St. Paul tells us we may give our body to be burned, and it may profit nothing. Martyrdom itself may be self-willed; in itself and by itself it is no passport into the kingdom of heaven. We speak of faith in God; we call it the sight of the soul, that by which God may be seen and known and understood; and we urge men to win this faith, and to grow in this knowledge. And yet we may have all faith, we may understand all knowledge and all mysteries, we may speak with the tongues even of angels, and yet be only as sounding brass or a tinkling cymbal.

The corruption of our best; the light that is in us darkness; the knowledge of God, the power and strength and insight of the intellect, that has never touched and purified the heart; outward self-surrender, devotedness, care for others—all these may be only the very subtlest form of self-seeking. How many a large subscription is given to this or that charity and the reward received in the full when popular applause acclaims the giver? How much is done for others from the mere pleasure in activity, or in consequence of the gratification we enjoy in the sense of superiority which is ours, when we are able to help or, as we almost unconsciously regard it, patronize others? How much, too, is done, which looks outwardly like the purest unselfishness, from that eagerness for popularity which is so great a snare to sensitive natures? Indeed, men who are thought to be, and who are, in the best sense of the words, good men, have need to remember the warning of our Lord, "Woe unto you, when all men shall speak well of you!"[1] Would men do many things they now do if the consequence was that they made themselves unpopular? Would they go on giving time, money, thought, if they gained by their actions no consideration? or if by what they did they positively lost caste in the eyes of others?

The Epistle for to-day, however, points us to one grace which, alone of all God's spiritual gifts to us, rises clear above every danger of degradation or misuse, and that gift is Charity, or Love. The Love of God Himself above all created things, and the Love of man in God and for God,—this, St. Paul says, never fails. All other gifts, even the greatest, as faith and hope, may be said, in a sense, to begin from ourselves, and to move out from ourselves towards God; but Love is the fire the Saviour came to kindle upon the earth. "Love is God Himself," I quote the words of one well remembered by some of us in this place,[2] "His very substance

---

[1] St. Luke vi. 26.
[2] The Rev. E. B. Pusey, D.D. Cf. Sermon xxxviii. of "Cathedral and Parochial Sermons."

the very bond of union of the Co-equal Trinity." Thus the Holy Spirit, who is God, and therefore is Love, sheds abroad in the hearts of men that Love which is Himself; and we learn to love God because He first loved us; and so from the hearts of men there flows back to Almighty God that Love which comes from Him; it is from Him, and it moves back to Him.

And therefore Love cannot fail. Faith will vanish for ever in the unveiled presence of God; it will be lost and swallowed up in sight: hope can have no place at all when the soul has received the full revelation of Him whom now it dimly longs for, yearns after, and moves towards: but it is not so with Love. Now it may be but poor and feeble at its best, but then it will grow ever richer and fuller and stronger. Love will then be all that the soul can ask or need. It will be, it is in itself, heaven. It is that fulness of joy which is in God's presence, those pleasures at His right hand which endure for evermore.[1] Therefore, Love is the touchstone of the spiritual life; so far as we have it, faith, hope, self-denial, self-discipline, knowledge of God, devotedness, if it may be even to death, these and all other Christian gifts and graces are placed beyond the reach of corruption or degradation or misuse. Without Love we may have every other

[1] Ps. xvi. 12.

virtue and grace, and yet, as St. Paul tells us, be nothing.

When Jesus our Lord—He who is God, and therefore is Love itself—was here among men in bodily presence, He tried them by this test; and it often happened that the learned, the intellectually brilliant, the outwardly strict, the careful keeper of the law, the Pharisee, failed to respond to it. Such men had knowledge, they gave alms, they were the distinguished for the external correctness and propriety of their conduct, they were—stress is often laid upon this point—quite free from gross outward sin: but in spite of all this they were nothing, while of the woman who was a sinner Jesus said, "Her sins, which are many, are forgiven; for she loved much."[1] In saying this no apology is suggested for a lax or careless life. We, at all events, in this place, are without excuse; shielded and protected during our childhood in Christian homes, guarded and fenced round in countless ways, so that we have almost of set purpose to seek out opportunities of open sin,—in us, if in any, the ordinary virtues of the Christian life must be found; uprightness, truthfulness, purity, unselfishness, sincerity, these and all such Christian graces should be simply matters of course with us. The point is this, and we should do well never to forget it, that we may

[1] St. Luke vii. 47.

possess all these graces,—we may be strictly honest, sober, temperate, chaste,—and yet be none of His. We, who perhaps think ourselves good men, and whom men about us think to be good, may be shut out of heaven, and others, who have been looked down upon as lost and outcasts in this world, the publican and the harlot, may be found among the number of the redeemed. "They shall come from the east, and from the west, and from the north, and from the south, and shall sit down in the kingdom of God,"[1] and we, the children of the kingdom, churchmen, baptized, communicants, may be for ever shut out. If Jesus Christ were to come among us to-day in visible form, is there no chance St. John's words would once more be fulfilled to the letter, "He came unto His own, and His own received Him not?"[2] Would it not probably be one series of surprises, as He rejected and upbraided some whom the world calls good and great; while He had compassion on and was welcomed and recognized by some poor and, as we think, degraded people who live surrounded by all the temptations of our crowded cities?

How, then, are we to win this Love towards God? The only answer is, as has been well said, learn to love by loving. We learn to run by running, and to row by rowing, so learn to love by loving. Teach yourself, therefore, to see God everywhere. This should not be

---

[1] St. Luke xiii. 29.   [2] St. John i. 11.

difficult for us; for about our favoured lives there is an untold abundance of goodness; goodness which surely must command our thankfulness, and through our thankfulness should lead us on to Love. All the wealth of knowledge, all the possibilities of happiness that come with good health, with those capacities and opportunities for pure enjoyment which God has given to so many of us, all the beauty of this world in which we live,—there is none of us in the place who has not a real share in some or all of these. Do they not call on us to be glad and thankful? All of us, I suppose, have stamped indelibly upon our memories pictures of nature's loveliness, which, if we lived for centuries, would be as vivid at the end of them as they are now, or were when we looked upon them, it may be, years ago; as we gazed then upon the radiant glory of the face of nature, we seemed for a time to stand within the very presence-chamber of Almighty God. The dullest of us cannot remain wholly unmoved at such moments as these; yet if we were only more thoughtful, we should realize that the meanest flower that grows upon the ground could teach us something of the eternal beauty. And God created all this wonder and glory, and has given us power and capacity to see them and to understand them and to rejoice in their beauty. Thank Him, then, with unfeigned hearts, for His priceless gifts. Acknowledge Him in everything; accept everything as coming from Him; and compel yourself, even when you feel most dull and hard, to say the "Gloria Patri," and as you say the words to remember what they mean. And if Love can grow up strong and clear from the recognition of God's gifts in nature, what should it become when men have learned the meaning of sin, and the mercy and the grace of forgiveness? when they have heard ever so faintly the voice that says, "Son, be of good cheer, thy sins are forgiven thee?" when they have begun to understand something of the hope given to mankind in the resurrection of Christ our Lord from the grave?

Train yourselves, then, to love God. Begin by loving Him because you need Him; He will accept even such selfish love as this. But do not rest here; it is indeed an impossible halting place. Press on and learn to love God because He is God; and to love all men, yes, and even yourself too—if it may be put so—for His sake. We indeed are often tired and out of heart; and sometimes we are sullen and ill-tempered, and then we feel we cannot continue to make the effort demanded of us; we begin to doubt whether we have in us any capacity of loving God at all. And yet we know that this Love is the goal of our life's journey, the end for which we were born, the purpose for which we came into the world; and, knowing this, we must utterly refuse to be turned aside from our purpose because we cannot always command our unstable feelings and emotions. In the dark days, whether they are many or few, as well as in the bright, in cloud as well as in sunshine, have one fixed purpose before you to learn something of this Love for God. The unswerving purpose is the proof of your sincerity, and the pledge of your success. And this Love, however feeble it may seem at times, will never wholly leave you; it lights up with its own brightness the face of the visible world, and shows us created things as a veil through which there shines out upon us something of the Infinite glory; it fills up with an untold wealth of meaning all the mysteries of music; it reveals itself through all true and pure and noble work in literature and in art; and then, when we reach the rough and difficult places of life's journey along which we must all of us sooner or later travel, this Love can make the rough places smooth, and reveal to us sorrow and pain and even death itself as the messengers of a peace of God which passes the understanding of men.

XVI.

The Anxieties of Life no Excuse for Failure of Courage.

"He that observeth the wind shall not sow; and he that regardeth the clouds shall not reap."—ECCLES. xi. 4.

(TWENTY-FIRST SUNDAY AFTER TRINITY, OCTOBER 30, 1887.)

WE may well feel a little astonished that a book like this from which the text is taken has ever been admitted into the sacred canon. The writer is one who has enjoyed a position of absolute power, such as is only possible to an Eastern despot. Every wish, every imagination of his heart, that it was in human power to gratify had received its gratification; he had been endowed with great gifts of intellect; the treasures of wisdom had been set within his reach, and he had made no bad use of his opportunities; wealth, power, knowledge—these, with all their varying interests, he had been allowed to make his own; and yet, as he looks back upon them all, he repeats over each in turn his one hopeless refrain, "vanity of vanities, all is vanity": and therefore he praises the dead, which are already dead, more than the living which are yet alive; and better than both, he declares, is he that hath not been, who hath not seen the evil work that is done under the sun.

There are, it is certain, some amongst us now who may learn very useful and very necessary lessons from this book; and who, therefore, may well be thankful that this phase of human experience is represented so fully in the Bible.

The century in which we live has been a time of unprecedented and marvellous growth in many different directions; perhaps the most marvellous of all the wonders we have seen is the extraordinary success which has attended men in their endeavour to develop the resources of the earth, with its consequent enormous increase of material wealth. Certainly we in these islands have not been slow to avail ourselves of the opportunities thus offered to us. For the time men seem to have forgotten everything else in their haste to take possession of the kingdom of wealth so opened out before them. In the first rush of these years of prosperity it was declared in words that have been often quoted, and which—so one said who heard them spoken—seemed in their jubilant exultation as the heralds of the handwriting on the wall against our nation, that "our prosperity was advancing by leaps and bounds." Now, at all events, we appear to have run through our fortune, and, under the influence of widespread commercial depression, other consequences of the vast movement of the present century are steadily and persistently forcing themselves to the front; and social and political problems, the extent and reach of which not the wisest man can foresee or estimate, are looming in the near future before us:—problems, too, which are certain and unavoidable, and for which some solution must be found; for we cannot turn back the stream of time, or rewrite the history of the world. There is enough going forward in this present year to give us food for serious thought; and the coming years must be years of anxious conflict between varying opinions and interests and necessities, as the old order changes, giving place to the new.

But the experience through which we have immediately come has been in many ways a bad preparation for the work before us; for our supreme need is faith. And yet in an age of material growth and material prosperity men's minds have been entirely diverted to the things that belong to the world of sense. All the modes of thought that have become habitual to them, all the principles that guide their decisions, and determine them to action or inaction,—all these turn on immediate and material consequences or experiences, on what they touch, and taste, and handle, and see. And more than this, our intellectual advance can be turned against us: it has been said that thought is fatal to action; that education deprives men of the ability to decide important issues, to form judgments at a great crisis; since, as a result of their education, they learn to look, or try to look, too far ahead. Their imaginations are quickened; they fear consequences, they foresee possible disaster, and therefore become nerveless and hesitating, and grow incapable of making the great ventures of faith that come naturally and easily to simpler minds. Without attempting to ascertain the value that should be attached to decisions that confessedly are what they are through the ignorance of those who make them, we need not hesitate to allow that the call made upon a man's faith is greater, in proportion to his capacity to understand how vital are the issues that depend upon his decisions or his actions. And herein lies the supreme necessity of faith at this moment. It is, indeed, a hard task to regain this virtue, to win it back in days when all that we have been taught about the unseen world, about God and the soul, as to the meaning and consequence of sin, as to the certainty of the judgment, all that belongs to the supernatural or preternatural is not so much denied, but seems rather in many cases simply to have vanished out of the sphere of human consciousness. Even when these things are recognized by the acceptance of outward practices or by the repetition of verbal formulæ, they are unconsciously denied and entirely set at nought by the manner of men's lives. All must know something of what this means, since the intellectual atmosphere in which we live cannot but influence our own life and conduct. The spirit that dominates the world has found its way within the Church, and has taken a far deeper hold than we like to acknowledge on those who in name and profession are servants of Jesus our Lord and our God. There are only too many who prefer not to put the matter too seriously to the test. The external difficulties of the Church, its political relations, party questions, party zeal—these provide outlets for activity—they recognize, in a way, the acknowledged claim of the Lord of the Church for personal devotion and personal love. Social problems, practical questions as they are called, are sometimes welcomed with an almost feverish eagerness; they do something to bring satisfaction to the deeper needs of the heart; in the excitement of their prosecution, and in the rush of action men lose and forget themselves, and no longer need to consider whether they can give an account of the faith that is in them, or whether there is in them any faith at all. And yet when the tide of enthusiasm slackens, in presence of mistake and failure, when face to face with hard questions that urgently demand an immediate answer, when looking forward to the many anxieties that surround the coming years, men find that they need something more than enthusiasm for hard work. Faith in the righteousness and love of God alone can stand us in good stead at the critical moments of life;

this alone can teach us to take no thought for the morrow, to say, not merely as a formula with the lips, but with the whole energy of the heart and will, "Though He slay me, yet will I trust in Him;"[1] this alone can rise to the sublime confidence of the Three Holy Children, and in whatever danger of the present or anxiety for the future, simply say, "Our God whom we serve is able to deliver us: but, if not, we will not serve thy gods nor worship the golden image."[2]

The writer of Ecclesiastes presses home this lesson. Live, he seems to say to us, for wealth or pleasure or knowledge as ends in themselves, and do so under the happiest and most favourable conditions, and the soul, at last satiated and weary, will find all to be but vanity and vexation of spirit. Man cannot live by bread alone: life means more than simply living; it is a trial, a discipline, by means of which character grows and shapes itself; and, when it is done, the soul passes on to the judgment. Whatever your present condition may be, whether you are rich or poor, glad or sorry, know assuredly that for all these things God will bring you to judgment. Therefore, whatever thy hand findeth to do, do it with thy might; therefore fear God and keep His commandments, for this is the whole duty of man. Never forget that if you dream and brood and murmur, if you give yourself up to the evil spirit of pessimism, the end can only be utter ruin and loss. The man

[1] Job xiii. 15.   [2] Daniel iii. 17, 18.

who does nothing but watch the wind and the clouds will never even sow his seed, much less reap his harvest.

Here, then, is our lesson: amid whatever perplexities, anxieties, or hesitations, we must keep a firm hold on our belief in the love and the goodness of Almighty God; we must trust Him, believe in Him, hope in Him; even if it seems quite impossible, yet we must still trust, still believe, still hope; we must look away from our little despondencies up to Him; He, "Deus rerum tenax vigor," alone guides and sustains the world through all its changes. To the Christian one thing, and only one thing, is certain, and that is the Will of God. He has set us here, in all this eager active life; He wills for us all this strain and stress of outward circumstances; we have received no promise of temporal success or temporal reward, no promise even that truth shall prevail, and error be destroyed; the very gifts He gives men may be turned against Him; men may win freedom, or knowledge, or power only through them to deny and reject Him who gave them all. But these are not reasons for one moment's hesitation. Admit, if it be so, that the forecasts of the most hopeless men amongst us are to be justified: even then the trial that is to try the Church is the will of God for her. In this trial is our discipline; under these conditions, and no other, our characters are to be formed and developed; here we are to be witnesses for Him; in this way to prove, or, perhaps I might say, to win our love for Him.

So far as we are true to the Creed of the Church of Christ, hopelessness, faithlessness, is an impossibility. No doubt it is hard to be so entirely true; but we may and must cling firmly to the faith we have, however poor and weak and halting it may be. "Lord, increase our faith," will be our daily, hourly, almost momentary prayer. Under all the pressing anxieties of this age in which we live, we, servants of our Incarnate Lord, dare not stand moodily aside, refusing to do our part, until we can see our way right on to an assured and certain end. While we are criticizing—and everything can be criticized—while we are hesitating, doubting, shuddering, the years of life are slipping past us, our opportunities are missed, and the days in which we might have worked for God are lost for ever. Come what may, the movement of the ages is, after all, the will of Almighty God, working out its one great purpose to one assured and perfect end. We must work in this living present. We dare not wrap the one talent He has given us in a napkin, and bury it away out of sight; we must set ourselves steadily to the duty which lies before us; we must be ready to risk something, to venture something, and then to leave the result in His hands. It is treachery to His goodness to allow His gifts to us of increased knowledge and increased insight to unnerve our hearts, or to paralyze our wills.

Faith, prayer, and hard work[1]—here lies the bounden duty of each member of the Body of Christ. We may make mistakes: as we get older we shall learn the truth of this by sad and sorrowful experience; but it is better, far better, so than, for fear of mistakes, to dream away the years of life. We are under no illusions; we are not the victims of a shallow optimism; we are fully aware of the dark side of life's picture; we cannot under-estimate the strength of sin, who see in it the power that nailed the Lord Jesus to His cross; we know the disasters it has worked in the past; we have no reason to think it will be less powerful in the future; we have seen the ruin it has made of many and many a life; we know it yet more clearly in the hand to hand struggle with the evil of our own hearts. But we believe and are sure that we have been set to take our part in this conflict by Perfect Love; and in this certainty we may learn, if we will, the lesson of patient endurance, of quiet steadfastness in duty; we may discover the secret of a power that will give us courage and cheerfulness through the difficulties and anxieties, whatever they may be, in which we are called upon to work; and so we may at last, by God's blessing, learn to make our own those words of St. Paul's, "We know whom we have believed, and are persuaded that He is able to keep that which we have committed unto Him against the day of Christ."[2]

---

[1] Cf. Gal. v. 6.   [2] 2 Tim. i. 12.

XVII.

The Life of the World to come.

"I saw a new heaven and a new earth."—REV. xxi. 1.

(SEPTUAGESIMA SUNDAY, JANUARY 29, 1888.)

IN the Church of England since the sixteenth century (in this continuing a custom that dates from the days of St. Chrysostom),[1] part of our preparation for the

---

[1] Cf. Bingham, vol. v. p. 57 (Oxford University Press, 1855). The sermon on Genesis i. 1, mentioned here, was preached (see "Tillemont Memoirs," vol. xi. 42) on February 16, 386, being the first day of Lent, the Monday after the seventh Sunday before Easter. This is the day on which Lent is still reckoned as beginning in the Eastern Church.

The author has not ascertained when Genesis i. was first read on Septuagesima Sunday. It is appointed for this day in the Benedictine Breviary and in all breviaries of the Roman type. No date can be assigned for its introduction; but as St. Chrysostom tells us that Genesis was always read during Lent, it is possible that, as the preparation for Lent in the West was pushed further back, the reading of Genesis was begun earlier; if so the question resolves itself into the fixing of the date when Septuagesima Sunday was first observed in its present form. The above suggestion is supported by the fact that the Ambrosian Breviary, which includes Septuagesima, begins Genesis the Monday after Septuagesima, while the Mozarabic, which has no Septuagesima, begins Genesis on the Monday after the first Sunday in Lent.

Duchesne (Origines du culte Chrétien, pp. 234, seq.) gives reason

season of Lent has been to read in public the earlier chapters of the Book of Genesis. And so this morning we have once more read how, in the beginning, God created the heavens and the earth—and created them pure and perfect and good, without any dark shadow of pain or sorrow; "God saw everything that He had made, and behold it was very good." But this is not

to suppose that Septuagesima and the two following Sundays were fixed, *i.e.* had proper Masses attached to them, at about the same time as the four odd days from Ash Wednesday to the following Saturday were added to make up the forty days of the Quadragesima. The latter were not observed in Gregory the Great's time, but they are found in the "Gelasian Sacramentary" of the Eighth Century, in which Septuagesima, Sexagesima, and Quadragesima are also found.

In "Edward VI. and the Book of Common Prayer," published by F. A. Gasquet, O.S.B., and E. Bishop, it is stated, on p. 384, that "the interest of the comparison (of the Lectionaries drawn up at the Reformation period) really lies in the proof afforded of the gradual tendency to substitute the civil for the ecclesiastical year; and for an arrangement which in some measure corresponded with the ecclesiastical seasons, a mechanical 'lectio continua' of the Scriptures"; and lower down the transference of Genesis (of course in the week-day lessons) to January is noted as an illustration of what is objected to. The Church of England has, however, practical justification from ancient sources for reading Genesis in January as well as in Lent. In the "Comes," which is sometimes, but erroneously, referred to Jerome (probably the date is two or three centuries later), Genesis ii. vers. 7-14 inclusive is ordered to be read on January 1, if a week-day, and allowing for holy-days, what may be called the history of man from the Book of Genesis is ordered to be continuously read in the week-day lesson (see "Comes," Editio Vallarsi, vol. xi., column 609). As March, which used to be the first month of the year, coincides practically with Lent, it is possible that one of the reasons for reading Genesis in Lent was that it coincided with the beginning of the year. The author is indebted to the Rev. Dr. Bright, Canon of Christ Church, and to the Rev. F. E. Brightman, for most of the above references.

the world we know; our thoughts run on at once to all that so quickly follows—the disorganization and dislocation of this fair and perfect work of God through the disobedience and rebellion of man. We see the entry into the sphere of human life of other and malignant forces which, but for the deliverance worked out by God himself, must in the end have destroyed those germs of goodness and righteousness that survived the first catastrophe, and so must have made this world, without protest and without opposition, the kingdom and the home of evil. This is the other law that St. Paul tells us he found warring against the law of God, in which after the inward man he delighted; so that, he exclaims, " the good that I would I do not : but the evil which I would not, that I do." [1]

This unending conflict with sin—with all its consequences, direct and indirect—this struggle that seems always to be beginning, and never to get one step nearer its end,—this is what is forced home upon our thoughts as we come once more within sight of Lent. There is a dreariness and hopelessness about it all, against which some of us have to put forth our whole strength ; and therefore it was a bit of real inspiration that led those who revised our Lectionary some twenty years ago to set beside the first chapter of Genesis the last chapter of the Book of Revelation, that, as we read of the completeness of the disaster, we may

[1] Rom. vii. 19.

also be reminded of the sure and certain hope of perfect restoration.

What is the motive power that gives steadiness and resolution to men in their life's work? That enables them to persevere in disagreeable or wearisome duties, to shun delights and live laborious days? No doubt, in God's goodness, there is a real happiness in activity for its own sake; but this will scarcely stand the test of the monotony and the tediousness that are apparently more or less necessary attendants upon all continuous work. Some, perhaps, will point to ambition; here certainly is a powerful force, especially with the young; one, too, that is able at times to dominate men even in extreme old age. But some of us never become the slaves of ambition; few, I hope, remain under its thrall in middle or later life. There is, it is certain, one influence that can carry men who are wholly under its guidance through fire and water, and that is greed: we need not, however, wait to speak of that now; we know its strength and we know its author; none would willingly acknowledge himself to be living his life under its inspiration. The question still remains, what is it that can give staying power to honest and unselfish work? There is, and we may well be thankful for the fact, a great deal of such work being done; there is a truer spirit of unselfishness, a more ready willingness to help others at the cost of personal comfort, than has, perhaps, ever before been seen in the world. It would be well if we allowed ourselves to recognize this fact more unhesitatingly; we should then be saved from the harsh and ungenerous judgments that men are only too apt to pass on those who are working on lines they do not understand or approve. Temperance, purity, education, social and political reform—these and similar subjects are occupying the attention and claiming the time and trouble of hundreds and thousands, clergy and laity alike, many of whom are working willingly and gladly with no thought of reward, no desire for public recognition, no expectation of personal gain. Why do they do it? What hope have they? For—

> "Work without hope draws nectar in a sieve,
> And hope without an object cannot live."[1]

When the collar begins to gall, when the wear and tear of life begin to tell, men are at last compelled to put to themselves the question which John Stuart Mill tells us was at one time forced upon his own thoughts: "Suppose that all your objects in life were realized; and all the changes in institutions and opinions which you are looking forward to could be effected at this very instant: would this be a great joy and happiness to you?"[2] And if they have no thought of anything beyond the present life, they will find, if they are honest, they must answer the question as he

---

[1] "Coleridge's Poems," p. 330. Moxon's edition, 1870.
[2] "Autobiography of J. S. Mill," ch. v.

did, with an unhesitating "No." The truth is that men are immortal beings, and that therefore they cannot make this world their one supreme object; if they do they only court certain failure. They see, for example, after long years of work and waiting, some change made or some reform carried which they have ardently desired, and the result is only disappointment: the world is little bettered by what has been done; indeed men almost seem to refuse the deliverance they have helped to win for them. Thus their gain becomes their loss; success has robbed them of the real source of their happiness, the enthusiasm for action, the excitement of the chase. But Christ's followers can answer this question with a decided "Yes;" "yes," because every position gained can only mean at best a starting point for renewed and even greater effort; "yes," because they are not careful to measure or appraise results, because in themselves success and failure are of no account at all. Come what may, Christian men and women must work for Him to Whose service they are pledged; the cause is His, not theirs; they must do the little they are able to do, to take temptation out of men's way, to open out before them, as far as may be, the possibility of clean and wholesome lives. They must do their part, but the result is in the hands of Almighty God; and, therefore, however complete may seem to be the failure of this or that which they once thought gave promise of solid achievement, they cannot be disheartened, they will not allow themselves to despair; for the end is not now, but far on in that day which their eyes shall at last behold—they look " for the new heaven and the new earth."

And if the best workers of the world know what it is to feel the necessity for the hope the Christian Creed can give, what shall we say of others? Of those, for example, whose life must be one long endurance of pain? We know there are such; many of us can say this from our own personal knowledge. Month after month, year after year, boyhood, youth, manhood, all passing away without any prospect of what we as men could speak of as happiness; with no deliverance possible for them, but that which death will bring. There is scarcely any possibility of exaggeration here. There can be few clergymen, at all events, who have not come in contact with suffering and disease, often intensified by the pressure of poverty, where, if they could not have said from the very bottom of their hearts,—yes, here is the weariness, the pain, the discipline of life, but under it all is love, and beyond it there is the sure and certain hope—it would have been impossible to refrain from a fierce and bitter outcry against the cruelty of the power, or fate, or chance which had thrust men into the world only that they may suffer. How people face these things whose outlook is bounded by the present day of suffering it is hard to understand; I can only suppose that they do their best to forget it, and to put it out of sight. No doubt it is true that the promise of happiness in a future life does not, in our ways of measuring things, set right the sorrow of the present world: but there is yet a further question to be answered. Can this trial be a preparation for the future life? Can this be the road by which, as perhaps by no other, men and women may reach the perfection of saintliness? We must indeed have kept our eyes very tightly closed if we have failed to learn that this discipline of pain creates, in God's Providence, characters among the most beautiful that we ever meet with. In some poor room, which the occupant, it may be, will only leave to be carried to rest in the churchyard, we may meet a quiet contentment, a trustfulness and thankfulness, yes, and even a radiant happiness, at which we can only look with wonder and amazement, if shame for the ingratitude and thanklessness of our own lives leaves room for any other thought at all. And this beautiful creation, this pure and true love to God our Father, this gentle, patient, faithful character, grown to be what it is through the very pain that seemed to be so wanton and so unintelligible, are we to think of it as a lovely and beautiful work, the offspring of chance or necessity, which a few months, or at most a few years hence will be crushed into nothingness? No indeed: Christian people are certain that all this pain has not been suffered without purpose. They know that souls are fitted by the discipline of pain for the work they have to do in the life of the world to come; that they are prepared through much tribulation for their place in the new heaven and the new earth in which even now by faith they live, and for whose advent they continually pray, "Thy kingdom come."

And then there are others, whom men of robuster mould are apt to treat somewhat scornfully, into whose wounds they have no oil that they can pour; those, I mean, who from conditions of birth or education, from faults of character, from mistakes and want of judgment, have travelled down the pathway to despair; those who are the failures of the world, dragging out a weary existence in some distasteful or monotonous work; shut in by narrow and sordid aims; visited with the consequences of their fathers' sin, tied and bound in the chains of their own; weary, incapable, without one glimmer of any real hope before them in life. You may organize and reform, and re-organize and re-reform the world till the end of time, such as these will never vanish from the earth. It is certain that the one thing that can by any possibility put strength into such stagnant lives is the hope that the Church of Christ proclaims; the hope that can speak to them with unfaltering accents, and tell them, in spite of everything that seems so dark, to be of good cheer, since they may, even in the failure and the disaster of the present, find the discipline of their character, the sanctification of their life. God's best and truest gifts are not reserved for the successful, for those whom we men account happy and prosperous. Saintliness, goodness, holiness, patience, gentleness, purity, love—these are out of the reach of none; and when this world and all the fashion of it are passed away, when so much that is now made great account of will have perished for ever, those who have won these graces shall have their place in the new heaven and the new earth.

And, if we may pass from characters which are, as we measure things, least attractive to us, to others which of all that we meet in life command our readiest sympathy, think for one moment of men who are richly endowed with various mental gifts, and who yet are hampered and held back by external circumstances, by failure of health and strength, and so are compelled to live apart from the full stream of life, their powers, as it seems to them, useless and unused. How can we help these? How can we sound the depths of their distress? Unless, indeed, we are able to say,—the cause is God's, not yours; the end is in His keeping; He made you, He needs you; He is, even here, training you, if you will but leave yourself in His hands; some day—though it may be not now—some day, in that far-off future, as we men in our limitation speak of time, every capacity and gift and power you possess shall have their full play in the perfect service of Him who is a God of perfect love. We can only read the riddle of life as we fall

> " with our weight of cares
> Upon the great world's altar stairs
> That slope thro' darkness up to God," [1]

and look on by faith to the day when the new heaven and the new earth shall be revealed.

We must learn that it is our duty and our happiness to bring our wills with no shadow of hesitation or reserve into accordance with the will of God: and as we do this we are taught the secret of the one principle that can give steady purpose to our work in life, whatever that work may be, whether it be found in active service or in patient endurance. Here we can find the courage which will enable us to wage the ceaseless conflict with sin; here, through all the irksome duties of our daily tasks, we can find the source of a patience which will endure when all lower motives have entirely spent themselves. We cannot flinch in the moral struggle, or consent to lead idle and frivolous and hopeless lives, if we "look for the resurrection of the dead and the life of the world to come."

[1] Tennyson's "In Memoriam," p. 78.

XVIII.

Faith.

"Then opened He their understanding, that they might understand the scriptures."—St. Luke xxiv. 45.

(Sunday after Ascension Day, May 13, 1888.)

We not unfrequently hear men speak with great satisfaction of what they call a "rational faith;" the words are used with perfect honesty, but the speakers seem to be altogether unconscious of the fact that this phrase, unless carefully guarded and explained, is little less than a complete contradiction in terms. If and so far as any subject matter is within the compass of our natural reason or can be understood and measured and formulated by its unaided guidance, it makes and can make no call on faith properly so called. If on the other hand it comes into the sphere of our consciousness through faith, which is "the assurance of things hoped for, the proving of things not seen,"[1] then reason must so far be content to stand aside; for questions are at issue with regard to which

[1] Heb. xi. 1.

it cannot claim to hold any final court of appeal. These two principles of faith and reason stand over against each other. The principle of faith loyally acknowledged, loyally followed, leading men steadily on through whatever dimness or uncertainty that may from time to time surround them to a fuller knowledge of the truths about God, the soul, and eternity; the principle of reason leading men, whatever may be the religious beliefs of particular persons or particular societies who from time to time submit themselves unreservedly to its guidance, farther and farther away from any hope that looks beyond the horizon of the present life.

The Church is pledged to the principle of faith. The kernel and heart of the Creed is that man was created with the endowment of powers and faculties which brought him into direct and conscious communication with Almighty God; that in the Fall he lost these capacities which had been his; that henceforward between himself and his Creator a great gulf was set, which he had no power to bridge; that only by God's revelation of Himself could he re-enter this vast world of thought and knowledge from which by sin he had been excluded. This revelation has been going on through all the ages of the world's history, until at last in the fulness of time God became Man; and in the Incarnation of our Blessed Lord, there was found on the one side the complete revelation of the Being and

Nature of God; and on the other side the means were provided by which man, though fallen, could be re-admitted into communion with his Father in heaven. This fact and all that it involves is known to us by the gift of God Himself; no principle of human reason could have worked it out, or proved or explained or guaranteed its truth to us. This mediatorial work of our Redeemer is the basis of the whole of the teaching of the Church; to Him she traces every gift she holds; her teaching is, as it were, only the continual repetition of His Name. "The Word was made flesh and dwelt among us full of grace and truth."[1] Full of grace,—every capacity of the soul, every thought of holiness, every gift of sanctification, all that makes for our highest moral and spiritual selves, comes from Him: and also full of truth,—the gifts of knowledge, the powers of the intellect are bestowed by Him; He opens the understanding of men that they may know.

Distinctly opposed to this idea stands out the conception of the sufficiency of natural reason. This principle is in our day accepted by many, in full consciousness of all the consequences that are involved in its acceptance; they are satisfied with it, and find their rest in it, although they know that it bars the gate of heaven, and leaves mankind to live their life in the world with no God in the present and with

[1] St. John i. 14.

no hope in the future. To these we have and can have at this point little to say; we can only sorrowfully acknowledge the completeness and consistency of the intellectual position they have assumed. But since the great upheaval of the sixteenth century, this principle of the sufficiency of human reason to deal with and to compass the things of the unseen life, has been only too largely adopted by Christian people and Christian societies, it would seem without any idea of its ultimate and necessary consequences. It is difficult to doubt that the Agnosticism of the nineteenth century is the lineal descendant of principles which came into prominence three centuries ago. It is not to the point to say that those who then adopted these principles held this, that, or the other larger or smaller portion of the Christian Creed; the question is not where they were able to stop, but whither the principles they adopted necessarily led them. Extreme Puritans, who objected that the Church obscured the Person and Work of Christ, are the ancestors of those who have adopted Socinian theories, and say that the Church leans far too much upon Him, and now deny His Godhead. One of the most popular outcries against the Church was that she ignored and neglected the Bible, and did not give God's revealed word the place and position to which it was entitled; the successors of these men in Germany and elsewhere are those who would have us regard the

Bible as an extremely interesting collection of Jewish literary productions, but as a Book which is in no intelligible sense an inspired book.

In this question of inspiration the lesson is written clearly enough for any one to understand. Men who ignored or denied the Church as a living witness to the truth of God, fell back in the sixteenth century, as a matter of necessity, on the written word: they were then compelled to construct theories of the infallibility of that written word, from which they could by logical process build up those schemes of Christian doctrine and belief which they, acting on their private judgment, deemed it well to retain. The present century has been watching the destruction of those theories, and the consequent tottering of the edifices constructed upon them. Now the historical Church as a whole is committed to no theory of inspiration; she declares the Bible to be the word of God, to contain the revelation of God's will for man, but she has never made the attempt to separate this divine element from the human, or to settle exactly and definitely when, where, and how the divine guidance was given. The Church draws her life from her Incarnate Lord; she is the extension into the sphere of the present of His Person and work; she is linked with her Lord through the power of the Holy Spirit, and, under the guidance of the same Spirit, she has enshrined in her creeds that body of revealed truth to which the Bible witnesses, and which, "whether men will hear, or whether they will forbear,"[1] she calls on all to accept, believe, and teach.

But, besides and beyond this body of external objective revealed truth, there is what has been called an infused gift of truth: since truth, in the same way as holiness, requires to be brought home to the inner life, there is the gift to all faithful members of the Body of Christ of right judgment, of insight into and recognition of revealed truth, which our Lord promised to all who would do His will. This knowledge, however, is not, any more than the Creeds themselves, the product of the natural reason; it is the gift of God through the mediation of Jesus Christ. "The gift of faith," says Archdeacon Wilberforce, "the power of understanding, the inward light of a higher reason, these are among the blessings which mediation obtains, and which flow in perfection from Incarnate Godhead into the members of His mystical body."[2] "The things of God knoweth no man, but the Spirit of God. Now," St. Paul adds, "we have received, not the spirit of the world, but the Spirit which is of God; that we might know the things that are freely given to us of God."[3] And

---

[1] Ezek. ii. 5.
[2] "Archdeacon Wilberforce on the Incarnation," 2nd edit., 1849, p. 500.
[3] 1 Cor. ii. 11, 12.

therefore our Lord "opened the Apostles' understandings, that they might understand the Scriptures."

In these two gifts of revelation, in the imparted treasure of truth, and in the engrafted principle through which that truth is apprehended, we find at once the limitation and the guide of reason as it can be exercised in relation to things divine. Faith, it is true, limits under one aspect the authority of reason; but faith, it is also true, extends infinitely the range of vision. The revealed truth of God in the Creeds sets the limits within which individual thought may be exercised in relation to subject matter which, but for the gift of God, would never have come within the sphere of human consciousness: and, further, in its action with regard to that truth, reason must act in subordination to the engrafted gift of heavenly guidance which the Mediator bestows on the body of His disciples.

A great deal of perfectly needless misunderstanding would disappear, and a great waste of power would be saved, if we once recognized the fact that people cannot be made Christians by argument. Men may expound with all conceivable brilliancy, and ingenuity, and eloquence, and incisiveness, the body of truth contained in the Creeds and the Bible, but only the Spirit of God can bring it home to the heart and conscience and will, and so to the intellect and the reason. He, not we, can open the understanding: so long as we act as though the strength of the Church lay in argument alone we must fail; for the Spirit of God works in the hearts of men in ways we cannot know, and by methods that lie beyond the reach of our subtlest analysis. I do not for one moment mean to say that we should not do our best to understand what the assumptions made by the Creed are; what relation they bear to general questions; what are the really essential and critical points in the Christian and the non-Christian positions; all this is, in its true place, of very great importance; but it is work that demands special training and special qualifications in those who are called on to undertake it. And even so, when all has been said and done in this regard, we can only look up to Him "who alone can order the unruly wills and affections of sinful men,"[1] and say from our heart of hearts Elisha's prayer, "Lord, I pray thee, open their eyes, that they may see."[2] Quietly, persistently, and steadily the Church is called on to proclaim the revealed truth which has been committed to her keeping by Almighty God; but He, and He alone, can be His own Interpreter. Of one thing we are sure, while sin and sorrow, and pain and death, remain amongst us, this teaching cannot be without its hold on human consciences and wills, and almost in spite of itself on human reason too.

[1] Collect for the Fourth Sunday after Easter.
[2] 2 Kings vi. 17.

I have spoken of the external gift of revelation, and also of the imparted illumination granted to the body of faithful people. But those of us who have accepted the principles of the Christian Creed as the basis of our thoughts in regard to the world in which we live now, and of the unseen future to which we are day by day hastening on, must never forget that it is possible to accept the Creed with the intellect, and to be uninfluenced by it in the heart and life. "The mere intellectual perception of truth," says a well-known member of this House, "is like the perception of form by those who are colour-blind. Without the spirit of love, the higher meaning and relationship of things is lost."[1] In such a case, the body of revealed truth stands, as it were, outside ourselves. We are able, perhaps, to exercise ourselves with infinite skill and cleverness in stating its various positions, in unravelling its manifold intricacies, we may defend it from attack with subtlety and ingenuity, but all the while its truths may be nothing more to us in our inner lives than mere propositions of the schools. Only when the light from the Eternal Source of all light breaks in upon our hearts and consciences can the Creed become to us what it really is, a vivifying, energizing force; only then can it give us the strength to fight our battle with the sin and selfishness that

---

[1] "The Life beyond the Grave," by the Rev. R. M. Benson, Student of Christ Church, p. 464.

so sorely beset us in our own hearts and in the world around us; only then can it give us a sure hope that is able to take away the sting of death, and to rob the grave of its victory. If we steadily keep this in mind, we shall pray with all earnestness that God would send us the light of His Holy Spirit through whom alone it can be given us, "to have a right judgment in all things,"[1] whose special office and work it is "to guide into all truth,"[2] "to take of the things of Christ, and to show them unto us."[3] If we think a little of these things this week, we shall perhaps next Sunday morning be able to say our Pentecostal prayer, "Veni Creator Spiritus," with some clearer insight into the meaning of what we ask, and some truer measure of the fulness of the gift which we may, if we are faithful, receive.

[1] Collect for Whit-Sunday.   [2] St. John xvi. 13.
[3] St. John xvi. 15.

XIX.

The Wise and the Foolish Virgins.

"Then shall the kingdom of heaven be likened unto ten virgins, which took their lamps, and went forth to meet the Bridegroom. And five of them were wise, and five were foolish."—St. Matt. xxv. 1, 2.

(Fifth Sunday after Epiphany, February 10, 1889.)

Among all our Blessed Lord's parables there is none of more solemn warning than this from which I have taken my text. For it is not a parable that tells us about the bad and the good, as we call them,—about those who are openly and sincerely the servants of their Lord, and those who, in outward act and life, show that they have chosen the service of the evil one. No; it is a parable of the visible Church, and of those within that Church between whom in outward appearance no difference can be made by men. The foolish virgins as well as the wise were looking forward to the coming of the bridegroom; the foolish as well as the wise understood the duty of making preparation for it; the foolish as well as the wise thought they were prepared. All alike had their lamps, and the vessels for the oil; all alike had their lamps burning; all alike fell into slumber; all alike were roused by the midnight cry, that told of the immediate coming of Him for whom they had all prepared and waited and watched. And, when they heard the cry, all alike knew what it meant, and what must forthwith be done; "then all those virgins arose and trimmed their lamps;" all alike set themselves to make at once the last hasty preparations, that they may be ready for the coming Lord. And at this supreme and fateful moment a difference never before seen or noted was found between them; five of them discovered that their lamps were flickering and dying out, and that they had no oil in their vessels with which to replenish them. Hastily they turn to the other five, with the request, "Give us of your oil, for our lamps are going out." But this is quite impossible; their defect cannot be remedied so; they therefore hurry away—if yet there may be time before He comes—to buy from those who have oil to sell; they make a supreme effort to supply their fatal want. But while they are gone the Bridegroom comes; the five who are prepared, and stand with their lamps trimmed and burning, take their place in the train of their Lord; the palace doors are flung open, and the great procession passes within its gates; and then the doors are shut. Later on the other five come back; they knock at the closed and barred doors, and from within, in reply to their summons, there is heard only those terrible words, "I know you not."

A day is coming when a great and final separation will be made between men who in the present life appear to be absolutely alike. They have all shared the same privileges; all alike are baptized members of the Church of Jesus Christ; all alike profess themselves His servants; all alike look forward to the same end, and prepare themselves for the same day of account. They worship in the same churches, they kneel at the same altars, where all alike receive the bread and the wine, which are the pledges of the Saviour's love for men: we see no difference between them, outwardly there is no distinction that can be marked; all, so far as we men are able to judge, are united in one purpose and animated by one hope; and yet hereafter a deep and impassable gulf will open between them; for "five of them are wise, and five of them are foolish."

This is a lesson which our Blessed Lord again and again enforces. "Two women shall be grinding together; the one shall be taken, and the other left. Two men shall be in the field; the one shall be taken, and the other left."[1] Outward conditions, outward professions, outward actions are all, without exception, the same; and yet one enters into the joy of his Lord, while the other hears only the fatal words, "I never knew you." Thou hast not known us! why, "we have eaten and drunk in Thy Presence, and Thou hast

[1] St. Luke xvii. 35, 36.

taught in our streets;" and again the only answer, "I know you not whence ye are; depart from me, all ye workers of iniquity."[1]

What is it, then, that Christ our Lord saw in the wise virgins that ensure for them a glad welcome in the day of His coming? What is it that He missed in those other five which shuts them out from hope? In one brief word, the former had, while the latter had not, learned the meaning of the love of God. The whole Bible, from first to last, is the gradual unveiling of this love; the birth of Jesus Christ is its perfect manifestation; the apostle and evangelist of the Incarnation sums up all that this doctrine means for us in the single phrase, "God is Love." This love we must have, if we would reach our rest in the world to come; he that loves is "born of God,"[2] he that loves not "does not know God."[3] Without love we are nothing; we can do nothing that is pleasing in the sight of God, or that is in any true sense helpful to ourselves. I am not exaggerating; it is indeed impossible to go beyond St. Paul's words, "though I bestow all my goods to feed the poor, and though I give my body to be burned, and have not love, it profiteth me nothing."[4] Church privileges, sacramental grace, abstinence even from evil—all nothing, all able to avail nothing where love is not found. Therefore, O

---

[1] St. Luke xiii. 27.
[2] 1 St. John iv. 7.
[3] 1 St. John iv. 8.
[4] 1 Cor. xiii. 3.

God, in Thy mercy give us love. Yes; but what can we do? In these self-analytical days, when old moorings are lost, when thought is quickened and anxious and nervous, when we can no longer tread the quiet paths of less self-conscious times, it is most perilous to many minds even to suggest the question, Do I in truth love God?—since the question, merely by being asked, seems to call for the answer, No.

A man need not have lived very long to have found out that, for only too many, life runs a steady course of complete and, it may seem to us, unmerited failure; and to have learnt besides something of the ruin that sin can work, it may be has worked, in lives that are very near his own; and if it were not that at the moment of his sternest and most rebellious outcry against the hardness of it all, there lay in the background of his thoughts, fixed and rooted immovably, the firm belief—or assumption or presupposition, if you will—that unintelligible and confused as everything may seem to be, yet, under all there is the unchanging love of the Eternal Father, life must sink down into the abyss of a hopeless despair. But if God is indeed love, then so far as we are shut out from that love it must be by our own perverseness or our own sin. So we do not ask ourselves the question, Do I love God? but having learned the entire necessity of this supreme gift, we set ourselves, by His grace, to win it; strive for it as we would for any earthly prize; fight on, even though we do not seem to make much way, only anxious that we may not falter through the strenuousness of the conflict, that nothing should rob us of the eagerness of our quest; convinced that, if we are faithful, we shall find the gift to be ours in the great day of His coming.

Yes; but again, How are we to strive? Let me speak of two things. First there is the sin of thanklessness. Fight against this, and compel yourself to be thankful: keep under stern control the tendency to look with envious eyes on what may seem to you the greater happiness or good fortune of other men, their superior position and opportunities, their greater abilities, their greater power of endurance or of work, their sounder, stronger health. Put all such thoughts resolutely aside, and thank God for the gifts you have: the least fortunate of us in this place have very many and very real gifts. Check firmly that sense of weariness, because talents you may be, perhaps quite rightly, conscious of have to lie by unused; because the opportunities that appear to come so readily to others are denied to you, because while they are active you must be idle, because while they are called to work, you are called to wait. Believe me, as long as any man indulges himself in wilful despondency, and is as a necessary consequence stained with the sin of rebellious ingratitude, he is cutting himself off from all knowledge of God's goodness; and unless he makes a real effort, and determines by prayer and self-discipline to crush and conquer this sin, he will never know the meaning of the love of God.

And then, my brothers, there is another enemy of love of which, if you will bear with me, I will dare to speak—and that enemy is impurity. I do not mean those outrageous and flagrant sins, in which if men indulge themselves, they cannot, with any truth, be reckoned as Christian even in name; but those more secret sins in thought and word and deed, which may lie, as we must sometimes learn, very near lives that outwardly seem to be even exceptionally devoted to the service of our Blessed Lord. If men habitually and wilfully hang round the galleries of their imaginations pictures of evil and of shameful sin, then they may be sure that, however outwardly devout they may be, or however regular in their religious duties, the love of God is a grace of which they cannot know anything at all: no, nor, indeed, can they understand in any true sense the beauty and dignity and tenderness of human love. It is not, as excuses are so often made, that our spiritual self is hampered by our lower nature, in which all the forces of sin are to be found. The sin is not to be looked for in what we call our animal nature; no, indeed; but as has been most truly said,[1] it finds its strength in our higher nature, in

---

[1] Cf. "On behalf of Belief," p. 278 *seq.*, by Rev. H. S. Holland, Canon of St. Paul's.

the endowments of the intellect, and in God's great gifts of reason and memory and imagination; these step down from their high throne in the heights that are the very presence-chamber of the All Holy, and revel in the thoughts and words and deeds of sin; and the sin is what it is by this wanton degradation. To the heart that is the home of such sin as this, in secret no less than in open form, the love of God can never be revealed: the least whisper of that love is checked and silenced in such an atmosphere as this; the blessing of the sight and the knowledge of God—and sight and knowledge is love—is promised and can be given only to the pure in heart. Yes; it was, believe me, a wonderfully true insight that taught those who drew up our Communion Office in its present form, to appoint among its opening prayers one of the most beautiful of all our collects: when, therefore, we come into the presence of our Lord in our solemn Eucharistic Service, we pray God, "so to cleanse the thoughts of our hearts by the inspiration of His Holy Spirit that we may perfectly love Him,"[1] since perfect love can only be found where there is perfect purity.

[1] This collect formed part of the Introductory Prayers of the Celebrant in the Sarum Missal.

XX.

The Resurrection.

"Then went in also that other disciple ... and he saw, and believed."
—St. John xx. 8.

(Fourth Sunday after Easter, May 19, 1889.)

Dr. Mozley, in the first of his Bampton Lectures,[1] points out how very really the difficulty of the belief in what we speak of as the miraculous is increased for us by the rapid growth of knowledge, more especially by the growth of the physical sciences, and by the development of the historical imagination. Past events now range themselves visibly before us; we have learned to project ourselves backwards into the surroundings of the scene that the historian describes; we are there in bodily presence; we see, we touch, we handle, and we find it correspondingly difficult to accept anything that does not fit in with the experience of our senses. We stand beside the empty tomb on Easter Day, and all that it connotes in the physical world is so foreign to that of which we have

[1] "Lectures on Miracles," Bampton Lectures for 1865, by Rev. J. B. Mozley, D.D.

personal knowledge, that, however real our faith—or, rather, it is almost true to say in proportion to our faith—we are conscious of the shock of a surprise, of the press of a difficulty, of the presentation to our thoughts of the serious demands made upon us by the Creed; and so, for the moment, there is pause or hesitation, or even doubt. The truth is that we carry with us in our historical retrospect, unconsciously but almost necessarily, an idea that our personal experience is the one test of what is possible; and, consequently, any event that does not find its verification in that experience appears strange and incredible, and is instinctively felt to be exaggerated, if not false. There are some who have founded their theory of history on the axiom that the past must be verified by the present; to whom, therefore, historical evidence for a miracle is an impossibility, unless and until miraculous events shall once more take place openly before our eyes, and, by their occurrence in the present, verify the possible truth of the accounts which have been given of their occurrence in the past. To minds set in such a mould as this, records of miraculous events are only interesting in that they offer problems for ingenious speculation, to ascertain what, if any, is the real substratum of historical fact that underlies the stories; and next to find some explanation of the particular form which the account of the miraculous takes in particular cases. It is true, no substratum of any such verifiable history has ever been suggested as underlying the statement of the fact of our Lord's resurrection. But a great deal has been said on the second question; and a very general method is to explain it in one way or another as a perfectly natural outgrowth from the account of His life on earth; and thus to find its parallel in the various legends and stories that surround the great national heroes who lived in the early days of the world's history. But, as has been ably insisted on in a book lately published,[1] the whole gist of these legends is that the life was so imposing, so masterful, so heroic, that men could not believe that it had ceased to be, and, therefore, bit by bit, dressed it up with legends of renewed activity after death. All the stories are built upon the events, or supposed events, of the life. There in the life is found the true centre of the story; everything that is told as to what happens after death is explained by it. The legends would never have taken the form they did were it not for the splendid deeds and actions of the years of life.

We need not have read the New Testament very carefully to know that when we come to deal with the history of our Lord we meet with exactly the reverse of all this. His Life was not, in the sense in which we ordinarily use the words, and as we men judge such things, a specially striking, or

---

[1] 'On behalf of Belief,' p. 17 *seq.*, by the Rev. H. S. Holland, Canon of St. Paul's.

specially heroic life. It was gentle, winning, patient, gracious, tender: there was sympathy with sorrow and pain and distress, sympathy such as men had never dreamed of before. There, combined with a purity that awed and silenced opponents, was found compassion for those entangled in the meshes of sin, such compassion as drew the penitents to His feet. There were, indeed, miracles: but it is true, as we are often told—and we Christians can use the fact as well as others—that they were worked in an age when miracles were as generally thought possible as they are generally thought impossible now, and consequently they were not in any sense as startling or impressive as they would be if they were worked in our own day.

The story of the life as given in the Gospels emphasizes this point; as we read the narrative we find that, in the estimation of the disciples, our Lord fails just at the point where they expect He will assert Himself, and put Himself forward. Step by step the apostles are disillusionized: they looked for a conqueror who would found a great earthly kingdom, but He disappoints their expectations; He does nothing that even suggests its advent. After thirty years, passed so far as we know in silence, there came possibly only three years of active work. In these years no doubt many deep and mysterious things were spoken about; but in them, it is true to say, under the conditions and circumstances of the time, very little was done that could impress the imagination with the prospect of a brilliant future. On the contrary, there continually emerged dark sayings that suggested only failure; and that, not only for Himself, but for all who were ranked among His followers. To the apostles who were closest to Him, the best He promised was that they should drink of His cup and be baptized with His baptism; and that cup and that baptism were clearly not the symbols of any immediate earthly triumph. There were, it is true, two occasions of a different significance: the first when the chosen three saw Him in His glory in the mystery of the Transfiguration; and the second, which alone really met the disciples' hopes and expectations, when the triumphant procession passed over the Mount of Olives on Palm Sunday, moving forward amid the exulting cries of the multitude, "Blessed be the king that cometh in the Name of the Lord."[1] This was what they had looked for, hoped for, longed for, and at last it seemed as if their hopes were to be fulfilled. But the excitement of that day only served to make the gloom and desolation, the failure and defeat, more utterly crushing on the following Friday morning.

Then came the Resurrection. The fact was met by doubt and unbelief; it was accepted after pause and hesitation: but, once accepted, it was seen to be the

[1] St. Luke xix. 38.

key to the life; this one fact revealed to the apostles for the first time all that the life had meant. The last period of confusion is to be found in the great forty days, when they asked our Lord, "Wilt Thou at this time restore again the kingdom to Israel?" The answer given them was the promise of Whit Sunday, "It is not for you to know the times or the seasons. But ye shall receive power after that the Holy Ghost has come upon you: and ye shall be witnesses unto Me."[1] After the day of Pentecost the outlook is entirely changed: the men are the same still,—the same and yet not the same: the St. Peter of the Acts is the St. Peter of the Gospels, there is no mistaking his identity; but where before uncertainty and hesitation were found, there is now a clear strong conviction, that never wavers and never flinches; and the heart of that conviction is that Jesus Christ who was crucified on Good Friday rose on the first Easter Day from the dead. The whole conception of our Lord's office and person and work, the explanation of all that up to this point had been so unintelligible in His actions, starts from this central fact. In view of this fact the Life becomes coherent and intelligible; without the Resurrection it would have been a miserable and disastrous failure. Yes, if Christ be not raised, we Christians, so St. Paul unhesitatingly affirms, "are of all men

[1] Acts i. 6, 7, 8.

most miserable:"[1] our faith is vain, we are yet in our sins.

We shall never reach the full conviction that should be ours of the fact of our Lord's Resurrection, if we go back in thought to stand beside His empty tomb with our intellectual conceptions shut closely up within the four walls of a physical laboratory, or with our moral ideas set only on making the best out of this best possible of all worlds; practising virtue, if it can be called so, on utilitarian grounds; our first and best thoughts given to obtaining for ourselves the largest share we can command of present comfort and luxury; our spiritual selves choked with the cares and business and pleasures of this life. In such an intellectual or moral atmosphere as this there is nothing that corresponds with eternal truth: and, after all, if we understand what we say, it is true that the Resurrection must be verifiable in our own experience. The question for us is, and it is a far-reaching one, what that experience is and has been.

The mere physical fact of the Resurrection in relation to life as we have known it, the returning to the world of one who had died, is embarrassing, unintelligible, and therefore so far inexplicable; but we are not asked to stop here. When St. John went into the empty tomb he had the evidence of his senses for the fact of the Resurrection; but the acceptance

[1] 1 Cor. xv. 19.

of this fact by itself is a small part of what is meant by the words, "he saw and believed." The fact had a significance beyond any limit of space or of time; St. John "saw and believed," and was the author of the fourth gospel, and of the Book of the Revelation. Life and everything connected with it had passed through a great and momentous change; a new and marvellous factor had entered into it, and the kingdom of heaven was open to all believers. He believed and saw the first glimpses of the new heaven and new earth of which he wrote in later years; he heard the first notes of his later message, "Behold, the tabernacle of God is with men, and He will dwell with them. And there shall be no more death, neither sorrow, nor crying, neither shall there be any more pain: for the former things are passed away."[1] He believed and caught the first echoes of the promise, "Behold, I make all things new."[2]

If our spiritual instincts are numbed and atrophied, then there is nothing in us that can correspond to, or leap out to welcome the truth of our Lord's Resurrection. Yes, to know its truth, the Resurrection must be to our own lives what it was seen by the apostles to be in a unique and supreme sense to the life of our Lord. "We have to ask ourselves," as we have been well reminded, "whether we are living a life which demands our resurrection in

[1] Rev. xxi. 3, 4.   [2] Rev. xxi. 5.

Christ as its only adequate solution. Would your ways and mine be incomprehensible if there were no Resurrection? Have we any motives, real and animating, on which we act, which would be meaningless if we were not to rise again? Have we made any moral venture on the strength of this assurance?"[1] In a word, do we bring our creed to the test of practise?

We find here both the littleness and the greatness of our life on earth: its greatness, in that it stretches away into an infinite and unknown future which we cannot understand, but of which we can only say that it shall never end; its littleness, in that we are set here for our brief moment to do our work and duty; to hold, in our turn, the lamp of truth, that others may kindle their torches at ours, and take our place, and do, God grant it! better far than ever we have done. And the Resurrection supplies the key to the problem; we know assuredly that there are men and women living amongst us to-day with as clear and firm a hold on this conviction as, we may venture to say it, was given to the apostles themselves. One such life has but lately ended in a distant island, where a Christian priest, with a devotion worthy of the great communion to which he belonged,—a communion so rich in the memories of saints and confessors and martyrs,—has just sealed with his death his living martyrdom among the lepers to whom he had given

[1] "On behalf of Belief," p. 21.

everything a man has to give. We, it may be, know others, some perhaps whom we have been privileged to call our friends. There are, too, many more, known only to God Himself, and perhaps also to one here and there to whom they have ministered; and looking at such lives when our faith falters, we do well to ask ourselves what we have ever done that we should be worthy to know God's truth as they have known it, fully and clearly, with no cloud or shadow of doubt to darken it. Such lives and examples give, however, strength and form and substance to our wavering faith, and beckon us on, by God's grace, to make our own venture on the truth of what we profess to believe, and to live a little more as men should live who are one day to rise again to a new and endless life.

XXI.

The Dangers of Externalism.

"These have no root in themselves, and so endure but for a time."—
St. Mark iv. 17.

(First Sunday in Lent, February 23, 1890.)

How little we know ourselves—this is an axiom that is universally accepted, a mere truism. A well-known writer[1] has pointed out that when one man is conversing with another, either represents three distinct persons—there is the man as his friend thinks him to be, there is the man as he conceives himself to be, and, thirdly, there is the man as he really is. There need be no intentional hypocrisy in this; it is the natural consequence of the conditions under which we are called to live. But, ultimately, each lives his life apart and alone.

> "Each in his hidden sphere of joy or woe,
>   Our hermit spirits dwell and range apart,
>   Our eyes see all around in gloom or glow,
>   Hues of their own fresh borrowed from the heart."[2]

---

[1] "The Autocrat of the Breakfast-table."
[2] "Christian Year," Twenty-fourth Sunday after Trinity.

"We touch," Bishop Samuel Wilberforce once said, "like spheres at a single point; strive as we may we can never touch at more." The two great realities for each of us, Cardinal Newman has taught us, are ourself and God; *solus cum Solo,*—each alone with God alone, we live our lives as if there were no other created thing. Few, I suppose, who accept the Christian Creed would deny that there is truth in such statements as these.

And yet it is only through the activities of the visible world that it is possible for us to give expression to the thoughts, the hopes, the purposes that are in us. We project ourselves out upon the scene, we throw ourselves eagerly into the work that lies before us: often we seem like children surrendering ourselves now to this and now to that enthusiasm, each for its turn occupying all our thoughts. And we find our happiness in this activity; in the dullest of us some pulse of life throbs and beats. We find ourselves, we scarcely know how, bound up with this or that party, pledged to this or that reform, anxious to oppose this or that change; we find our work in this place or in that; and the duties which consequently fall upon us call into play all our reserves of strength and will and steadiness of purpose. There are, indeed, some men who are unhappy enough to have no duties, or, as it would be more true to say, to think that they have none; they consequently live for pleasure, sometimes of a higher sometimes of a lower kind; and thus they, too, are lost, perhaps even more completely than others, in the rush of external interests. There is, therefore, a real spiritual danger that besets us all—those who set before themselves a high standard of active duty as their ideal, no less than those who think only of living pleasantly and comfortably—and it is this: we soon begin to live for the things we care for and think about; in the bustle and confusion and noise the external world becomes the one all-sufficing reality. "Earth, these solid stars, this weight of body and limb,"[1] become in sober earnest the sign and symbol of our division from Almighty God. We have but little time, in the midst of our busy work or our eager pursuit of pleasure, to remember that true life within us, which once begun can never cease to be; which, under all this external excitement, is being shaped and moulded and fashioned for an end of which we rarely think: we remember it, perhaps, in a way when we kneel down in the morning or evening to say our prayers; but otherwise it has small place in our thoughts, and very little influence over our actions.

Recall for one moment what the motives and aims are that generally influence and guide us in our work in the world: pleasure, self-gratification, ambition, the desire to get on, or to stand well among men,

[1] Tennyson's "Higher Pantheism."

loyalty to our party, to those with whom we are more immediately associated, respect for some leader to whom we have given our allegiance, admiration for some one with whom we have been brought into close contact, and for whom we have, it may be, a sincere and true affection. Some of these—ambition, for example—are almost wholly bad; some, like loyalty, a curious compound of good and evil; none is wholly and unreservedly good. Think how mixed the motives are which influence men in their religious life. They attach themselves—they could scarcely tell you why—to parties or to sects: if they do this, as it is to be feared they too often do, without a sincere devotion to the service of Almighty God, they bring with them a purely political element, with all its fuss and noise and passion; and the consequence is that outward acts of devotion or reverence or ceremonial, which should be the natural expression of a true religious life, are made the badges of a party and the flags of a faction fight; and men, as they quarrel about these poor shadows of the visible world, lose sight of the growth in holiness, and the realization of the nearness of God's presence and of the infinite depths of His love; and yet without these all external acts of devotion and service are entirely worthless. Real religious life will, we allow, of necessity find its expression in outward ceremony and outward act; but these external acts are not the life. Where the life is, there they will be found: but, unfortunately, it by no means follows that where they are to be found there is of necessity the life also.

Again, men sometimes pay to a leader or teacher the devotion and homage which are due to God alone. All their abilities, capacities, and endowments are placed unreservedly at their hero's disposal: and, now and then, the most wonderful gift that life can give us, the grace of friendship, is misused in this way. Men take up opinions and accustom themselves to use phrases, without thinking that they only mimic, it is well if they do not caricature, the teaching, and sometimes the very tone of voice of their leader. Admit that he may be most worthy of admiration; allow that all his words and acts are the natural and almost necessary expression of a true life with God; unfortunately, this does not ensure reality in the imitation; the customs, observances, and acts which are in the one case the spontaneous expression of true faith and devoted love, are only too likely to become in the other the empty mockery of mere ceremonial.

We live, I repeat, our true lives hidden from the observation or the criticism of our fellowmen; if we are not honest with ourselves, we live them masked and screened even from ourselves. To all of us, no doubt, opportunities are given when we may, if we will, understand this more clearly. We find ourselves at times carried aside out of the stream of life's business, caught in some back eddy of its restless current; and there alone, it may be even without the help that external religious rites could afford us, we are able to learn, if we will, what are the things that are of eternal worth. Then all that finds its strength and stay in the confusion and bustle and excitement of our everyday life vanishes like "a dream when one awaketh."[1] At such times we can, in some sense, answer the question whether there is any root in ourselves,—anything that, given to us by God, is dependent solely upon Him, and is therefore able to endure though the heavens should be destroyed, and the world and all that is in it should pass away for ever; or whether, on the other hand, the religious ideal in which we have put our trust represents nothing but political or social enthusiasm, or is only the expression of personal friendship or of unreal sentiment. If we find only too real reason to fear that much that we thought of sterling worth is mere straw and stubble, it is for the moment sad enough for us; but it is also good for us to get an insight into the possibilities of unsuspected and unconscious hollowness and unreality that have been concealed under our external professions and actions. We are thus compelled to fix our thoughts steadily on that which is

[1] Ps. lxxiii. 19.

the beginning and the end of all true religion, the increase of the knowledge of God, the growing sense of His Presence, the certainty of His goodness and His love, the reality of our life in Him.

Such opportunities of careful thought are suggested to us by the course of the Christian year; certainly something like this is the call that is made upon us by Lent; we are bidden to put aside, at least for a few hours now and then in the next six weeks, the amusements and pleasures, the cares and anxieties of our eager, hurrying life; to go apart even from friendship; to leave everything, and look steadily at life as we should see it, if we were called on here and now to die. To do this quietly and humbly is to bring our everyday life to the test of an unfailing standard; here we can find, and especially we who are clergy and those who in future years intend, God willing, to take on themselves the great responsibility of the priesthood, some protection against those serious dangers of externalism which only become greater and more pressing as our responsibilities increase and multiply.

We do well to draw aside when we hear glib discussions of the minutiæ of outward observances; we are right instinctively to turn away when we hear clergy counting up their communicants, or numbering their confirmation candidates, when they are, to use a commercial phrase, taking stock of their success;

for we know that success cannot be measured by these things;—"The wind bloweth where it listeth, and thou hearest the sound thereof, but canst not tell whence it cometh, and whither it goeth : so is every one that is born of the Spirit."[1] The work of God's grace within the soul of man is known only to God Himself; when the end of this age has come we shall learn something of the great things He has done for men. It must be allowed, however, that these considerations have a value if they are regarded as negative, and not as positive tests. Those who come to the Holy Communion do not merely by their coming prove themselves to be true and loyal servants of Jesus Christ: but when out of a large congregation only a scanty remnant come to the altar of God; when many come rarely, and many more not at all; then we may rightly fear—as sometimes is sadly felt in this place as the little band of communicants gathers here on Sunday mornings at eight o'clock—that religious life is not very clear or deep or strong; then we may well begin to ask ourselves what our responsibility in the matter is; for we who come to the Holy Table may be living so inconsistently with our outward professions as actually to repel others from their religious duties.

The gifts of the Church are, thank God, real and true gifts; they are the channels and the means of

[1] St. John iii. 8.

grace. We are sent to bless; we are sent to absolve; we are sent to give into the hands of men the bread and the wine, the Sacrament of the Body and Blood of the Lord; but the sphere within which the grace so given is effectual and availing is beyond the reach of our penetration, far away out of our ken. We, laity and clergy alike, can judge only superficially. Right belief, right actions, almsgiving, prayers, fasting,—these all will be found where true love is; but they give us no sure key by means of which we may enter into the secrets of the inner life, where alone the root of true religion can grow and strengthen, and bring forth fruit for the eternal world. There in the silence of our own separate life, we do not appear as we fondly imagine ourselves to be, or as friends in their kindliness or good nature estimate us, or as strangers or cynics caricature or depreciate us, but as we really are, as we shall know ourselves to be when we come to die, as we shall be known to be when we stand before the Judge.

XXII.

Excuses.

"They all with one consent began to make excuse."—St. LUKE xiv. 18.

(SECOND SUNDAY AFTER TRINITY, JUNE 15, 1890.)

To make excuses for ourselves comes quite naturally to all of us; indeed we may almost make this habit our definition of man. In the great allegory with which the Book of Genesis opens, in which is summed up the story of the Fall, this characteristic comes out with perfect directness and simplicity. The tragedy is completed, and sin has entered into the world; and at once the man excuses himself by throwing the blame on the woman, while the woman in her turn throws the blame on the tempter. The silence in which these excuses are passed by is more impressive than any condemnation could be; the original source of the evil is indeed acknowledged, but no attention is paid to the defence put forward by the offenders against God's law: they have themselves sinned and therefore they must suffer; so the man receives his sentence of painful and weary effort in the sustaining of life, in the sweat of thy face shalt thou eat bread; while to the woman the pains of childbirth are assigned, as at once the penalty of her sin, and also the pledge of future deliverance, since in the time to come the seed of the woman shall bruise the serpent's head. The story has all the simplicity of childhood about it; but the world has long outgrown its childhood. Excuses, however, by no means come to an end on this account; they only run into some other channel; the circumstances of their education and the peculiarities of their temperament, and even the whole realm of nature itself provide men a wide area in which they can always find broad and deep courses for the floods of apology and excuse.

It is, indeed, a large question to attempt to follow out in all its details. We may, however, dismiss at once all excuses that indirectly as well as directly take the form of falsehood or untruth. We all agree about this: none of us would tolerate any touch of falsity here. But in passing it is worth while to mark how, in spite of this, the anxiety to escape trouble or discomfort, the lazy slipping along the line of least resistance, creates a practice of excusing or apologizing for conduct without sufficient regard for accuracy or sincerity: when this happens the sense of the stern necessity for truthfulness grows dull, and sometimes there grows up a habit of mind which feels no shock or distress at a direct lie. Strange as it seems, there are people who have reached such a mental and moral condition that they simply cannot be straightforward; an indolent, easy-going nature that never wilfully intended to deceive or mislead has, through the constant practice of making unreal excuses to others, and worse still to itself, become radically unreal, insincere, untruthful.

Let us pass on to consider two characters which on very different grounds find it necessary to offer explanations or apologies for themselves. First, there are men of a somewhat sensitive, mobile nature, who spend a great deal of their time in the disastrous amusement of what is called castle-building. They are conscious—and it may be quite rightly—that they have gifts in this direction or in that; but then, instead of doing with heart and soul the duties, insignificant and trivial as they may seem, which lie before them to be done, they live in a world of their own creation; in all the scenes they picture they naturally hold a prominent place, for success and not failure is the subject of their dreams—success and the applause won by success forms the background of all their thoughts. The chance they look for may never come to them, and then their life slips from them with nothing done: or it may be the opportunity is given them—they get their desire, and as the Psalmist says, it brings "leanness withal into their soul."[1] The good that is in

[1] Ps. cvi. 15.

them—and there is good—rebels against the conditions of success now it is won; the men of whose applause they had dreamed are, they discover now, just those who have no plummet with which to sound the depth of serious purpose, which, in spite of their self-absorption, had a place in all their dreams. After all, they had some true measure of the real needs of the human soul, and this keener, truer insight soon tells them what a hollow mockery their success is; it shows them that, in past neglect of the work that they ought to have done and in dreaming their life away, they have lost irrevocably their one opportunity of preparation for the duties now before them. They have reached a prominent position, and they might have had something to say to these people who look up to them; they might have been ready to help on the work they now see has to be done; they might have been and they are not, and never can be. Well indeed for them if indolent self-appreciation gives way at this point. Unfortunately men are too apt to accept the present conditions, and to make the best of their hollow success. It is true, they quite allow it, that they might have been ready for the opportunity which has come to them: but, after all, the fault is not so much in themselves, as in the conditions and surroundings of their past lives; they never really had a fair chance of preparation; for they were so completely misunderstood by all the people who had to deal with them.

But there is a danger in the opposite direction; there is the possibility summed up for us in the well-known phrase about those who make the great refusal. Indolence urges the refusal, and suggests that humility absolutely consecrates inactivity. An opportunity is given that demands sincere effort, and it may be real self-sacrifice; it comes in different ways to different people; it calls one to a position of prominence, another to a post of danger, another to duties and responsibilities in some obscure corner of the world. However it may come the man is called by the Lord and Master of us all to do the best he may in this particular sphere of duty; to go out and meet his work in faith and trust in God, who alone can enable the strong to be really strong, and in whom the weak may be made strong. The call has come: how it is so, or why it is so, he may not be able to say; but it has come, and he has not courage to meet its responsibilities. He finds a ready ground of excuse in the ordinary cares that come in some shape to all; he has bought a field, he has bought some oxen, or he has married a wife; excuses enough are close at hand, and in the end if they do not serve him, plainly he will not obey the call. No one can refuse a real opportunity of useful work without moral strain, even if the refusal be—as it sometimes is—a right refusal; but if it is based on indolence or faithlessness, the man will henceforward live his life not merely with the sense of what he might have been, but through misdirected effort failed to become, but of what he might have been and would not even try to be.

Translate these suggestions into practice. A man has intellectual gifts of a fair order; he is, and in no way wrongly, conscious of them. He has an interest in metaphysics or theology, in mathematics or scholarship, in the problems of the world of nature, or in those of social and political science. But he is bent on running before he can walk; he refuses to face what a great teacher,[1] whom some of us remember here, used to speak of as the underground work, the drudgery which all must go through if they would prepare themselves to use rightly and effectively any gifts whatever of mind as well as of body. This man, versatile enough, with only too ready an aptitude for catching up phrases and theories, dreams away his days reading things he cannot properly master, ignoring the accurate training of grammar or logic or mathematics, secure in the ready excuse when he fails in them that the men who have to deal with him are narrow and unsympathetic, and in their curious insistence on the petty details of moods and tenses, and the simple duty of accuracy of thought, are quite unable to appreciate the flights of genius. Do men never make shipwreck of fair abilities by the refusal to submit to this discipline of preliminary and necessary drudgery? Do they, or their friends for them, never make the flattering

[1] The Rev. J. B. Mozley, D.D., Regius Professor of Divinity.

excuse that their failure is not so much due to themselves as to the incapacity of others to understand originality?

Again, all admit the responsibility attaching to the choice of a profession. Think for one moment of the clerical office. The due supply of persons qualified to serve in God's Church is an anxious question for all of us, and, it is to be hoped, is one we at times make the subject of our prayers. It is true enough all are not intended to be clergymen, and there are many to whom such a future has never suggested itself as a possibility in their own case. But suppose that the possibility has presented itself; that as the question of Trinity Sunday morning is asked, "Whom shall I send, who will go for us?" the answer, "Here am I, send me," has risen to our lips. We are so apt to think that in determining such a question all the responsibility is on the side of saying "Yes," while no responsibility attaches to the answer, "No." Clerical life involves in any case some self-denial and self-restraint: but beyond this there are those to whom it presents itself as a call, accompanied by special claims for endurance and self-forgetfulness; work in the mission field, or work at home in places and under conditions where the hope of worldly advancement is small, where the work itself is not likely to attract much attention or to make much stir. It may be right, this is admitted, on consideration to turn aside, but it is a grave responsibility to do so.

To leave such a high purpose and to set one's self in one of the ordinary grooves is manifestly to accept a lower ideal of life. It is useless to say,—after all, I am but as other men, and they do not make this sacrifice; this is to miss the whole point. These others must meet their own responsibilities at their own time. No one of us can be as any other; each is in a sense a law to himself; no man can put his hand to the plough and look back without moral loss. I do not mean that all who in some moment of enthusiasm think of becoming clergymen are truly called to the priesthood. Some rightly say "No"; but others also, to their own untold loss, make what is in their case "the great refusal." There is always, when a decision has to be made, a responsibility in the refusal to undertake a serious duty only less grave than that which attaches to its acceptance.

Other illustrations of the refusal of the higher ideal and the acceptance of the lower one of ease and, as it seems, success, might be taken. The artist who neglects his art and paints to sell; the musician who leaves his great themes and truckles to popular fancies; the statesman who barters righteousness for popular applause; the preacher who speaks, not what he believes, but what he fancies others would like to hear; all who sell themselves and their powers, whether great or small, for popularity or success, for gold or the equivalent of gold—all these are, in their measure and degree, refusing the good and choosing the evil. For all the excuse is ready, you must not ask too much of people: it is made until it becomes a matter of course; and men sum it all up in what they regard as a sort of moral truism, that no one can be expected to be so quixotic as to give up his chance of success in life, in obedience to simple faithfulness to a high ideal of duty.

Life, we are sometimes told, is meant to be happy and prosperous. Seriously this cannot be true. There are lives in which the great temptations, the main springs of disaster, are to be found in their uniform success. Difficulty, failure, struggle—these, even in severe forms, may be the greatest blessings that can be given to men. No doubt passionate rebellion against God's will is sometimes only too possible under these conditions; but it is also true that character is moulded by adversity as it can be in no other school: we never know what is in us, for good as well as for evil, till the waves and storms of life have gone over us. But through this discipline we are trained for the things which are unseen and eternal; hereafter we shall learn that lives reckoned by us to be great successes have been disastrous failures, and some that we have reckoned failures to have been the truest successes: the small man aiming at small things and scoring his hundreds; the great soul filled with a great purpose and breaking down, and, as we say, failing; but there is no need to speak of this, we all know Browning's Grammarian's Funeral.

The failures as we think them: as we watch a young life that has achieved nothing, broken and wasted with disease; or as we call to mind him [1] who spent one brief term as an undergraduate in this House, and then last January was struck down with the fatal illness from which in God's mercy his release came some three weeks ago; are these and such as these failures? When we look at the Cross of our Lord, and realize who He is, and why He hung there, we know that these seemingly complete failures are not always the lives that ask for defence or apology or explanation. The indolent, dreaming, self-centred life, that sometimes attains success in virtue of inherited gifts of intellect or of social position—a success, however, for which no preparation has been made, no foundation laid that enables the man to do his duty as a leader or teacher or guide; and the selfish, faithless, cowardly life that refuses to accept the sterner duties and responsibilities that are offered to it; the hollow prosperity of the former, the lazy self-indulgence of the latter—these even now are seen to demand apology and justification. In the day when the secrets of all hearts are laid bare, both will be found to be without possibility of defence or excuse; while truthfulness, sincerity, courage, and

[1] A. G. Haselfoot, scholar of Christ Church, matriculated October, 1889, and died in the course of the following spring.

their correlatives purity, unselfishness, faith, though in this world they may be found in lives that have never known what we men think of as success, will alone stand men in good stead when they are face to face with their Lord and Judge.

XXIII.

Esau and Jacob.

"Jacob have I loved, but Esau have I hated."—Rom. ix. 13.

(Second Sunday in Lent, February 22, 1891.)

Most of us, I suppose, are somewhat surprised at this emphatic sentence: indeed, for ourselves, we are almost prepared to reverse its terms. We do not, it is true, regard Esau as an exactly lovable character; but his distress commands our sympathy, while his brother's cunning and deceit and duplicity go far in our estimation to justify our hatred of so mean a character. No doubt our idea of the two men is largely based on the well-known chapter of Genesis,[1] which has been read once more to us in this morning's first lesson; and it may be at once allowed that our judgment, so formed, is a perfectly right judgment. It is, however, formed on incomplete evidence. If we study the characters more carefully, and follow them throughout the whole course of their lives, we shall, I think, find reason to modify our opinion, and to acknowledge the justice of the words

[1] Gen. xxvii.

of the text in their approval of Jacob, and their condemnation of Esau.

Physically, as in every other way, the two brothers are complete contrasts. Esau, on the one hand, is vigorous and athletic, a cunning huntsman, disdaining the more peaceful occupations of the pastoral life, and choosing rather to live by his spear and his bow. Jacob, on the other hand, is physically weaker, sensitive, with keener intellect, seeing more what things mean, better able to look before and after in the struggle for existence, finding in his brain a source of strength which is denied him by his physical organization. In primitive, less ordered conditions of life, skill soon degenerates into cunning; and duplicity, emphatically the besetting sin of Jacob's character, becomes, in early days, an important factor in his life. Esau returns one evening from his hunting, fagged and worn out and hungry; he desires some food that Jacob has prepared, and recklessly careless about everything but the immediate gratification of his appetite, sells to his astuter brother his place as the senior in his father's house; surrenders his birthright to the younger for a mess of pottage. "Thus," in the words of the book of Genesis, "Esau despised his birthright."[1]

In this morning's lesson we have the second act in the drama, when Jacob, his falsehood aided and abetted by his mother, secures the formal declaration of the

[1] Gen. xxv. 34.

blessing from his father Isaac, now old and blind. It is a shameful story of lying, deceit, and fraud, and there would be something wrong about us if we had no sympathy with Esau's bitter cry. But, that which Jacob had gained by such crooked means, Esau had thrown away through contempt and self-indulgence; and now, stung to passionate fury by his disappointment, he gives free rein to his vindictive nature, and lays his plans, so soon as his father dies, to take his brother's life, and in this way to recover the position he had lost. Sin brings suffering to all but the hopelessly bad: none are so surely deserted by God as those who sin and never pay the penalty. Jacob and Rebecca have to learn this. The mother sees what is in store for her favourite son, and avoids it in the only possible way by sending him into a distant country to her brother Laban. So far as the story tells us, she never saw him again.

On the journey he rests at Bethel, and there we learn something of another side of Jacob's character, his belief in the unseen world, and in a God to whom his service is due. We all know, since our child days, the story of the ladder he saw in his dream, set up between earth and heaven, with the angels of God ascending and descending upon it, while God revealed Himself as the God of Abraham, and the God of Isaac his father. His faith, indeed, is not very clear: when he wakes he knows that he has been at the very gate of heaven. But in spite of this he must make a sort of bargain with God; if God will bring him safely back to his father's house in peace, then shall the Lord be his God: and he sets up a pillar or cairn of stones as a token of his vow. Not very high, or pure, or strong, this faith; but faith is there, and that is something now, and may be everything in future days.

Arrived at his uncle Laban's house, he enters into his service; there he finds that he has no monopoly of deceit. The devices he used against his brother Esau, are now, in some sort, turned against himself. In the end, however, Jacob appears to get the better of Laban; in one way or another, by hard work, and certainly not without a good deal of his natural craftiness, he becomes a very wealthy man at Laban's expense. At last the inevitable quarrel between them came about, and Jacob, with his family and all his large possessions, sets out on his return to his father's country.

On the return journey, the strong and the weak sides of Jacob's character are equally well illustrated. There is first the wonderful vision of God, in which he gained the victory in the mysterious struggle with the angel, and by tenacious importunity, "I will not let Thee go, except Thou bless me," won the signal blessing and the title Israel, Prince of God; "for as a Prince," it was said to him, "hast thou power with God and with men, and hast prevailed." [1] And then in contrast

[1] Gen. xxxii. 28.

with this there is his pusillanimous fear of Esau, his care to propitiate him by magnificent presents, and by abject submissiveness: as we think of Esau's rough good-natured reception of a brother, whom he naturally considered to have defrauded him of what should have been his own, it is difficult to give Jacob credit for any special nobility of character in comparison with his brother Esau.

Years pass on, and in Jacob's family the wild tempers of the Eastern nomad tribes, and the guile and cunning which were part of their natural inheritance, do their work in Jacob's home. On one memorable occasion a gross wrong done to the family by a prince of the Shechemites was avenged by two of Jacob's sons with savage brutality and treachery that could hardly be surpassed. Jacob, indeed, condemns their act, but he has no word of condemnation for its deceit or its falsehood. As he querulously puts it, "Ye have troubled me to make me to stink among the inhabitants of the land: and I, being few in number, they shall gather themselves together against me, and slay me."[1] The safety of himself, his property, and his belongings—his mind runs on these, and not on outraged truth and good faith. It is, indeed, but a poor figure he makes; it is, however, the last story of his weakness.

In later years we see him with all kinds of home

[1] Gen. xxxiv. 30.

troubles thick upon him; mourning for his loved wife Rachel, heartbroken at the loss of his favourite son Joseph: and then towards the end of his days we meet him a stranger in the land of Egypt, where the son he supposed dead is a leading and prominent official. In all the pages of the Old Testament there is no more dignified or gracious figure than Jacob, as he stands, in his old age, in the presence of Pharaoh and gives his blessing to the Egyptian king. He was an old man then, trained and disciplined and chastened by the storms and vicissitudes of life: his sins have found him out; they have all borne their bitter and appointed fruit; but he has come through the fiery furnace, and has reached a strong and beautiful old age. There is little in his speech or bearing that recalls the weakness of the past. He finds himself a stranger in a strange land, among a people to whom he and his are an "abomination"; and, as he looks back over the long past, he sums it all up, in answer to Pharaoh's question, in the words, "Few and evil have the days of the years of my life been, and have not attained unto the days of the years of the life of my fathers." [1] But, whatever the evil days had been, they had done their work for him; and the treacherous youth had grown into the steadfast and brave old man, who looked in faith to the Eternal Lord, "for whose salvation he had waited," [2] who peered dimly into those far distant days when

---

[1] Gen. xlvii. 9.   [2] Gen. xlix. 18.

Shiloh[1] should come; and whose name is, therefore, rightly added to the great roll of the heroes of faith drawn up for us by the author of the Epistle to the Hebrews, the long roll of those who "out of weakness were made strong,"[2] and who died in faith of promises which they did not themselves receive, but only beheld afar off.

Of Esau, we know but little, except as the victim of his brother's misdeeds; otherwise there would not be much about him that would attract our sympathies. He stands before us wild, headstrong, impetuous, without stability, without reverence,—witness his carefully laying himself out to vex and annoy his father's old age—a character summed up in the Epistle to the Hebrews by the single epithet "profane."[3] His life is, from a worldly point of view, successful; he, no less than Jacob, attains to wealth and power: but there is in his case no sense of failure or incompleteness, no hint that it ever occurred to him that he might do wrong, or that he could sin as well as be sinned against. He remains the type of a character that is sometimes mistakenly thought generous, because the man, if at the moment his own interests are untouched, is reckless and indifferent, and so outwardly good-natured; a character with no respect for duty and no thought of

---

[1] Gen. xlix. 10. [2] Heb. xi. 34.
[3] Heb. xii. 16. βέβηλος. Bishop Westcott says the word describes a character which recognizes nothing as higher than earth: for whom nothing is sacred; no divine reverence for the unseen.

responsibility, seeking only at each moment to get its own way, and to gratify its own selfish desires.

My brethren, we dare not play with our responsibilities; although to do so may win for us ease, or secure for us popular applause and temporary goodwill. When life is too full, too complete, too satisfying, we may well be made very thoughtful: never to know ourselves in the wrong, never to have any suspicion of failure, never to feel the potter's hand [1] or to be conscious of the whirling of the wheel, never to surrender ourselves to that unseen Power which, through the press and push of outward circumstance, is fashioning and moulding us; this, however pleasant it may seem at the time to avoid the discipline of life, is to miss the purpose for which we are here in the world.

But, to most of us, I trust, in these weeks of Lent, the lesson of Jacob's life comes home. If we know only little of ourselves, we know too well, I fear, much that degrades and stains our lives as fatally and as persistently as Jacob's falsehood stained and degraded his. The fact that, in spite of his weakness, he is set before us in our Bibles as one whom God could commend and love, should be of real help to us when we feel, as we so often do, how wearisome, how utterly hopeless our struggle seems to be with the sins that so easily beset us. Only remember this: Jacob did not win his pre-eminence because he was deceitful,

[1] Cf. Browning's "Rabbi ben Ezra."

but because he fought against the evil, and after long years conquered it. His story illustrates, in those long-past days, all our Blessed Lord taught His Apostles as to endurance being the first condition of safety, "He that shall endure unto the end, the same shall be saved."[1] The lesson is the old lesson, old and well worn, but yet always to be steadily insisted on; the lesson of the duty of perseverance in spite of all failure and all weakness, and, if I may say it without danger of being misunderstood, even in spite of all lapses into sin.

[1] St. Matt. xxiv. 13.

XXIV.

God's Voice must be Heard in the Claims of Present Duties.

"And he said, Nay, father Abraham: but if one went unto them from the dead, they will repent. And he said unto him, If they hear not Moses and the prophets, neither will they be persuaded, though one rose from the dead."—St. Luke xvi. 30, 31.

(First Sunday after Trinity, May 31, 1891.)

One of the special characteristics of the days in which we are living is the vast increase of knowledge. When we say this we do not mean merely that men have learned more facts or accumulated large additional stores of information: the change goes much deeper than this; it is a change of method quite as much as of material: the last fifty years have seen what amounts to a practical revolution in our ways of thinking. The consequences of this affect us all, unlearned as well as learned; all at least who live in a University must perforce breathe this quickened keener atmosphere; we are the children of our age, and we share all that it has to give us, whether we turn its gifts to our gain or to our loss.

Think only of two points: first, the great development of historical research. The past that seemed so far away has been brought very close to us. Whole nations, as we have been well reminded, have been called out of their graves; and as we have been brought into closer contact with them we have found the men and women of those long-past times to be, after all, of the same flesh and blood, the same capacities, the same weaknesses as ourselves—to be, indeed, in all things men of like passions with ourselves. No doubt we can point to many and great differences between ourselves and them; but these lie often on the surface of things and lose something of their prominence as we better understand the conditions of that older life. One thing, however, we have learned with perfect certainty; and that is that all national and social growth and development that have in themselves real elements of stability or permanence are universally very gradual and very slow, and can only be measured and understood when they are followed through many years, and even ages, of silent and progressive change. And then, secondly, side by side with this development of historical insight, there has been given us a clearer idea of the evolution of the world in which we live; and while the past we can reach in written record has been bridged over and brought so much nearer to us, the past written in rocks and stones, in the hills and valleys around us has revealed itself as far more complex than men used to suppose: so that while historical time has appeared to contract, geological time has stretched itself out into ages that are often difficult for us to grasp or even conceive.[1] But here again, as we have learned the story of our planet, we have found one note dominant through all its changes, and that is their slowness and gradualness: nowhere is there any hurry or confusion or suddenness; all moves onward in quiet orderliness, here a little and there a little; the result, unseen and imperceptible at the time, discernible only after long waiting—the unnoticed, unmeasurable, and yet ceaseless movement bringing, in the lapse of time, its certain growth, modification, and development.

There are two classes of minds who, in different ways but with the same practical result, are always ready to throw the blame of their failure, whether intellectual, or moral, or spiritual, on the particular circumstances of the special time in which they live, and to find in these the complete excuse for their breakdown. The fault is not in themselves: with their temperament the conditions of their lives gave them no real chance. Men of one cast of mind decorate

---

[1] At present geological speculation on the physical side suggests that we cannot draw upon a past of quite indefinite duration, and that probably some reduction must be made in the very long periods of time that have hitherto been suggested as necessary to explain the development of the world. But, however this may be, geological time must remain enormously great compared with historical time.

the past with every kind of ideal virtue; and as they dream of the ages of faith in which they would have lived, find excuses for their unbelief and faithlessness in the difficulties that belong specially to their days, and press with such severity on men of their peculiar characteristics: while others, as they look on to a future, entirely visionary and ideal, imagine that there are in themselves possibilities of moral and spiritual development, which would be realized if only this or that or the other obstacle which is just now in their way could be removed; if the world, or the church, or society, could be at once re-organized according to their ideas of what each should be. The latter are impressed with the idea that they are born too soon, the former are sure that they have lived too late in the world's history.

If nothing else were to be said, the utter futility of all such hypothetical positions should be their complete condemnation for healthy minds. And all that we have learned as to the conditions of growth around us, all that we have learned in our fuller knowledge of the days that have gone before us, as we have been brought into closer contact with them, teaches us, and that with no uncertain voice, the same lesson our Lord teaches in the words of the text—a lesson which should silence for ever all such vain imaginings. Men are themselves and themselves only: in the historical and spiritual spheres no less than in the physical, the old saying holds good, "Coelum, non animum, mutant, qui trans mare currunt." Dives pleads for his brothers that something startling should be done in their behalf, lest they, too, should wreck their lives as completely as he had wrecked his own; and the answer is not as to what they would have, or should have, or might have, but as to what they have—"They have Moses and the prophets, let them hear them." Dives objects that this is not enough, and implores that more might be done for them; for, he says, "If one went unto them from the dead they will repent." And once again the same reply is given him, "If they hear not Moses and the prophets, neither will they be persuaded though one rose from the dead."

When we speak of the difficulties that belong to particular times and circumstances, we forget that even in the darkest days God has never left Himself without a witness; that each age has its peculiar graces and gifts as well as its peculiar dangers; that God in sundry places and in divers manners has spoken in times past to men, and that the same God who spoke in the past reveals Himself now in our own day to us; and if we cannot hear His voice now we may be sure that, even if one came to us from the dead, we should still refuse to hear it.

When our Lord lived in bodily form on earth, men felt considerable wonder as they saw who they were who received and acknowledged Him, and who they were who rejected Him. In fact, under the surface of visible things a new and mysterious force began to act, a new line of cleavage began to show itself in human society;[1] it knew nothing of social or ecclesiastical distinctions, it ignored the test of external respectability; the law of its action men could not trace then, nor have they been able in the centuries that have since elapsed to determine its course; on the one side were those who, in the words of the Gospel, had faith, on the other side were those who had it not. Now, as then, there are the faithful and the faithless; now, as then, if we could see below the surface, we should be astonished to know who belonged to the former, and who to the latter. These are matters into which we cannot penetrate: but to those who will hear, God's voice speaks to-day as clearly as it has spoken in the past. If we cannot hear it now, then neither the thunders of Sinai nor the miracle of the first Easter Day could teach us anything.

The living power of God in this living, breathing present, as surely as in the hour of creation or the day of redemption—this is the truth the Church of Christ has to insist upon. To-day, as surely as when St. Paul preached at Athens, God is not far from any one of us; now, as then, in Him we live and move and have our being. If we cannot read the pages set wide open around us and within us, if the heavens do not

---

[1] Cf. Ecce Homo, Christ's winnowing fan.

declare His glory, if His voice has no message to our hearts and consciences, then, even though one rose from the dead we should not repent. The fault is not in our circumstances, it is in ourselves; carry us whithersoever you may, mere change in space or time will never give us that gift of sight without which we cannot recognize the kingdom of God.

The lessons of the past are given us to guide and strengthen us for our work in the present; they are not given us to make us discontented, or that we may cast wistful eyes back to a condition of things that appear to us so much more to our taste than the days in which we live. The impulse and enthusiasm of hope are ours that we may be ready to work for a future we shall never see; they are not given us that we may build magnificent castles in the air, and then grow listless and dissatisfied because we may not live in them. We may be certain it is indolence or pride that whispers to us that we are so greatly superior to the days in which we are called on to live and work; that excuses our inaction on the ground that everything is wrong and that we can do little or nothing to right it; that bids us stand aside in lazy despair while we soothe our discontent with cynical epigrams.

We are, many of us, almost of necessity bound to the past by the closest ties; changes are distressing to us and sometimes bring a pain that must be felt to be understood. This is our peculiar tone and cast of mind; we can no more help it than we can help the length of our arms or the colour of our hair. Still these very circumstances assign us our work and our duty, for the conservative forces have a true place in the evolution of life. But, because changes come about that we do not like, to lose faith and hope and to find excuse for bitterness and despondency, is to deny in act the words we Sunday by Sunday repeat with our lips, "I believe in God the Father Almighty, Maker of heaven and earth, and of all things visible and invisible."

To see one's own cherished fancies set aside; to feel the set of some strong current of thought and action against one; to be generous and fair, and at the same time true to the side of truth which God has taught us; to be sympathetic without being flabby; to be considerate and open-hearted and yet true to principle; to work heartily for the many—as was once finely said from this place—while we think with the few;[1] to be true to the last word of what we believe, and yet to understand that God does not work as we men work; to know that much we build, much, it may be, on which we spend years of thought and energy, may yet be unable to stand the trial by fire that shall try each man's work of what sort it is—that there is much of wood, hay, straw, and stubble, that will and ought

[1] In a sermon preached at a college service by the Bishop of Lincoln when he was Canon of Christ Church.

to perish, although, in God's mercy, through the fire and the loss the man shall reach his own purification; to understand something of all this, and then with sincere and steady purpose to do the work which God has given us to do; this surely is the duty laid upon us as the servants of Jesus Christ. It is, no doubt, a high ideal, and we may well ask, who can be sufficient for these things? But we are not left to work in our own strength; we have the witness of God our Heavenly Father with us, if only we will receive it; His witness in the long story of His dealings with past ages of our race; His witness in the book of Nature spread open round us; and, far more than these, His witness in our hearts and consciences. He has given us all we need; and we may rest assured of this, that if we cannot hear His voice that speaks to us now, then no miracle, no catastrophe, however it may thrill or horrify or appal us, could bring us to a true repentance or rouse us to a clear knowledge of what are the real issues of life and of death.

XXV.

The One Lord.

"Jesus Christ is the same yesterday and to-day, yea and for ever."
—HEB. xiii. 8 (R.V.).

(SECOND SUNDAY IN LENT, MARCH 13, 1892.)

OUR creed has come to each of us in some special outward dress, and under definite external conditions and circumstances; and we, not unnaturally, attach great importance to these surroundings. The more sincere and true our faith, the more keenly shall we reverence all that is linked with our religious life in the past; especially all that belongs to child-days, and brings, it may be, before the thoughts the memory of some one, now lost to us, who first taught us to think of God as our Father in Heaven. And yet—and we do well to remember it—much that we value so highly may be, after all, of no vital moment; we may be making the mistake of setting things that are accidental in the place of things that are essential; we may, in our blindness, be substituting for God's truth human inventions and human ideals; in our care and zeal for the casket we may be in danger of forgetting the jewel for the protection and safety of which it was ordained.

Does not this explain why some people are so easily persuaded that the faith of Christ is in jeopardy and that the foundations of the Church are being undermined? They are alarmed because a movement is going forward which threatens their cherished fancies; because a change is impending which interferes with their prejudices. Perhaps, in the course of time, that which they dreaded so much comes about, and when the storm of controversy has passed by, they find that, after all, the Church of Christ stands as secure as it ever did. It may be the march of events has shown them, that this which they thought so great an aid to faith was rather a stumblingblock in its way, while that which was supposed to supply motive power was only a drag and a hindrance. Others, again, sanguine men, born reformers, have their peculiar moods and fancies. They are apt to think that the world would be a very good place if they could have the ordering of it: in the re-constituted Christian society of their imagination all problems and difficulties solve themselves. Perhaps they live to see reforms they wished for carried out; but, after all is done, things are much the same as they were before. Certainly the offence of the Cross has not ceased, as it certainly never will cease, while time shall last. The conservative and the reformer alike have misunderstood the conditions of the problem: each, no doubt, has his part and place in the movement of the world, each can give his mite to the common stock; but both have to learn that they must look for the realities that are the life of the Faith in other things than those which, in their hope or their despair, they had thought of such paramount importance. We need not be disheartened by our mistakes; we have this treasure, St. Paul teaches us, in earthen vessels:—

> "Our little systems have their day;
> They have their day and cease to be;
> They are but broken lights of Thee,
> And Thou, O Lord, art more than they." [1]

But we make a mistake if, on this account, we think lightly of the systems: through them each one of us, if he is in earnest, has learned something of the truth that God has been teaching us; the vessels are earthen, but they bear the revelation of God Himself to the human soul. Sir Walter Scott, in one of his most powerful books, has painted with a master's hand the blind fanaticism of the covenanters' army that fought at Bothwell Bridge. Not many pages later in the story we are given an account of the trial, the torturing, and the condemnation to death of one of the leaders, Macbriar, who accepts his

[1] Tennyson's "In Memoriam."

sentence with these noble words; "I forgive you, my lords, for what you have appointed and I have sustained—and why should I not? Ye send me to a happy exchange—to the company of angels and the spirits of the just for that of frail dust and ashes; ye send me from darkness into day, from mortality to immortality, and, in a word, from earth to heaven! If the thanks, therefore, and pardon of a dying man can do you good, take them at my hand, and may your last moments be as happy as mine."[1] The contrast between this scene and the fanatical excesses that precede it is so marked, that it is not easy at first sight to connect them with the same people: but pain and death are two great touchstones of human character and test men to the quick; under all that may seem so wild and grotesque, there can grow, by the grace of God, as the result of the discipline of life, a faith that can make men heroes and martyrs, and prepare them to meet even death itself.

To a large extent, it is true, we are not responsible for the external circumstances which go so far to mould and determine our lives; whether they are hopeful or the reverse, whether they are bright or cheerless, they are so far quite independent of us. But if we are inclined to be despondent about our own peculiar anxieties arising out of these conditions, we may well remember we are not the first

[1] "Old Mortality," chap. xxxv.

who have felt thus, as we certainly shall not be the last. In Bishop Butler's days, men supposed Christianity to be now at last dead, and thought and spoke as if nothing remained but to give it a decent and respectful burial. Those who held to their faith at that time can have had no easy task: they never dreamed then that, before many years were over, the faith of Christ would once more assert, as successfully as ever, its unique and supreme claim on the lives and consciences of men. The Wesleys, and all the great movement associated with their name, first within the Church, and afterwards, alas! without it; Mr. Simeon and the evangelical school which set so clear a mark on our sister university; and then, here in Oxford, the Tractarian movement, the energy and impetus of which is, in God's mercy, still unspent amongst us: these things men, in Bishop Butler's day, could not foresee. As we look back on them and think of those who, under God, were the leaders in these revivals, so different, so widely different as they have been, and yet all alike such powerful instruments in moulding the religious life of this century, we may well ask what is the connecting link that binds them into one? What is the peculiar secret of their influence? What is it that unites together Wesley and Keble, Simeon and Newman? What is it that gives a place beside them to the great Nonconformist preacher we have but just now lost, Charles Spurgeon? What is this gift which, while it adorns and sanctifies intellectual eminence, can exist in fullest vigour where learning is not? The answer is, I believe, not far to seek: these men all alike have a firm unwavering faith in the Living Christ; they are His servants, they spend themselves and are spent in His service. He is near them and with them in all they think or do. He speaks through them and in them; their gifts and endowments, whatever they may be, great or small, are as nothing and less than nothing, since self is lost and swallowed up in devotion to Jesus, their Master and their Lord. It is no uncommon thing to hear Churchmen and Catholics contrasted with Puritans and Protestants, by saying that the religion of the former is that of a Church, while the religion of the latter is that of a book. Both these estimates are incomplete and unfair. So far as the Puritan or the Catholic is true to his creed, the religion of either is the religion of a Person, of the Incarnate Son of God. To so convinced a Protestant as Mr. Spurgeon the book is nothing, save only for the sake of Him who speaks by it to men; who in its pages is brought near to hearts and consciences that are weighed down with the load of sin, or broken and bowed under the crushing weight of pain or bereavement. The living Christ revealed in the pages of the gospels; this was the core of the message he had to deliver. Christ our Lord spoke through him; of this he never doubted;

and therefore week after week he was able to draw together the thousands who depended on him for their spiritual instruction, for the external support and guidance of their spiritual life.

And the Church, and Church organization and ritual, even the very Sacraments themselves—take away the thought of Jesus Christ, and what remains? Nothing but empty and meaningless forms and ceremonies. The Church and the Sacraments are what they are to us because, and only because, they are the channels to our souls of the grace of God; because in them and through them He, the living Lord, comes near to us to heal and to save: He comes to us in all our weakness and foulness and sin with His gift of pardon and cleansing; He comes to sanctify all our joys, and to sustain us in the day of pain and sorrow. Dr. Pusey's sermons and teaching and Mr. Keble's "Christian Year" do not set before men a barren ritual system, a Church organization that is merely external: they speak of the needs of the soul of man, of sin, and of suffering the necessary consequence of sin, of purity that has been lost but which may be regained, and of holiness, of peace, of joy, of love in the communion of the Holy Spirit; and then of the way open to all to attain these graces through the Cross of the Lord Jesus Christ. The Church is what she is because she represents her Lord: the Church is His Body; the Sacraments are the channels of His grace, the means by which men are united to His death and share His risen life; in which He comes to men and dwells with them and they with Him; in which He makes them members of Himself, of His Body, of His Flesh, and of His Bones. And the same is true of the teaching of our great Oxford Cardinal: when he passed within the Roman communion, he no doubt accepted doctrines and practices that seem to us to obscure the essential truths of the Creed which he and we alike are anxious to defend. But let us at least be just; although doctrines and practices are accepted by the Roman communion, which we hold to be doubtful and dangerous, and likely to do positive harm to men and women who make use of them, still the prominent place in every church is given to the Crucifix, and to Him Who died upon the cross for men; we find, it is true, litanies and special devotions to saints and angels which we think it quite impossible to use, but the great service of all is the daily and continual pleading of the Memorial of the one Sacrifice once offered for the sins of the whole world.

I do not mean to say that all such things can be treated as matters of indifference by serious people. We must be honest in dealing with these questions; we must not palter with the truth as we have learned to know it; but we may do all this and yet live in charity with others. It is not, I allow, easy for us to understand how vast and many sided truth must be, and yet to be absolutely faithful to those aspects of it which we have learned; to hold this truth without any reserve, while we realize that God's word is wider than we can grasp or comprehend: the task is a hard one, but we may by God's grace fulfil it. We know the gifts of the living Christ are bestowed on men who are outside the borders of the historical church; we can only deny this if we resolutely shut our eyes and refuse to look upon what God has done in the world. But this does not lessen our responsibilities: we are linked, as we believe, in unbroken historical descent with the Church of Apostolic days, and therefore have a great trust committed to our charge to guard and to use: if we would use it rightly we must never forget that in all we teach and in all we do we are powerless, except we, steadily forgetful of everything else, proclaim to men Jesus Christ and Him crucified; since only in His name and in His living present power can we fulfil the duty that has been so solemnly laid upon us to advance His kingdom in the souls of men.

We are living in an age when numbness and deadness seem again to have stolen over the spiritual world: here in Oxford, where the atmosphere quivers with the least breath of hostile movement, it needs some tenacity of purpose to hold firm to Christian truth. In the conversation of some of those with whom we associate, in reviews and general literature, there has again grown up a way of speaking about Christianity as if it were a thing of the past. No doubt, as a rule, it is spoken of respectfully and given a very prominent place in the story of the world's development; but its claim, at least, as a revelation of the supernatural, is supposed to be entirely set aside; its interest lies in the leading part it has played in the evolution of Western civilization. We are not careful to answer this: we read the Church's history differently, and we know that, however carefully men may seal the stone and set the watch, the Lord of Life cannot be held in the bonds of death. "Jesus Christ is the same yesterday, to-day, yea, and for ever;" the storms of to-day will pass away, as the storms of years long gone from us have spent themselves before, and Christ our Lord will be again acknowledged the Lord of the intellect, as He is the Saviour of the souls of men. For us, it remains only that we be found faithful—faithful to what we have learned, faithful to what we may yet, if we will, learn of His way and of His purpose for us. And if it be so, if we seem to see nothing, to learn nothing, to understand nothing, if no ray of certain light breaks through the shadows that have gathered about our path, we can still, " in our patience possess our souls ; " we can wait and to the best of our power do the work that lies before us waiting to be done. God knows the task is at times a heavy one for some amongst us—God forgive us that we are so often ready to despair, that so often we will not and cannot trust Him; God pardon those of us who are so prone to think hard thoughts of Him.

XXVI.

The Love of God.

"As the Father hath loved Me, so have I loved you."—St. John xv. 9.

(Twentieth Sunday after Trinity, October 30, 1892.)

The love of God; none of us, believe me, know God at all except so far as we know Him to be Love. God is Love. This is the supreme revelation given us by Jesus Christ. In this one sentence we find the sum of the teaching of the New Testament as well as the key to the Old. There is much in the Bible—we need not hesitate to admit it—just as there is much in the world we see about us, that is confusing and perplexing, and very hard to understand; much that at times overwhelms us with almost unbearable doubt, that hides away God's face from us, that seems to turn His word into a threat and His world into a dungeon; but still He is Love. And yet how utterly impossible, unthinkable, unprovable many will say; look round you at the men, women, and children that may be found any day within but a small radius of our own homes; how many a life is crushed under a load of intolerable distress. Here is one halting through the world with a broken and maimed body; here is another stretched on a bed of sickness—sickness that shall only end in death; here is a third in the midst of all his busy, eager work, pushing his way on as best he may, bravely doing what he can, though stricken with mortal disease. There is everywhere pain and want; there is weakness pitiful—oh, so pitiful!—there is sin so grim and so ghastly—sin that far more often than we care to remember wraps the child about from the hour of its birth, welcomes it into the world, and then never leaves it, but steadily stunts, pollutes, and at last destroys its life, without, as far as man can see, giving it one smallest, slenderest chance of any escape—and still, God is Love.

It is no wonder men find it hard to believe it; that at times they turn round in almost fierce rebellion against any who would bid them receive such a doctrine as this. In one sense, our strength becomes our weakness, and our gain our loss. In the days in which we live now, we have passed away from those old conditions in which it was possible for men to be satisfied to enjoy their own happiness and their own comfort; and, secure themselves, to give no heed to the voice that bade them think how their brothers and sisters in this great human family were living their lives. We have passed, and we may be thankful for it, far away from that smug Pharisaic contentment that could actually dare to thank Almighty God that some had what others had not. The reason of this is obvious: the world is smaller than it was; it is closer to us. I do not mean that the people who live in the same village or street or town are closer to us; nor even our own countrymen, the inhabitants of the densely crowded quarters of our over-populated cities; we have leaped over the narrow barriers of seas and of oceans, and the sorrows of all who suffer on the face of the whole earth are present to men's minds with a force and a vividness that make them only too oppressive realities. We understand and feel for the mass of human suffering and sorrow and sin as men have never felt before; we know, as St. Paul scarcely knew, the meaning of the words he spoke when he declared that "the whole creation groans and travails in pain."[1] It is not that we are so much better than our fathers were; it is the necessary consequence of the increase of possibilities of intercourse, through which mankind has been presented to our thoughts as one great family huddled together on this tiny planet, as it careers with inconceivable velocity through the abysses of never-ending space.

The old question, "What is man, that Thou art mindful of him?"[2] is asked now with an emphasis impossible in simpler days. Human life is present to our thoughts in all its pathetic weakness; we know

[1] Rom. viii. 22.   [2] Ps. viii. 4.

how infinitesimally small we are; we know the earth, our present home, to be but a tiny speck among the stupendous order of created things; and then, with every fibre of our thoughts quivering with the sense of man's utter insignificance, and so often, too, of his hopeless and miserable failure, we are still bidden to say that God is Love, and to believe Him to be in deed and truth our Father in Heaven, full of most tender pity for all His children.

When such questionings threaten to overwhelm us, how can we find an answer that shall give us, I do not say their solution—that may be impossible—but that shall give answer enough to enable us to pause, and be quiet and stand firm until the storm has passed away. There is no answer that can be given, I firmly believe, but that which is found in the clear assurance of the reality of the life of the world to come. In the assertion of a future life we reach—it is a mere truism— the core of the Christian creed: in all ages of the Church, apostles, martyrs, saints, confessors have borne witness to their steadfast belief in this by dying, and, which is sometimes far harder, by living for the things that are unseen. How often and how sadly Christian people at large have lost sight of this truth is only too painfully evident. Men and women come to church and make the solemn declaration, "I look for the resurrection of the dead, and the life of the world to come," and then go away and prove up to the hilt by the way they live that what they have said with their lips is a formula and nothing more. When illness comes upon them, or in the hour of danger or difficulty, they perhaps turn to their Creed; but they do so mainly with the thought that they may, if possible, escape the danger, or that they may regain their health; and, to put it quite bluntly, the Church seems to be regarded rather as a means of obtaining comfort or well-being in this life than, as it is in fact, the extension into the sphere of visible things of the unseen world in which Christ gives His spiritual gifts to men.

During the past summer most of us have been reading something about the pilgrimage-trains which have been carrying their sad burden of sick and dying to the shrine at Lourdes. The unspeakable pathos of the sight lay, it seems to me, in two things: firstly, that they seemed to be in a sense sad and sorrowful representatives of humanity in its pain, distress, and suffering; and, secondly, that the appeal made to the Mother of our Lord was not so much that she would aid them with spiritual gifts and graces, in order that they may reach their home in the eternal world, but rather that she would give them healing for their bodies, and so enable them to enjoy their present life on earth.

I repeat, we need at this moment, perhaps as never before, to hold fast to the belief in the world to come. There are, it is true, those who do not think this:

they look forward to a millennium of perfect sanitation, of widespread education, and of undisturbed social equality, when life in the present shall be so full and so satisfying that men will need to give no thought to anything beyond it. It may be said that such complete felicity is perhaps more problematical than enthusiasts imagine: but, however this may be, it is at least certain that no one alive now will live long enough to see it. Reckless or desperate people may try and hasten its advent; but revolutions hinder as much as they advance the progress of the world. They destroy obnoxious rulers, they break up what are called the governing classes; they give the rein, too, to the fiercest passions of envy and greed and hate; they have been sometimes the agents of a terrible vengeance—a vengeance that seems to be almost justified as men recall the provocation that led up to it. Nevertheless, whether they are with or without possibility of excuse, when the din and confusion and tumult have cleared away, things are found to be but little different from what they were before. Some who were rich have become poor; and some who were poor have become rich; that is all, or nearly all. Violence such as this does little, often less than nothing, to hasten forward the slow and silent movement through which the will of God for man is being done.

And time which brings its social changes very slowly brings with it also mental and moral development;

they are equally slow, but they have to be reckoned with: so far there has come with our progress an increase of sensitiveness; our eyes are opened and our ears unstopped, and we see and hear as men could not in older days; and it may well be that hereafter, as man advances, the earthly millennium, with the hope of which he cheats himself, will appear to recede as he goes forward; and if so, then the creed of the Church of Christ will be more than ever his only escape from the wretchlessness of a more complete despair than we have ever known as yet.

Certainly, without the belief in the reality of the world to come, the problem life puts before us is for the men and women now living round us, so far, at all events, as their own lives are concerned, simply insoluble; with such a belief I do not say that it is solved, only that its solution ceases to be practically unthinkable. No doubt two wrongs do not make a right; no doubt cruelty and injustice suffered in this life cannot be, as we say, made up in another: but we Christians are, in one sense of the word, "Agnostics:" we frankly admit that the problem is too complex for us to grasp or to understand, and that the threads are tangled beyond hope of our unravelling them; only, since He in whom we believe is Love, we are able to commit ourselves, all our despairing thoughts, all the pain, sorrow, distress we feel and know, all the far greater, far heavier burden which we do not know, to the

Love of God, who we are convinced has cared and will care for all the creatures He has made.

Recall once more the words of my text, and remember who they were to whom they were spoken. "As the Father hath loved Me, so have I loved you." Jesus Christ spoke these words to His dearest, truest friends. How did He fulfil them? He did not call the Apostles to honour, but to dishonour; not to wealth, but to poverty; not to success, but to disaster; some, at least, among them to the death of martyrdom. Listen to the words of one who was not numbered with them at the time, but who in suffering for Christ came not one whit behind any among them: "Thrice was I beaten with rods, once was I stoned, thrice I suffered shipwreck; in journeyings often, in perils of waters, in perils of robbers, in perils in the city, in perils in the wilderness, in perils among false brethren; in weariness and painfulness, in watchings often, in hunger and thirst, in fastings often, in cold and nakedness."[1] And in the end, St. Paul gave his life for the cause of Christ, and, if the tradition may be trusted, died with St. Peter a martyr's death at Rome. Through all they suffered these men never doubted the love of God, never doubted that Christ had given them all, and more than all, He promised. "The love of Christ constraineth us,"[2] St. Paul cries; that they may "know the love of Christ, which passeth

---

[1] 2 Cor. xi. 25. [2] 2 Cor. v. 14.

knowledge,"[1] is his dearest hope for the Ephesian Christians. Can we ask more for ourselves than they received? "O Lord, in Thee have I trusted; let me never be confounded"—this must be our prayer; for, as has been well said,[2] to remain quite steady and unmoved, a man must be either very brave or very insensible: not all of us are very brave; none, I hope, are quite insensible. The confusions are before us, and we may not wholly escape them; and so we have the difficult task of holding fast to beliefs and hopes under conditions of anxiety and strain that may at times seem almost more than we can bear; but if we, even in our greatest weakness, will dare to trust in God, we shall not be altogether confounded.

Let me end as I began: God is Love; we know Him only so far as we know Him to be Love. This, if we think a moment, will be the measure to us of how little we know Him, perhaps it will teach us that we do not know Him at all. The preacher's lips may well falter as he speaks of such things as these; but in the faithful discharge of his commission he is called to speak of much which he can but dimly understand, which is again and again the measure to him of his own completest failure. But, it may be, his words may kindle others, and aid them in their struggle up to heights he sees afar off, but may never

---

[1] Eph. iii. 19.
[2] "Village Sermons," by Dean Church, p. 163.

reach himself: should this be so for one single life, his prayer is more than answered; if only in the end, when the work of life is done, he who speaks and they who hear may one and all reach the eternal fruition of the Love of God, himself in the last and lowest place, as God wills and when God wills, but only without shame and without sin.[1]

[1] Bishop Andrewes' "Devotions."

XXVII.

Thanksgiving.

'O all ye works of the Lord, bless ye the Lord: praise Him and exalt Him above all for ever."—Song of the Three Holy Children, 35.

(TWENTY-SECOND SUNDAY AFTER TRINITY, OCTOBER 29, 1893.)

"LET us sing the song of the Three Children which they sang as they blessed the Lord in the furnace of fire."[1] These are very familiar words to many of us: they are the opening words of the thanksgiving which we are accustomed to use when we have been present at the service of the Holy Communion; with this thought set prominently before us we are wont to summon all the energies of our souls to render thanks to Almighty God for His great mercies vouchsafed to us in the Sacrament of our Lord's Body and Blood. "They blessed the Lord in the furnace of fire;" here in one single sentence is summed up a whole philosophy of the Christian life. Trial, temptation, distress, affliction, pain, suffering—these or some of these are always present with us, and we must bow our heads

[1] "Treasury of Devotion," Thanksgiving after Communion.

and thankfully accept them. Through them all, if we are called on to endure them, we must be patient; and for the trial and the discipline, whatever it may be, however it may meet us, we must be ready to thank and bless God.

This certainly is no very easy or obvious view of life. To many in this place, in full health and strength, and under the favoured conditions they enjoy, it may well seem an impossible one. Of the ordinary anxieties and troubles of many of our fellow-men we know practically nothing. All the necessaries, and many even of the luxuries of life, come to us we scarcely know how or think how. We have never known the stern experience of hundreds—or rather thousands—of men, women, and children around us, who cannot tell from day to day where their next meal is to come from. The simple primary meaning of the petition, "Give us this day our daily bread," is one that does not occur to us as we use it: we have never been starving; we have never been in distress for want of necessary clothing, or in actual suffering because we could not afford a fire in the biting cold of winter. Again, like all other men, we have capacities for pleasure and amusement, and the days as they come bring to us, with the minimum of forethought and anxiety on our part, our full share in these. We are fond of sport, or we are fond of games, and opportunities abound to us which we may rightly use in satisfying our desires. And then, once more, to rise to higher things, there are all the gifts that belong to a place of culture; those great intellectual interests which all of us who are members of this House, by our presence here, at least profess to set some store by. These the wonderful wealth of opportunity that Oxford sets within our reach gives us ample means to enjoy to the full.

No doubt in all such things there is a share of real and true discipline. We can do nothing without some effort. If we would play a game well, we must give time and thought to practise it. Certainly, in intellectual matters, if we will not face the drudgery of hard work we shall never win the gift of wide and sound learning. Besides this there is also the real discipline of failure, the sometimes almost severer discipline of success. But making as full allowance as we can on grounds such as these, it must of necessity remain true that we have as yet done little more than touch the fringe of the stern ordeal which life will surely mean for us. All our activities seem to realize themselves without let or hindrance; the happiness of success is only not less than the happiness of failure. We are trying our powers in a new and unknown world; its possibilities seem unlimited, nor can its hopes just now be clouded by disappointment. Rejoice, O young man, in thy youth; but do not entirely forget the added warning, for all this God will bring thee into judgment. Remember, therefore, now thy Creator before the evil days come.[1]

Yes; hitherto we have learned very little of what our probation here means; we have sunk no plummet into the hidden and secret depths of life; we have little idea of its possibilities, little conception of the demands it will sooner or later make upon us. So far, for most of us, life has been steadily prosperous, and Christianity has no message but one of serious and solemn warning to the successful and prosperous man. "Woe to you rich! for ye have received your consolation."[2] "Woe unto you, when all men shall speak well of you!"[3] "When thou shalt have eaten and be full; then beware lest thou forget the Lord."[4] "Man's life consisteth not in the abundance of the things which he possesseth."[5] "This night shall thy soul be required of thee: then whose shall those things be?"[6] Be glad, then, and rejoice in all the happiness life brings you. Yes; but take care sometimes, if only for an hour now and then, to be still, and to think and to remember whose you are and whom you serve. Use the gifts that are poured out upon you in such unstinted measure; but each morning pray for grace to use them unselfishly. The sorrows of life, if they do not actually touch you,

---

[1] Eccles. xi. 9 and xii. 1. [2] St. Luke vi. 24.
[3] St. Luke vi. 26. [4] Deut. vi. 11, 12.
[5] St. Luke xii. 15. [6] St. Luke xii. 20.

are near enough round about you, close by the homes in which you live so happily and lie so softly. In many ways, direct and indirect, you may if you will share them, and in sharing them win discipline for yourselves and lighten the burden for those who are called upon to suffer.

The successful, smooth, prosperous life is not the normal life: here and there—more seldom probably than is generally imagined—it is found; but sooner or later the years must bring the trials that will test us to the quick. There is the discipline of pain. As we grow older there is rarely a single day in our lives when we have not present to our thoughts one or another known to us, perhaps very close to us, cast down bound into the midst of the fiery furnace of physical pain, and called upon,—impossible, inconceivable as it may seem,—to thank God for what they have to bear. And there are men and women who can thank God, and do thank Him, in their pain. The parish priest who knows his people has seen them; not often, perhaps, but one here and another there; and they are his evidences of Christianity; he needs no other; and as he watches the patience and the faith that grace can bestow, he thanks God and takes courage.

But we may, at all events for some years, escape the discipline of pain; from the moment we become responsible agents we cannot escape the discipline of temptation. If it seemed an impossible demand on us when we are told to thank God for physical suffering, it will seem a far more impossible demand that we should be called upon to thank Him for temptation. "My brethren, count it all joy," St. James writes, "when ye fall into divers temptations: knowing this, that the trying of your faith worketh patience. But let patience have her perfect work, that ye may be perfect and entire, wanting nothing."[1] "Think it not strange," writes St. Peter, "concerning the fiery trial which is to try you, as though some strange thing happened unto you."[2] "We glory in tribulations also:" says St. Paul, "knowing that tribulation worketh patience."[3] Temptation, probation, is the will of God for us, and we must bow our heads and thankfully accept it.

This is no doubt a hard saying; but there are two considerations that may help us to receive it. First, the innocence of childhood is very pretty, very winning, and very graceful; but it is fragile, and has no strength or vitality in it. The innocence of the man who knowing evil has conquered it—or, as it is truer to say, is with steady determination fighting the battle of holiness, and striving all he knows, under every difficulty, by God's grace to bring every thought into captivity to the obedience of Christ—this has strength and substance and reality in it; it is innocence, not ignorance; and it is ours, and can only be ours,

---

[1] St. James i. 2–4. [2] 1 St. Peter iv. 12. [3] Rom. v. 3.

when we have passed through the fiery ordeal of the temptations of life.

And next, as we read the story of the life of Jesus Christ, and remember who He was, and what He did for us, as we place ourselves in thought once again at the foot of His Cross, we surely take close home to ourselves that old reproach, "All this I have done for thee, what hast thou done for Me?" If any earthly friend is very dear to us, our first thought is, how can we most simply, most unobtrusively and, therefore, most sincerely, prove our love. Christ our Lord bids us prove our love for Him; and the one way to do so is to give Him ourselves; the one answer to His question is something like this:—For Thy sake, and for love of Thee, I have striven after goodness; I have held steadily on my way in my struggle with the assaults of the flesh, and with the many temptations that beset me and goad me on to sin; I have striven to forgive, as I pray to be forgiven; I have done what I could to follow among men the things that make for peace, that lead to holiness. Not many of us, perhaps, can dare to say such things as these; rather we must say,—we have tried to live the life which by God's grace we should, but we have failed, often sadly, sometimes ruinously; still at least we have tried, and in the strength of His unchanging love we will try again and again as long as our probation lasts.

"They sang as they blessed the Lord in the furnace of fire." The triumphant cry of the Benedicite, "O all ye works of the Lord, bless ye the Lord, praise Him and exalt Him above all for ever," can only be ours when our thoughts take a wider range than our eyes can see or our senses understand, when the seen is lost in the unseen and the temporal in the eternal; in a word, when we can make our own the bright hope of immortality set before us in our Bibles. Then the trials of the present hour vanish away from our thoughts as we look on, with longing but patient hope, to the day when St. John's words shall at last have their complete fulfilment, "Behold, the tabernacle of God is with men, and He will dwell with them, and they shall be His people, and God Himself shall be with them, and be their God. And God shall wipe away all tears from their eyes; and there shall be no more death, neither sorrow, nor crying, neither shall there be any more pain: for the former things are passed away. And He that sat upon the throne said, Behold, I make all things new. It is done. I am Alpha and Omega, the Beginning and the End. I will give unto him that is athirst of the fountain of the water of life freely. He that overcometh shall inherit all things; and I will be his God, and he shall be My son."[1]

[1] Rev. xxi. 3–7.

XXVIII.

The Bearing of the Cross.

"If any man will come after Me, let him deny himself, and take up his cross, and follow Me."—St. Matt. xvi. 24.

(Second Sunday in Lent, February 18, 1894.)

"The idea of these words," says Mr. Ruskin, "has been *exactly* reversed by modern Protestantism, which sees in the Cross, not a furca to which it is to be nailed; but a raft on which it, and all its valuable properties, are to be floated into Paradise."[1] We need but superficial knowledge of current ways of speaking and writing among some religious people to know that there is much that goes a good way to excuse or to justify this very severe criticism. It may, perhaps, be worth while to consider for a moment how this comes to be so.

St. Paul is emphatically the preacher of the Cross; and, as we think of him, there are, it seems to me, two characteristics which stand out most obviously, and at once challenge our attention. The first of them is his sense of sin. St. Paul's idea of sin cannot be expressed

[1] "Bible of Amiens," J. Ruskin, p. 124.

in negative terms. To him it is no abstract idea, no negation of good, no mere absence of qualities that are useful or meritorious, no mere contradiction of prudential considerations, no mere disobedience to natural laws. Sin is something real, positive, I had almost said tangible; it clings about men, tainting, defiling, degrading them. It is an enemy close to them, personal, overmastering, holding them fast bound in fetters and chains, a power to which they are by nature sold to be bondslaves. Recall his description of moral evil in the Gentile world in the first chapter of the Epistle to the Romans; it gives one of the most appalling pictures of human degradation that we can imagine. But the Jew is found to be no better than the Gentile; St. Paul passes on at once to show that the former, with all his privileges, was the bondslave of the same master: Jews and Gentiles, both alike, are found to be fast bound in the chains of sin. No one escapes the slavery; "I," he cries, "am carnal, sold under sin":[1] and, in one of his latest Epistles, he says, Christ Jesus came to save sinners, of whom I am chief;—ὧν πρῶτός εἰμι ἐγώ [2]—in his mouth this is no conventional phrase; it is the natural and necessary expression of a perfectly candid and sincere soul.

And next, over against his conception of sin there is set the possibility of deliverance from sin through the Cross of our Lord Jesus Christ. Here was the heart of

---

[1] Rom. vii. 14.   [2] 1 Tim. i. 15.

his Gospel; the glad tidings, to carry which throughout the world, he willingly gave all that he had—and that was much—of energy, enthusiasm, and intellectual and moral gifts. "Being justified," he writes, "freely by His grace through the redemption that is in Christ Jesus: whom God set forth to be a propitiation, through faith, by His Blood;"[1] and, again, "In Christ Jesus ye that once were far off are made nigh in the Blood of Christ";[2] and, again, "Having blotted out the bond written in ordinances that was against us, which was contrary to us: and He hath taken it out of the way, nailing it to the Cross."[3] Sin and the redemption from sin—they stand over against each other. "The good which I would I do not: but the evil which I would not, that I practise. But if what I would not, that I do, it is no more I that do it, but sin which dwelleth in me. Oh, wretched man that I am! who shall deliver me out of the body of this death? I thank God through Jesus Christ our Lord."[4] Man as man could not help himself; he was tied and bound in the chains of his sins. The deliverance came, as it only could come, of the free gift of Almighty God in the mercy of the Incarnation, in the life and death of Jesus Christ. The sense of wonder and astonishment at this gift never leaves the Apostle; it thrills and penetrates his whole being; and again and again he turns aside in

---

[1] Rom. iii. 24.
[2] Eph. ii. 13.
[3] Col. ii. 14.
[4] Rom. vii. 19, 20, 24, 25.

the midst of his argument to pour out, in one doxology or another, his thanks to God, the Giver of all good; "Oh, the depth of the riches both of the wisdom and the knowledge of God! how unsearchable are His judgments, and His ways past tracing out!"[1]

When men think of sin as St. Paul thought of it, when the death on the Cross means to them all it meant to him, then, no doubt, you have in these two doctrines the essence of the Christian Creed. But, if the glow and warmth of life have gone out of them, if men accept them with the intellect alone as complete and formal summaries of the Christian Creed, they may only too quickly degenerate into the lifeless formulæ of a narrow and meagre presentation of St. Paul's teaching. The time was when they moved men's hearts and moulded their lives, but they can do so no longer. The fineness of religious touch has been dulled, and the fervour of self-devotion has been lost, as the world through selfishness and indolence has regained its old mastery over thought; and, consequently, propositions which were at one time the expressions of vital truths, are so manipulated and interpreted as to suggest some such wild travesty of the Creed as that which called forth Mr. Ruskin's unsparing but perfectly just criticism.

"Believe on the Lord Jesus, and thou shalt be saved."[2] This, rightly understood, is the heart of

---

[1] Rom. xi. 33.   [2] Acts xvi. 31.

the Apostle's message. But what did he mean by "believe?" No doubt he meant intellectual assent to definite historical and theological propositions; but he meant a great deal besides this. "Thou believest, thou doest well: the devils also believe, and shudder,"[1] St. James writes. We must turn to St. Paul's Epistles for the full answer to the question. Listen to what he says about himself: "I buffet—or bruise—my body, and bring it into bondage: lest by any means, after that I have preached to others, I myself should be rejected;"[2] "I have been crucified with Christ;"[3] "I die daily;"[4] "the sufferings of Christ abound unto us;"[5] "that I may know Him and the fellowship of His sufferings";[6] "not that I have already obtained or am already made perfect";[7] "they that are of Christ Jesus have crucified the flesh";[8] "the Cross of our Lord Jesus Christ, through which the world hath been crucified unto me, and I unto the world";[9] "now I rejoice in my sufferings for your sake, and fill up on my part that which is lacking of the afflictions of Christ in my flesh."[10] No; be sure of this, redemption is not in the Cross of Christ without you as an external objective fact, but in the power of that Cross brought home to you, penetrating and pervading the whole moral and spiritual life, through the grace of the Holy Spirit,

---

[1] James ii. 19. [2] 1 Cor. ix. 27. [3] Gal. ii. 20.
[4] 1 Cor. xv. 31. [5] 2 Cor. i. 5. [6] Phil. iii. 10.
[7] Phil. iii. 12. [8] Gal. v. 24. [9] Gal. vi. 14.
[10] Col. i. 24.

perfected in you during the whole of life on earth in the constant struggle with sin and temptation.

> "Let no man think that, sudden, in a minute,
>   All is accomplished and the work is done;
> Though with thine earliest dawn thou shouldst begin it,
>   Scarce were it ended in thy setting sun.
>
> "How have I knelt with arms of my aspiring
>   Lifted all night in irresponsive air,
> Dazed and amazed with overmuch desiring,
>   Blank with the utter agony of prayer!
>
> "Ay, and for me, there shot from the beginning
>   Pulses of passion broken with my breath;
> O thou poor soul, enwrapped in such a sinning,
>   Bound in the shameful body of thy death!
>
> "Well, let me sin, but not with my consenting,
>   Well, let me die, but willing to be whole;
> Never, O Christ,—so stay me from relenting,—
>   Shall there be truce betwixt my flesh and soul."[1]

But, more than this: it was impossible for St. Paul to imagine that he would travel through life here by some easier path than that which his Master had trodden. Christ Himself was made perfect through the things that He suffered; surely the servant cannot be greater than his Lord; surely the sorrows of the Master shall be and must be shared by all His followers. Each who will take up this service must be ready, by the terms of the service, to travel along the way of the Cross, to drink of the cup his Master drank of, and to be baptized with the baptism that He was baptized with.

[1] "St. Paul," by F. W. H. Myers.

St. Paul's teaching is a consistent whole; you cannot take it to pieces and rearrange it to suit your fancy. Accept his teaching, as indeed you must, about sin and redemption from sin by the Cross of Christ; but you must also accept all he tells you as to the means whereby, through the power of the Holy Spirit, that redemption is worked out in each individual soul. True, no doubt, had Christ never died, there would be no Cross to which we could be nailed; true, no doubt, the redemption is all His; but, if we would have it for ourselves and make it our own, we can only do so in the one way which St. Paul points out, that is, by taking our share, as God shall show us, in the Cross.

For, after all, St. Paul is only teaching what our Lord had taught in the words of the text, "If any man will come after me, let him deny himself and take up his Cross, and follow Me"; deny himself, take up his cross, follow Me. Deny himself as Christ did; Love, Divine pity and compassion, was the motive of that self-emptying, that humiliation—and our self-denial is of no value save as it honestly seeks to find itself in love, love to God shown and testified to by love to man.

And let him take up his cross; again take it up as Christ took His; carry it as He carried His; and in the end be nailed to it as He was nailed to His.

To bring these things home to our dull hearts is no easy task, for, as Dr. Hort has said, "we are slow to believe that the Cross of anguish can be a Tree of Life." [1] When the hand of God is heavy upon ourselves, when the discipline and anxieties of life are heavier than we know how to bear, when the cross laid on us is weighing us down, seeming to crush us beneath its weight, we find out how very far we have come short of the life of faith that should be ours. Shall we, therefore, give up the struggle in despair? God forbid! All we need then ask is patience to be quiet and still, to bear and to endure; and strength and courage to do the work that has been put into our hands to do. For round us on every side are the sheltering arms of the Christian Church; before thousands upon thousands of Christian altars the Eucharistic pleading is continually made, the pleading of the one Sacrifice once offered, the holding up before heaven and earth of the one true Cross. It may be that for the moment we have lost sight of everything; that faith seems a delusion, and hope a far-off echo of some bygone dream or fancy. But we can still throw ourselves, as we may and must, upon the faith of the whole Church of God, and, in the strength of that companionship, live and work, endure the hardness, and when the time comes, if need be, die. It is easy—God pardon us who preach!—to say such things as these, but hard—God only knows how hard!—to live them through in our lives. Still, there lies our path, and we must do our best steadily to

[1] "Hulsean Lectures," by the Rev. Dr. Hort, p. 218.

make our way along it. It will help us if we remember that, perhaps in the very stress of the confusion, in the crushing and, as it seems, the fatal maiming of our present life, unknown to us, in ways we cannot now conceive or understand, the life that never has an ending may be gathering strength and fulness and power within us, and so for us too, as we pray in God's mercy we may one day know, the Cross is indeed the Tree of Life.

XXIX.

Covetousness.

"Take heed, and beware of covetousness: for a man's life consisteth not in the abundance of the things which he possesseth."—St. Luke xii. 15.

(Quinquagesima Sunday, February 16, 1896.)

We are, I fear, only too ready to imagine that the command to beware of covetousness is one that is not of any special importance for people placed as we are: it applies, we think, rather to those whom we often call, in not very happy phrase, the lower classes; to those who are poor and in want, and are therefore naturally tempted to cast covetous eyes on the things they see in the possession of others. Perhaps the words of the Church catechism, in which we were taught as children that we must not covet or desire other men's goods, have some share in emphasizing this very restricted view. No doubt it is a sin to covet that which belongs to another; let us admit this as fully as we can—and let us admit, too, that those who are in very impoverished circumstances of life are peculiarly liable to this particular temptation; but we must also admit, if we are capable of dispassionate thought, that under these conditions we meet the sin in its least heinous form ; that again and again there is in the surrounding circumstances, when we come to know them, only too much that goes far to palliate if not even to condone the wrong desire. When we hear well-to-do people solve all the problems presented by the struggles of political and social life by the simple dictum that it is only a question between " the haves " and " the have nots," implying, as they usually do by the words, that most of the greed and most of the selfishness is on the side of the latter, we may well pause a moment, and think ; and the result of our thought will be, I feel perfectly clear, to convict " the haves " of the greater guilt of covetousness.

Most people, however, get one step beyond this very elementary view of the question : they recognize that covetousness in the abstract, the burning desire to add to one's possessions, is ignoble and debasing, is in a word sin ; that, as Christian men and women, we are bound to be contented with the conditions in which we find ourselves placed, and to do our duty thankfully in that state of life to which Almighty God has called us ; that the undisciplined desire to double or treble our incomes, or to add to what is ours of wealth or power, denotes a sordid mind ; that the man who indulges these thoughts lives in continual sin. Here we reach a point that is, it may well be feared, only a too serious one for Englishmen. We speak of national sins, and we do so rightly, for societies, no less than individuals, have a moral conscience ; it is, therefore, a fair question to ask, whether covetousness is not a national sin amongst us. I would I felt I could answer this question unhesitatingly in the negative. He that makes haste to be rich, the Bible tells us, shall not be innocent.[1] There is an old saying, quoted in a sermon some two centuries ago by one who held office as a Canon in this Church ;[2] "there is no man," it runs, "very rich, but is either an unjust person himself, or the heir of one or other who was so." "I dare not," the preacher adds, " pronounce so severe a sentence universally : but the general business and corruption of men's practices has verified this harsh saying of too many ; and it is every day seen how many serve the god of this world to receive the riches of it."

If Dr. South could say this in his day, what would he think if he saw things as they are now ? What are hundreds and hundreds of Englishmen, yes and Englishwomen too, doing to-day but wildly, passionately, hasting to be rich ? And what are the means they are using to attain their end ? Stock Exchange operations no doubt attract a great many ; but the excitement of these is equalled, possibly surpassed, by the methods that obtain nowadays in commercial

---

[1] Prov. xxviii. 20.
[2] South's Sermons, vol. iv. p. 473. Edition, 1715.

transactions. One sometimes hears it questioned whether there is any sound, legitimate business left; so much of it has become wild speculation, or, to put it in quite plain words, betting and gambling. And the game, disastrous as it is, I believe, in itself, is too often made infinitely worse because it is not played fairly. Men form rings, companies, syndicates, and seem at times to recoil from nothing that can compass their one end—gain: false news, bogus telegrams, political complications, even national troubles,—any method may be used, and any risk run that will bring about the desired object, a rise or a fall in the market; and then those who are behind the scenes sell or buy at the critical moment, that moment being the time when, to put it quite bluntly, the opportunity occurs to steal as much as possible from other people. We have seen the closing of the gambling tables at many of the places of popular resort; we hope before long to see the end of the tables at Monte Carlo; and we are inclined to congratulate ourselves on the moral advance we have made. Are we not a little too hasty? With the growth of intercommunication, linked together as the human race now is by the telegraph, the world has become one vast gambling house; the counters lie about at every large Stock Exchange and at every great commercial centre, and the wildly exciting maddening game is played almost without cessation.

One man's gain is another man's loss. This system does not create wealth; it does not beneficially distribute it; it forcibly wrenches it from one and flings it to another. The thousands a successful speculator sweeps into his coffers come of necessity out of the pockets of others: it would be well if they came only from those who gambled as he does: unfortunately at times, and only too often, innocent people suffer, and the old man's savings, the widow's income, and the money that should educate and feed the children pay their tax to these unscrupulous operators. God's law for man is the merciful beneficent law of labour—"in the sweat of thy face shalt thou eat bread."[1] All the earth has to give us is the reward of toil, and only by toil can any of its wealth be honestly gained or honestly held. Those who work immediately and directly in the production of the fruits of the earth, those who work indirectly in the duties of government, or healing, or teaching, or any of the manifold tasks which may be allotted men,—not primarily for their own profit, but that the world may be the better because they have lived in it,—all these earn their living honestly as the Bible bids them do. Those who amass wealth by preying upon their fellow-men, whether on a large and magnificent scale, where success wins admiration and applause, or in those less splendid ways which never win popular approval,

[1] Gen. iii. 19.

and very often end in jail, earn their livelihood dishonestly—in one word, they steal it.

It will, perhaps, be thought that all this is very remote from our lives here; it may be so, I trust it is so; but there are other ways in which the same sin, the same deadening unholy worship of the god of this world, may be brought much nearer home to the life of a University. No doubt the sin appears in less obvious ways; it does not flaunt itself so openly and so unblushingly; but its consequences are none the less fatal, perhaps they are even more disastrous. It shows itself under decent outward pretences, it puts on the guise of moral purpose, it assumes at times the cloke of religion. Think only of one aspect of it; how industriously, and sincerely too, during these many years past, well-meaning people have preached the great gospel of "getting on"; do this and avoid that, choose the one and refuse the other and you will "get on"; not meaning that you will be better men, truer, braver, more generous; that you will have learned more kindness and consideration for others, more control over yourself; that you will have won some clearer hold on all that is meant by goodness; that you will know more of the love of God; not this at all, or anything like this; but that you will have some chance of a decent balance at your bankers. "Get on" means get wealth, get power, get honour, get position, get money; here is the ideal; here is the golden image set up for the worship and adoration of Christian people. Surely the god of the world has blinded their eyes; surely they are being taught to spend their strength for nought, and their labour for that which shall never profit them. It would have seemed possible that the things with which this place is chiefly concerned, the things that belong to the mind and intellect might escape the contamination, and yet they have not done so. Many are working steadily and unselfishly in the cause of education, and it is one of the most hopeful signs of our times that this should be the case: but it will save some from bitter disappointment if they remember, that education may be made a mere engine for profit and social advancement; that it is only too often sought and desired, not for its own sake, but for the price it will fetch in the world's market. It, too, is compelled to bow the knee to Mammon, and as it pays its worship it loses utterly and for ever all that gives it its worth; it loses its soul.

Compare with these low standards the aims set before us in the pages of the Gospels, and you will see how practically fathomless the gulf is that opens out between the ideals, moralities, and respectabilities of modern society and the teaching of Jesus Christ. Try and think of Him on earth in bodily form again; and ask yourself how He would bear Himself in Throgmorton Street? What would He do or say among the hurrying crowds of speculators?

among the men who are busy bartering their gifts of intellect for money, or power, or place? or among those who, having the key of knowledge, neither enter in themselves nor suffer others who would do so to enter in? We know, indeed, where He would be found. He would be with the ploughman as he drove his furrow through the field; He would bless the husbandman as he sowed his seed; the reaper as he gathered his sheaves; He would acknowledge His true merchants,[1] as they fulfilled their beneficent mission in providing for the wants of men, by distributing the fruits of the earth or the products of labour. No honest work sincerely done for others' good would be beyond the reach of His benediction. He would be found where sickness and pain were, in the wards of our hospitals and by the bedside of the dying; He would be found, too, let us never forget it, among the poor. We think of Him as tender, compassionate, gracious; but we forget, willingly, perhaps wilfully forget, that He said some very stern things; sternest of all of the rich and the well to do, the Pharisees and the rulers. Would He, think you, in this our day, be less severe than He was of old in Palestine? Would He call to Himself now the rich, the Church people, the well to do? Would He bless those that sit in the seats of the teachers now? Are they all no longer blind guides? Are the dangers of wealth less now

---

[1] Cf. Ruskin's "Unto t' is Last," 6th edition, p. 33.

than they were then? Have the sins and selfishness that shamed it then in His presence become impossible now? Would His temple need no cleansing now? Are there no longer usurers and money-changers to be cast out? Would He readily find a home in churches frequented by rich and fashionable people? In our great cathedrals, with their stately magnificence and dignified services, would He now be at once welcomed and recognized? or would He be again rejected, again scorned, again crucified? It may help us, as we enter once more into Lent, if we each try to answer these questions so far as they concern ourselves personally.

XXX.

Covetousness.

"Take heed, and beware of covetousness: for a man's life consisteth not in the abundance of the things which he possesseth."—St. Luke xii. 15.

(First Sunday in Lent, February 23, 1896.)

Last Sunday I spoke of covetousness under some of its very obvious aspects; to-day I pass on to consider it in its more subtle and indirect forms.

It will perhaps sound somewhat oddly, and yet it is entirely true, to assert that we may covet that which is, as children say, our very own, that which we have won by our own honest labour, which is morally as well as legally our own. We may use it selfishly; we may wrap ourselves up in comfort and self-indulgence; we may say to our souls that we have worked hard and now it is quite right that we should take our ease and enjoy the fruits of our toil; not necessarily at all in coarse or vulgarly selfish ways; selfishness may be, and very often is, quite refined, outwardly decorous and even graceful, and none the less it is wholly base. The selfish, self-regarding use of the wealth that is in our keeping is at bottom the same deadly sin with the sin of covetousness.

And we cannot stop even here: as we go on to think it all out, this sin of which we are speaking is found to extend over all the circumstances and conditions of life; it covers the whole of our relations with the visible world. Yes; covetousness in veiled forms may stain and taint the noblest gifts we possess—gifts of intellect, gifts of art, the magic power and wonder of music, and, lastly, the greatest gift of all, friendship, love, the ties of home, the source and spring of so much that is best in us.

I often recall a story, I believe a well-known one, told some years ago from this pulpit by one of our greatest preachers, who has since then passed to his rest. Cardinal Mazarin was lying on his death-bed; his attendants thought him asleep. For some reason or other they went out of the room, and left the old man alone. A minute or two later, as they were passing out of the picture gallery into which the bedroom opened, they heard a shuffling movement behind them, and, turning round, they saw the Cardinal, with a loose gown thrown round him, standing in front of his favourite pictures, and kissing his hand to them, and saying, "Good-bye, dear pictures!"[1]

---

[1] "Passiontide Sermons," by the late Rev. H. P. Liddon, Canon of St. Paul's, Sermon xvii. p. 266. The story as told here is somewhat

In a brief account of the career of one of our greatest Oxford scholars, it is told how, in his last illness, when he could no longer read or write or attempt any intellectual work at all, he had his beloved books gathered round him on his bed; and as he laid his feeble hands on them, he said fondly and sadly, "Ah, I am to leave my books!"[1]

It may, perhaps, be said, Are we not to admire beautiful pictures? Are we to close our ears to the subtle charm of music, to distrust and despise our intellectual gifts? Are we even, for it seems to be so implied, to put a restraint upon our affection for our friends?

Follow me for one moment in another line of thought; it will seem as if we were passing right away from all of which we are speaking, but we shall, I believe, be brought round to the answer we must make to all such questions as these. What do we mean by beauty? We shall best find an answer in brief compass by asking, what do we mean by beauty in nature? We have all watched an autumn sunset,—many of us have seen it in the clear warm air of Southern Europe,—the sky brilliant with colours of purple and crimson and gold that no tongue can describe and no pencil can paint. As the vision of the glory rises upon our wistful gaze, as it gathers strength and majesty and fulness,

---

altered. It was told from memory, and is left in the form in which it was given at the time.

[1] "Stones of Stumbling," by Hon. L. A. Tollemache, p. 124.

and then by slow degrees grows dim and at last fades altogether from our sight, can we say whether the feeling of which we are conscious is one of pleasure or of pain? There is the sense of stretching out far away from our ordinary selves to some great good only very dimly seen and very dimly understood, which yet we would fain, if we could, gather in and make our own. But we cannot do so; the light and the glory pass away and are gone, and there remains with us the sense of incompleteness and loss. We seem to have been close up to some vision of those things which eye has never seen nor ear ever heard; it was near us, and now it is gone, and we have lost it. Something of this I always imagine Wordsworth, with that intuitive sense he had of the Infinite veiled under nature everywhere, meant, when he said—

> "To me the meanest flower that blows can give
> Thoughts that do often lie too deep for tears."

This that we have tried to say of natural beauty is true of all beauty. All beauty is the reaching towards an ideal, the endeavour to realize to the outward senses something which is of necessity in its perfection wholly unattainable. What is it that makes a picture great? Certainly not the skill, wonderful as it may be, of the worker. We have all learned that the moment art becomes self-conscious, and is proud of what it can do and of its skill in doing it, it is smitten with sure and certain decay and death. That which makes the artist what he is, so we have been taught, is to be found in his gifts of sympathy and imagination—imagination, that is, in the highest, noblest sense of the word; imagination in the strength of which he may climb the height of heaven and reach thoughts words will not express. And having heard and seen and pondered, he needs must try to speak, and with the finite means at his command suggest something of that which lies beyond the bounds of time and sense. Impossible! Yes, of course it is impossible; and he is always telling us how impossible it is. But—and this is my point—his work is noble in so far as it lets us into his secret, and shows us that he has seen things which pass beyond his power of description. His true greatness lies just where he cannot but in one sense fail; that is, in his attempt to present to men truths that are beyond representation, to reveal that which never can be plainly said by any human tongue or distinctly limned by any human hand.

The same is true of music. Much of it is intricate and puzzling, and the satisfaction found in it at times appears to be chiefly akin to the arithmetician's interest in his clever puzzles. But the secret of the mighty power of music cannot be found in these; music in its turn must be the interpreter of all that is noblest in its age, and to be such an interpreter it must be able to rise infinitely above it and to reveal something of the divine ideals which lie hidden beneath the seemingly chaotic movement of the whole; it must have caught some echoes of the choirs of heaven, some thoughts that in their fulness lie far beyond our reach; in its attempt to present these it fulfils the conditions of its greatness in the certainty of its failure.

Intellectual gifts, intellectual genius, whether devoted to the world of outward nature or the world of thought, pass under the same law. The wisest men know how little they really know; how at their very best they are but as children picking up the shells and stones on the shore of an infinite sea. The things they find tell them wonderful stories, open out marvellous depths, seemingly boundless spaces for the imagination to penetrate: but with the increase of knowledge comes always a keener juster appreciation of the stupendous unknown: however complete some momentary advance may seem to be, the infinite beyond them always beckons men on; in the moment of greatest achievement they realize most acutely how infinitesimally small they are; how they also triumph only to measure their failure.

There remains the greatest gift of God to man, one which, however remote some of the things of which we have been thinking may seem from many of us, is close up to and within the reach of all, the gift of companionship, of friendship, of love. Life [1] we have been

---

[1] "For life, with all it yields of joy and woe,
Is just our chance o' the prize of learning love,
How love might be, hath been indeed, and is."
BROWNING, *A Death in the Desert.*

taught to think of as just the opportunity of learning this priceless lesson of love. Those who have failed to learn it have never really lived. Love, the purest and the most unselfish, has been given, God grant it! to each of us in the homes of our childhood, in the mother's tender patient care, and in the father's strong affection. There are, it is true enough, people to whom the words father and mother, one or both of them, never call up any gracious memories or any wondering gratitude; on them in God's inscrutable purpose for them has been allowed to fall one of the greatest of human sorrows; only those who have passed through it can know what that sorrow is. Love, however, comes to men and women in other ways; and the life must have been indeed a hard one to which it has never revealed itself in something of the strength and grace that have been given to it by God. Through it men learn what are the depths of human tenderness, the possibilities of human self-sacrifice, the miracles of entire and whole-hearted friendship. All these are wonderful gifts, wonderful beyond power of words to speak of; and yet they are, even while we hold them, ready to perish: misunderstanding may mar them; death will surely sever them; they pass from us, and we are left alone; they were, and now they are not, and we—what can we do to save ourselves in the day of our despair?

My brothers, what does it all mean? This constant stretching out of ourselves to seize upon the marvels revealed in art and in the mystic wonder of music? this leaping up of intellectual enthusiasm as the visions of the past and the hopes of the future, the mysteries of life and thought and consciousness, seem ready to unfold themselves? this amazing strength of friendship, these miracles of love? and then over them all, ringing out clear and strong, this sad pathetic note that tells of incompleteness, inadequacy, and failure? We Christians have our answer; "My soul is athirst for God, yea, even for the living God: when shall I come to appear before the presence of God? Why art thou so vexed, O my soul: and why art thou so disquieted within me? O put thy trust in God: for I will yet thank Him which is the help of my countenance, and my God."[1] Yes, it is all true. The day will come when you must leave your books, when you must say good-bye to your pictures, when love and friendship will pass from you, and you, stripped bare of all that now seems to hold your life together, must pass away alone into the mysterious, unseen, and unknown world that lies behind the veil of the things that are seen. Alone, and yet, God grant it to each of us! not alone: for when that day comes you do not leave Him Who is the Strength and Stay of all things made by Him; Who is Himself the supreme, unchanging beauty; Who has revealed Himself as perfect Love; Who is Himself the Giver of all human friend-

[1] Ps. xlii. 2, 14, 15.

ship, and the Source of all human love. In Him all things consist and are; they speak to us of His glory, and they tell us of His praise.

Here is the sum of the whole matter; only learn to see God's Presence revealed, dimly indeed but still most really, in all the world of nature round you, and you must of necessity learn to use His gifts rightly. So far as you live consciously in His sight, covetousness, the selfish desire for or the abuse of any one of His gifts, will become utterly impossible. So living you can thank Him with full hearts for all the gladness He has poured out upon your lives; you can praise Him for all His gifts of health and strength and intellect, and for all the dear ties of love and affection; you can never then forget the Giver, or as you receive His gifts use them selfishly. See His Hand everywhere; see Him revealed in every glory of earth and sky and sea, in every noble work of human skill, in every pure gift of human imagination. See Him, too, He knows how almost impossible it is, in the great mysteries of pain and sorrow and death: it may be a day will come for some of us when we shall be able to make our own the Psalmist's words, "It is good for me that I have been in trouble: that I may learn Thy statutes."[1]

At many different times, but twice on very solemn occasions, our Lord declared Himself to be the Life of men; "I am the Way, the Truth, and the Life;"[2] "I

[1] Ps. cxix. 71. [2] St. John xiv. 6.

am the Resurrection, and the Life."[1] Here in contrast with the words of the text which tell us that "a man's life consisteth not in the abundance of the things which he possesseth," is that in which our life in deed and in truth consists. "I am the Life;" this is the theme of St. John's Gospel, the sum of the Revelation he has to unfold; "In Him was Life; and the Life was the Light of men;"[2] the whole of the fourth gospel is a comment on, and an explanation of, these words. And in those wonderful chapters with which the New Testament closes he once again repeats and enforces the same truth; "And he shewed me a pure river of water of life, clear as crystal, proceeding out of the Throne of God and of the Lamb."[3] "And the Spirit and the Bride say, Come. And let him that heareth say, Come. And let him that is athirst come. And whosoever will, let him take of the water of life freely."[4] If we could once learn this lesson, if we could once realize that our true life is "hid with Christ in God,"[5] we should no longer need the continually reiterated warning of the New Testament, "take heed and beware of covetousness."

[1] St. John xi. 25. [2] St. John i. 4. [3] Rev. xxii. 1.
[4] Rev. xxii. 17. [5] Col. iii. 3.

THE END.

PRINTED BY WILLIAM CLOWES AND SONS, LIMITED, LONDON AND BECCLES.

A Selection of Works
IN
THEOLOGICAL LITERATURE
PUBLISHED BY
Messrs. LONGMANS, GREEN, & CO.

London: 39 Paternoster Row, E.C.
New York: 91 and 93 Fifth Avenue.
Bombay: 32 Hornby Road.

Abbey and Overton.—THE ENGLISH CHURCH IN THE EIGHTEENTH CENTURY. By Charles J. Abbey, M.A., Rector of Checkendon, Reading, and John H. Overton, D.D., Canon of Lincoln and Rector of Epworth. *Crown 8vo. 7s. 6d.*

Adams.—SACRED ALLEGORIES. The Shadow of the Cross—The Distant Hills—The Old Man's Home—The King's Messengers. By the Rev. William Adams, M.A. *Crown 8vo. 3s. 6d.*
The four Allegories may be had separately, with Illustrations. 16mo. 1s. each.

Aids to the Inner Life.
Edited by the Rev. W. H. Hutchings, M.A., Rector of Kirby Misperton, Yorkshire. *Five Vols. 32mo, cloth limp, 6d. each; or cloth extra, 1s. each.*
OF THE IMITATION OF CHRIST. By Thomas à Kempis.
THE CHRISTIAN YEAR.
THE DEVOUT LIFE. By St. Francis de Sales.
THE HIDDEN LIFE OF THE SOUL.
THE SPIRITUAL COMBAT. By Laurence Scupoli.

Bathe.—Works by the Rev. Anthony Bathe, M.A.
A LENT WITH JESUS. A Plain Guide for Churchmen. Containing Readings for Lent and Easter Week, and on the Holy Eucharist. *32mo, 1s.; or in paper cover, 6d.*
AN ADVENT WITH JESUS. *32mo, 1s.; or in paper cover, 6d.*
WHAT I SHOULD BELIEVE. A Simple Manual of Self-Instruction for Church People. *Small 8vo, limp, 1s.; cloth gilt, 2s.*

Bathe and Buckham.—THE CHRISTIAN'S ROAD BOOK.
2 Parts. By the Rev. Anthony Bathe and Rev. F. H. Buckham.
Part I. Devotions. *Sewed, 6d.; limp cloth, 1s.; cloth extra, 1s. 6d.*
Part II. Readings. *Sewed, 1s.; limp cloth, 2s.; cloth extra, 3s.;* or complete in one volume, *sewed, 1s. 6d.; limp cloth, 2s. 6d.; cloth extra, 3s. 6d.*

Benson.—THE FINAL PASSOVER: A Series of Meditations upon the Passion of our Lord Jesus Christ. By the Rev. R. M. BENSON, M.A., Student of Christ Church, Oxford. *Small 8vo.*
Vol. I.—THE REJECTION. 5*s.*
Vol. II.—THE UPPER CHAMBER.
Part I. 5*s.*
Part II. 5*s.*
Vol. III.—THE DIVINE EXODUS. Parts I. and II. 5*s.* each.
Vol. IV.—THE LIFE BEYOND THE GRAVE. 5*s.*

Bickersteth.—YESTERDAY, TO-DAY, AND FOR EVER: a Poem in Twelve Books. By EDWARD HENRY BICKERSTETH, D.D., Bishop of Exeter. *One Shilling Edition*, 18mo. *With red borders*, 16mo, 2*s.* 6*d.*
The Crown 8vo Edition (5*s.*) *may still be had.*

Blunt.—Works by the Rev. JOHN HENRY BLUNT, D.D.
THE ANNOTATED BOOK OF COMMON PRAYER: Being an Historical, Ritual, and Theological Commentary on the Devotional System of the Church of England. *4to.* 21*s.*
THE COMPENDIOUS EDITION OF THE ANNOTATED BOOK OF COMMON PRAYER: Forming a concise Commentary on the Devotional System of the Church of England. *Crown 8vo.* 10*s.* 6*d.*
DICTIONARY OF DOCTRINAL AND HISTORICAL THEOLOGY. By various Writers. *Imperial 8vo.* 21*s.*
DICTIONARY OF SECTS, HERESIES, ECCLESIASTICAL PARTIES AND SCHOOLS OF RELIGIOUS THOUGHT. By various Writers. *Imperial 8vo.* 21*s.*
THE BOOK OF CHURCH LAW. Being an Exposition of the Legal Rights and Duties of the Parochial Clergy and the Laity of the Church of England. Revised by Sir WALTER G. F. PHILLIMORE, Bart., D.C.L., and G. EDWARDES JONES, Barrister-at-Law. *Crown 8vo.* 7*s.* 6*d.*
A COMPANION TO THE BIBLE: Being a Plain Commentary on Scripture History, to the end of the Apostolic Age. *Two Vols. small 8vo. Sold separately.*
THE OLD TESTAMENT. 3*s.* 6*d.*   THE NEW TESTAMENT. 3*s.* 6*d.*
HOUSEHOLD THEOLOGY: a Handbook of Religious Information respecting the Holy Bible, the Prayer Book, the Church, etc., etc. *Paper cover*, 16mo. 1*s.* *Also the Larger Edition*, 3*s.* 6*d.*

Body.—Works by the Rev. GEORGE BODY, D.D., Canon of Durham.
THE LIFE OF LOVE. A Course of Lent Lectures. 16mo. 2*s.* 6*d.*
THE SCHOOL OF CALVARY; or, Laws of Christian Life revealed from the Cross. 16mo. 2*s.* 6*d.*
THE LIFE OF JUSTIFICATION. 16mo. 2*s.* 6*d.*
THE LIFE OF TEMPTATION. 16mo. 2*s.* 6*d.*

Boultbee.—A COMMENTARY ON THE THIRTY-NINE ARTICLES OF THE CHURCH OF ENGLAND. By the Rev. T. P. BOULTBEE, formerly Principal of the London College of Divinity, St. John's Hall, Highbury. *Crown 8vo.* 6*s.*

Bright.—Works by WILLIAM BRIGHT, D.D., Regius Professor of Ecclesiastical History in the University of Oxford, Canon of Christ Church, Oxford.

THE ROMAN SEE IN THE EARLY CHURCH: And other Studies in Church History. *Crown 8vo. 7s. 6d.*

WAYMARKS IN CHURCH HISTORY. *Crown 8vo. 7s. 6d.*

MORALITY IN DOCTRINE. *Crown 8vo. 7s. 6d.*

LESSONS FROM THE LIVES OF THREE GREAT FATHERS: St. Athanasius, St. Chrysostom, and St. Augustine. *Crown 8vo. 6s.*

THE INCARNATION AS A MOTIVE POWER. *Crown 8vo. 6s.*

Bright and Medd.—LIBER PRECUM PUBLICARUM ECCLESIÆ ANGLICANÆ. A GULIELMO BRIGHT, S.T.P., et PETRO GOLDSMITH MEDD, A.M., Latine redditus. *Small 8vo. 7s. 6d.*

Browne.—AN EXPOSITION OF THE THIRTY-NINE ARTICLES, Historical and Doctrinal. By E. H. BROWNE, D.D., formerly Bishop of Winchester. *8vo. 16s.*

Campion and Beamont.—THE PRAYER BOOK INTERLEAVED. With Historical Illustrations and Explanatory Notes arranged parallel to the Text. By W. M. CAMPION, D.D., and W. J. BEAMONT, M.A. *Small 8vo. 7s. 6d.*

Carter.—Works edited by the Rev. T. T. CARTER, M.A., Hon. Canon of Christ Church, Oxford.

THE TREASURY OF DEVOTION: a Manual of Prayer for General and Daily Use. Compiled by a Priest.

18mo. 2s. 6d.; cloth limp, 2s.
Bound with the Book of Common Prayer, *3s. 6d.*
Red-Line Edition. *Cloth extra, gilt top. 18mo, 2s. 6d. net.*
Large-Type Edition. *Crown 8vo. 3s. 6d.*

THE WAY OF LIFE: A Book of Prayers and Instruction for the Young at School, with a Preparation for Confirmation. Compiled by a Priest, *18mo. 1s. 6d.*

THE PATH OF HOLINESS: a First Book of Prayers, with the Service of the Holy Communion, for the Young. Compiled by a Priest. With Illustrations. *16mo. 1s. 6d.; cloth limp, 1s.*

THE GUIDE TO HEAVEN: a Book of Prayers for every Want. (For the Working Classes.) Compiled by a Priest. *18mo. 1s. 6d.; cloth limp, 1s. Large-Type Edition. Crown 8vo. 1s. 6d.; cloth limp, 1s.*

THE STAR OF CHILDHOOD: a First Book of Prayers and Instruction for Children. Compiled by a Priest. With Illustrations. *16mo. 2s. 6d.*

[continued.

Carter.—Works edited by the Rev. T. T. CARTER, M.A., Hon. Canon of Christ Church, Oxford—*continued.*

NICHOLAS FERRAR: his Household and his Friends. With Portrait engraved after a Picture by CORNELIUS JANSSEN at Magdalene College, Cambridge. *Crown 8vo.* 6s.

THE LIFE AND TIMES OF JOHN KETTLEWELL. With Details of the History of the Non-Jurors. With Portrait. *Crown 8vo.* 6s.

Conybeare and Howson.—THE LIFE AND EPISTLES OF ST. PAUL. By the Rev. W. J. CONYBEARE, M.A., and the Very Rev. J. S. HOWSON, D.D. With numerous Maps and Illustrations.

LIBRARY EDITION. *Two Vols. 8vo.* 21s. STUDENTS' EDITION. *One Vol. Crown 8vo.* 6s. POPULAR EDITION. *One Vol. Crown 8vo.* 3s. 6d.

Devotional Series, 16mo, Red Borders. *Each* 2s. 6d.

BICKERSTETH'S YESTERDAY, TO-DAY, AND FOR EVER.
CHILCOT'S TREATISE ON EVIL THOUGHTS.
THE CHRISTIAN YEAR.
FRANCIS DE SALES' (ST.) THE DEVOUT LIFE.
HERBERT'S POEMS AND PROVERBS.
KEMPIS' (À) OF THE IMITATION OF CHRIST.
WILSON'S THE LORD'S SUPPER. *Large type.*
*TAYLOR'S (JEREMY) HOLY LIVING.
*——— ——— HOLY DYING.

* *These two in one Volume.* 5s.

Devotional Series, 18mo, without Red Borders. *Each* 1s.

BICKERSTETH'S YESTERDAY, TO-DAY, AND FOR EVER.
THE CHRISTIAN YEAR.
FRANCIS DE SALES' (ST.) THE DEVOUT LIFE.
HERBERT'S POEMS AND PROVERBS.
KEMPIS (À) OF THE IMITATION OF CHRIST.
WILSON'S THE LORD'S SUPPER. *Large type.*
*TAYLOR'S (JEREMY) HOLY LIVING.
*——— ——— HOLY DYING.

* *These two in one Volume.* 2s. 6d.

Edersheim.—Works by ALFRED EDERSHEIM, M.A., D.D., Ph.D., sometime Grinfield Lecturer on the Septuagint, Oxford.

THE LIFE AND TIMES OF JESUS THE MESSIAH. *Two Vols. 8vo.* 24s.

JESUS THE MESSIAH: being an Abridged Edition of 'The Life and Times of Jesus the Messiah.' *Crown 8vo.* 7s. 6d.

HISTORY OF THE JEWISH NATION AFTER THE DESTRUCTION OF JERUSALEM UNDER TITUS. New Edition (The Third). Revised by the Rev. HENRY A. WHITE, M.A., Fellow of New College, Oxford. With a Preface by the Rev. WILLIAM SANDAY, D.D., LL.D., Margaret Professor of Divinity and Canon of Christ Church, Oxford. *8vo.* 18s.

IN THEOLOGICAL LITERATURE. 5

Eland.—THE LAYMAN'S INTRODUCTION TO THE BOOK OF COMMON PRAYER: being a Short History of its Development. By the Rev. EDWIN H. ELAND, M.A., Balliol College, Oxford. *With Facsimile. Crown 8vo. 5s.*

Ellicott.—Works by C. J. ELLICOTT, D.D., Bishop of Gloucester and Bristol.

A CRITICAL AND GRAMMATICAL COMMENTARY ON ST. PAUL'S EPISTLES. Greek Text, with a Critical and Grammatical Commentary, and a Revised English Translation. 8vo.

1 CORINTHIANS. 16s.	PHILIPPIANS, COLOSSIANS, AND PHILEMON. 10s. 6d.
GALATIANS. 8s. 6d.	
EPHESIANS. 8s. 6d.	THESSALONIANS. 7s. 6d.
PASTORAL EPISTLES. 10s. 6d.	

HISTORICAL LECTURES ON THE LIFE OF OUR LORD JESUS CHRIST. *8vo. 12s.*

Epochs of Church History.—Edited by MANDELL CREIGHTON, D.D., LL.D., Bishop of Peterborough. *Fcap. 8vo. 2s. 6d. each.*

THE ENGLISH CHURCH IN OTHER LANDS. By the Rev. H. W. TUCKER, M.A.

THE HISTORY OF THE REFORMATION IN ENGLAND. By the Rev. GEO. G. PERRY, M.A.

THE CHURCH OF THE EARLY FATHERS. By the Rev. ALFRED PLUMMER, D.D.

THE EVANGELICAL REVIVAL IN THE EIGHTEENTH CENTURY. By the Rev. J. H. OVERTON, D.D.

THE UNIVERSITY OF OXFORD. By the Hon. G. C. BRODRICK, D.C.L.

THE UNIVERSITY OF CAMBRIDGE. By J. BASS MULLINGER, M.A.

THE ENGLISH CHURCH IN THE MIDDLE AGES. By the Rev. W. HUNT, M.A.

THE CHURCH AND THE EASTERN EMPIRE. By the Rev. H. F. TOZER, M.A.

THE CHURCH AND THE ROMAN EMPIRE. By the Rev. A. CARR, M.A.

THE CHURCH AND THE PURITANS, 1570-1660. By HENRY OFFLEY WAKEMAN, M.A.

HILDEBRAND AND HIS TIMES. By the Rev. W. R. W. STEPHENS, M.A.

THE POPES AND THE HOHENSTAUFEN. By UGO BALZANI.

THE COUNTER REFORMATION. By ADOLPHUS WILLIAM WARD, Litt. D.

WYCLIFFE AND MOVEMENTS FOR REFORM. By REGINALD L. POOLE, M.A.

THE ARIAN CONTROVERSY. By H. M. GWATKIN, M.A.

Fosbery.—Works edited by the Rev. THOMAS VINCENT FOSBERY, M.A., sometime Vicar of St. Giles's, Reading.

VOICES OF COMFORT. *Cheap Edition. Small 8vo. 3s. 6d.*
The Larger Edition (7s. 6d.) may still be had.

HYMNS AND POEMS FOR THE SICK AND SUFFERING. In connection with the Service for the Visitation of the Sick. Selected from Various Authors. *Small 8vo. 3s. 6d.*

Gore.—Works by the Rev. CHARLES GORE, M.A., Canon of Westminster.
    THE MINISTRY OF THE CHRISTIAN CHURCH. 8vo. 10s. 6d.
    ROMAN CATHOLIC CLAIMS. Crown 8vo. 3s. 6d.

Geikie.—Works by J. CUNNINGHAM GEIKIE, D.D., LL.D., late Vicar of St. Martin-at-Palace, Norwich.
    HOURS WITH THE BIBLE: the Scriptures in the Light of Modern Discovery and Knowledge. *New Edition, largely rewritten.* Complete in Twelve Volumes. Crown 8vo. 6s. each.

OLD TESTAMENT.
In Six Volumes. Sold separately. 6s. each.

CREATION TO THE PATRIARCHS. *With a Map and Illustrations.*

MOSES TO JUDGES. *With a Map and Illustrations.*

SAMSON TO SOLOMON. *With a Map and Illustrations.*

REHOBOAM TO HEZEKIAH. *With Illustrations.*

MANASSEH TO ZEDEKIAH. *With the Contemporary Prophets. With a Map and Illustrations.*

EXILE TO MALACHI. *With the Contemporary Prophets. With Illustrations.*

NEW TESTAMENT.
In Six Volumes. Sold separately. 6s. each.

THE GOSPELS. *With a Map and Illustrations.* 2 vols.

LIFE AND WORDS OF CHRIST. *With Map.* 2 vols.

LIFE AND EPISTLES OF ST. PAUL. *With Maps and Illustrations.*

ST. PETER TO REVELATION. Completing the New Testament Series. [*In the Autumn.*

    LIFE AND WORDS OF CHRIST.
        Presentation Edition. With Map and Illustrations. 2 vols. Imperial 8vo. 24s.
        Cabinet Edition. With Map. 2 vols. Post 8vo. 12s.
        Cheap Edition, without the Notes. 1 vol. 8vo. 7s. 6d.
    A SHORT LIFE OF CHRIST. *With numerous Illustrations.* Crown 8vo. 3s. 6d.
    OLD TESTAMENT CHARACTERS. *With many Illustrations.* Crown 8vo. 3s. 6d.
    LANDMARKS OF OLD TESTAMENT HISTORY. Crown 8vo. 3s. 6d.
    THE ENGLISH REFORMATION. Crown 8vo. 3s. 6d.
    ENTERING ON LIFE. A Book for Young Men. Crown 8vo. 2s. 6d.
    THE PRECIOUS PROMISES. Crown 8vo. 2s.
    BEN AMMI: being the Story of the Life of Lazarus of Bethany, told, reputedly, by Himself. [*Preparing for publication.*

Hall.—THE VIRGIN MOTHER: Retreat Addresses on the Life of the Blessed Virgin Mary as told in the Gospels. With an appended Essay on the Virgin Birth of our Lord. By the Right Rev. A. C. A. HALL, D.D., Bishop of Vermont. *Crown 8vo.* 4s. 6d.

Harrison.—Works by the Rev. ALEXANDER J. HARRISON, B.D., Lecturer of the Christian Evidence Society.
PROBLEMS OF CHRISTIANITY AND SCEPTICISM. *Cr. 8vo.* 7s. 6d.
THE CHURCH IN RELATION TO SCEPTICS: a Conversational Guide to Evidential Work. *New and Cheaper Edition. Crown 8vo.* 3s. 6d.
THE REPOSE OF FAITH, IN VIEW OF PRESENT DAY DIFFICULTIES. *Crown 8vo.* 7s. 6d.

Holland.—Works by the Rev. HENRY SCOTT HOLLAND, M.A., Canon and Precentor of St. Paul's.
GOD'S CITY AND THE COMING OF THE KINGDOM: *Crown 8vo.* 7s. 6d.
PLEAS AND CLAIMS FOR CHRIST. *Crown 8vo.* 3s. 6d.
CREED AND CHARACTER: Sermons. *Crown 8vo.* 3s. 6d.
ON BEHALF OF BELIEF. Sermons. *Crown 8vo.* 3s. 6d.
CHRIST OR ECCLESIASTES. Sermons. *Crown 8vo.* 2s. 6d.
LOGIC AND LIFE, with other Sermons. *Crown 8vo.* 3s. 6d.

Hutchings.—SERMON SKETCHES from some of the Sunday Lessons throughout the Church's Year. By the Rev. W. H. HUTCHINGS, M.A., Canon of York. *Vols. I and II. Crown 8vo.* 5s. each.

INHERITANCE OF THE SAINTS; or, Thoughts on the Communion of Saints and the Life of the World to come. Collected chiefly from English Writers by L. P. With a Preface by the Rev. HENRY SCOTT HOLLAND, M.A. *Crown 8vo.* 7s. 6d.

Jameson.—Works by Mrs. JAMESON.
SACRED AND LEGENDARY ART, containing Legends of the Angels and Archangels, the Evangelists, the Apostles. With 19 Etchings and 187 Woodcuts. *2 vols. 8vo.* 20s. *net.*
LEGENDS OF THE MONASTIC ORDERS, as represented in the Fine Arts. With 11 Etchings and 88 Woodcuts. *8vo.* 10s. *net.*
LEGENDS OF THE MADONNA, OR BLESSED VIRGIN MARY. With 27 Etchings and 165 Woodcuts. *8vo.* 10s. *net.*
THE HISTORY OF OUR LORD, as exemplified in Works of Art. Commenced by the late Mrs. JAMESON; continued and completed by LADY EASTLAKE. With 31 Etchings and 281 Woodcuts. *2 Vols. 8vo.* 20s. *net.*

Jennings.—ECCLESIA ANGLICANA. A History of the Church of Christ in England from the Earliest to the Present Times. By the Rev. ARTHUR CHARLES JENNINGS, M.A. *Crown 8vo.* 7s. 6d.

Jukes.—Works by ANDREW JUKES.

THE NEW MAN AND THE ETERNAL LIFE. Notes on the Reiterated Amens of the Son of God. *Crown 8vo.* 6s.

THE NAMES OF GOD IN HOLY SCRIPTURE: a Revelation of His Nature and Relationships. *Crown 8vo.* 4s. 6d.

THE TYPES OF GENESIS. *Crown 8vo.* 7s. 6d.

THE SECOND DEATH AND THE RESTITUTION OF ALL THINGS. *Crown 8vo.* 3s. 6d.

THE MYSTERY OF THE KINGDOM. *Crown 8vo.* 2s. 6d.

THE ORDER AND CONNEXION OF THE CHURCH'S TEACHING, as set forth in the arrangement of the Epistles and Gospels throughout the Year. *Crown 8vo.* 2s. 6d.

Knox Little.—Works by W. J. KNOX LITTLE, M.A., Canon Residentiary of Worcester, and Vicar of Hoar Cross.

SACERDOTALISM, WHEN RIGHTLY UNDERSTOOD, THE TEACHING OF THE CHURCH OF ENGLAND. *Crown 8vo.* 6s.

THE CHRISTIAN HOME. *Crown 8vo.* 3s. 6d.

THE HOPES AND DECISIONS OF THE PASSION OF OUR MOST HOLY REDEEMER. *Crown 8vo.* 2s. 6d.

CHARACTERISTICS AND MOTIVES OF THE CHRISTIAN LIFE. Ten Sermons preached in Manchester Cathedral, in Lent and Advent. *Crown 8vo.* 2s. 6d.

SERMONS PREACHED FOR THE MOST PART IN MANCHESTER. *Crown 8vo.* 3s. 6d.

THE MYSTERY OF THE PASSION OF OUR MOST HOLY REDEEMER. *Crown 8vo.* 2s. 6d.

THE WITNESS OF THE PASSION OF OUR MOST HOLY REDEEMER. *Crown 8vo.* 2s. 6d.

THE LIGHT OF LIFE. Sermons preached on Various Occasions. *Crown 8vo.* 3s. 6d.

SUNLIGHT AND SHADOW IN THE CHRISTIAN LIFE. Sermons preached for the most part in America. *Crown 8vo.* 3s. 6d.

Lear.—Works by, and Edited by, H. L. SIDNEY LEAR.
   FOR DAYS AND YEARS. A book containing a Text, Short Reading, and Hymn for Every Day in the Church's Year. 16mo. 2s. 6d. *Also a Cheap Edition*, 32mo. 1s.; *or cloth gilt*, 1s. 6d.; *or with red borders*, 2s. 6d.
   FIVE MINUTES. Daily Readings of Poetry. 16mo. 3s. 6d. *Also a Cheap Edition*, 32mo. 1s.; *or cloth gilt*, 1s. 6d.
   WEARINESS. A Book for the Languid and Lonely. *Large Type.* Small 8vo. 5s.

   CHRISTIAN BIOGRAPHIES. *Nine Vols. Crown 8vo. 3s. 6d. each.*

MADAME LOUISE DE FRANCE, Daughter of Louis XV., known also as the Mother Térèse de St. Augustin.	THE REVIVAL OF PRIESTLY LIFE IN THE SEVENTEENTH CENTURY IN FRANCE.
A DOMINICAN ARTIST: a Sketch of the Life of the Rev. Père Besson, of the Order of St. Dominic.	A CHRISTIAN PAINTER OF THE NINETEENTH CENTURY.
HENRI PERREYVE. By PÈRE GRATRY.	BOSSUET AND HIS CONTEMPORARIES.
ST. FRANCIS DE SALES, Bishop and Prince of Geneva.	FÉNELON, ARCHBISHOP OF CAMBRAI.
	HENRI DOMINIQUE LACORDAIRE.

   DEVOTIONAL WORKS. Edited by H. L. SIDNEY LEAR. *New and Uniform Editions. Nine Vols.* 16mo. 2s. 6d. *each.*

FÉNELON'S SPIRITUAL LETTERS TO MEN.	THE HIDDEN LIFE OF THE SOUL.
FÉNELON'S SPIRITUAL LETTERS TO WOMEN.	THE LIGHT OF THE CONSCIENCE. Also *Cheap Edition*, 32mo, 6d. cloth limp; and 1s. cloth boards.
A SELECTION FROM THE SPIRITUAL LETTERS OF ST. FRANCIS DE SALES. Also *Cheap Edition*, 32mo, 6d. cloth limp; 1s. cloth boards.	SELF-RENUNCIATION. From the French.
	ST. FRANCIS DE SALES' OF THE LOVE OF GOD.
THE SPIRIT OF ST. FRANCIS DE SALES.	SELECTIONS FROM PASCAL'S 'THOUGHTS.'

Liddon.—Works by HENRY PARRY LIDDON, D.D., D.C.L., LL.D., late Canon Residentiary and Chancellor of St. Paul's.
   LIFE OF EDWARD BOUVERIE PUSEY, D.D. By HENRY PARRY LIDDON, D.D., D.C.L., LL.D. Edited and prepared for publication by the Rev. J. O. JOHNSTON, M.A., Principal of the Theological College, and Vicar of Cuddesdon, Oxford; and the Rev. ROBERT J. WILSON, D.D., Warden of Keble College. *With Portraits and Illustrations. Four Vols.* 8vo. *Vols. I. and II.*, 36s. *Vol. III.*, 18s.

[continued

Liddon.—Works by HENRY PARRY LIDDON, D.D., D.C.L., LL.D., late Canon Residentiary and Chancellor of St Paul's.—*continued.*

CLERICAL LIFE AND WORK: Sermons. *Crown 8vo. 5s.*

ESSAYS AND ADDRESSES: Lectures on Buddhism—Lectures on the Life of St. Paul—Papers on Dante. *Crown 8vo. 5s.*

EXPLANATORY ANALYSIS OF PAUL'S EPISTLE TO THE ROMANS. *8vo. 14s.*

SERMONS ON OLD TESTAMENT SUBJECTS. *Crown 8vo. 5s.*

SERMONS ON SOME WORDS OF CHRIST. *Crown 8vo. 5s.*

THE DIVINITY OF OUR LORD AND SAVIOUR JESUS CHRIST. Being the Bampton Lectures for 1866. *Crown 8vo. 5s.*

ADVENT IN ST. PAUL'S. Sermons bearing chiefly on the Two Comings of our Lord. *Two Vols. Crown 8vo. 3s. 6d. each. Cheap Edition in one Volume. Crown 8vo. 5s.*

CHRISTMASTIDE IN ST. PAUL'S. Sermons bearing chiefly on the Birth of our Lord and the End of the Year. *Crown 8vo. 5s.*

PASSIONTIDE SERMONS. *Crown 8vo. 5s.*

EASTER IN ST. PAUL'S. Sermons bearing chiefly on the Resurrection of our Lord. *Two Vols. Crown 8vo. 3s. 6d. each. Cheap Edition in one Volume. Crown 8vo. 5s.*

SERMONS PREACHED BEFORE THE UNIVERSITY OF OXFORD. *Two Vols. Crown 8vo. 3s. 6d. each. Cheap Edition in one Volume. Crown 8vo. 5s.*

THE MAGNIFICAT. Sermons in St. Paul's. *Crown 8vo. 2s. 6d.*

SOME ELEMENTS OF RELIGION. Lent Lectures. *Small 8vo. 2s. 6d.*; or in paper cover, *1s. 6d.*
The Crown 8vo Edition (5s.) may still be had.

SELECTIONS FROM THE WRITINGS OF H. P. LIDDON, D.D. *Crown 8vo. 3s. 6d.*

MAXIMS AND GLEANINGS FROM THE WRITINGS OF H. P. LIDDON, D.D. Selected and arranged by C. M. S. *Crown 16mo. 1s.*

Luckock.—Works by HERBERT MORTIMER LUCKOCK, D.D., Dean of Lichfield.

THE HISTORY OF MARRIAGE, JEWISH AND CHRISTIAN, IN RELATION TO DIVORCE AND CERTAIN FORBIDDEN DEGREES. *Crown 8vo. 6s.*

AFTER DEATH. An Examination of the Testimony of Primitive Times respecting the State of the Faithful Dead, and their Relationship to the Living. *Crown 8vo. 3s. 6d.*

THE INTERMEDIATE STATE BETWEEN DEATH AND JUDGMENT. Being a Sequel to *After Death. Crown 8vo. 3s. 6d.*

[continued.

IN THEOLOGICAL LITERATURE. 11

Luckock.—Works by HERBERT MORTIMER LUCKOCK, D.D., Dean of Lichfield.—*continued.*
FOOTPRINTS OF THE SON OF MAN, as traced by St. Mark. Being Eighty Portions for Private Study, Family Reading, and Instructions in Church. *Crown 8vo.* 3s. 6d.
THE DIVINE LITURGY. Being the Order for Holy Communion, Historically, Doctrinally, and devotionally set forth, in Fifty Portions. *Crown 8vo.* 3s. 6d.
STUDIES IN THE HISTORY OF THE BOOK OF COMMON PRAYER. The Anglican Reform—The Puritan Innovations—The Elizabethan Reaction—The Caroline Settlement. With Appendices. *Crown 8vo.* 3s. 6d.
THE BISHOPS IN THE TOWER. A Record of Stirring Events affecting the Church and Nonconformists from the Restoration to the Revolution. *Crown 8vo.* 3s. 6d.

LYRA GERMANICA. Hymns translated from the German by CATHERINE WINKWORTH. *Small 8vo.* 5s.

MacColl.—Works by the Rev. MALCOLM MACCOLL, M.A., Canon Residentiary of Ripon.
CHRISTIANITY IN RELATION TO SCIENCE AND MORALS. *Crown 8vo.* 6s.
LIFE HERE AND HEREAFTER : Sermons. *Crown 8vo.* 7s. 6d.

Mason.—Works by A. J. MASON, D.D., Lady Margaret Professor of Divinity in the University of Cambridge.
THE FAITH OF THE GOSPEL. A Manual of Christian Doctrine. *Crown 8vo.* 7s. 6d. *Cheap Edition. Crown 8vo.* 3s. 6d.
THE RELATION OF CONFIRMATION TO BAPTISM. As taught in Holy Scripture and the Fathers. *Crown 8vo.* 7s. 6d.

Maturin.—SOME PRINCIPLES AND PRACTICES OF THE SPIRITUAL LIFE. By the Rev. B. W. MATURIN, Mission Priest of the Society of S. John the Evangelist, Cowley, Oxford. *Crown 8vo.* 4s. 6d.

Mercier.—OUR MOTHER CHURCH : Being Simple Talk on High Topics. By Mrs. JEROME MERCIER. *Small 8vo.* 3s. 6d.

Milne.—THE DOCTRINE AND PRACTICE OF THE EUCHARIST as deduced from Scripture and the Ancient Liturgies. By J. R. MILNE, Vicar of Rougham, Norfolk. *Crown 8vo.* 3s. 6d.

Moberly.—REASON AND RELIGION : Some Aspects of their Mutual Interdependence. By R. C. MOBERLY, D.D., Regius Professor of Pastoral Theology, and Canon of Christ Church, Oxford. *Crown 8vo.* 4s. 6d.

Mortimer.—Works by the Rev. A. G. MORTIMER, D.D., Rector of St. Mark's, Philadelphia.

HELPS TO MEDITATION: Sketches for Every Day in the Year.
Vol. I. ADVENT to TRINITY. 8vo. 7s. 6d.
Vol. II. TRINITY to ADVENT. 8vo. 7s. 6d.

STORIES FROM GENESIS: Sermons for Children. *Crown 8vo.* 4s.

THE LAWS OF HAPPINESS; or, The Beatitudes as teaching our Duty to God, Self, and our Neighbour. 18mo. 2s.

SERMONS IN MINIATURE FOR EXTEMPORE PREACHERS: Sketches for Every Sunday and Holy Day of the Christian Year. *Crown 8vo.* 6s.

NOTES ON THE SEVEN PENETENTIAL PSALMS, chiefly from Patristic Sources. *Fcp. 8vo.* 3s. 6d.

THE SEVEN LAST WORDS OF OUR MOST HOLY REDEEMER: with Meditations on some Scenes in His Passion. *Crown 8vo.* 5s.

LEARN OF JESUS CHRIST TO DIE: Addresses on the Words of our Lord from the Cross, taken as Teaching the way of Preparation for Death. 16mo. 2s.

THE LAWS OF PENITENCE: Addresses on the Words of our Lord from the Cross. 16mo. 1s. 6d.

Mozley.—Works by J. B. MOZLEY, D.D., late Canon of Christ Church, and Regius Professor of Divinity at Oxford.

ESSAYS, HISTORICAL AND THEOLOGICAL. *Two Vols.* 8vo. 24s.

EIGHT LECTURES ON MIRACLES. Being the Bampton Lectures for 1865. *Crown 8vo.* 3s. 6d.

RULING IDEAS IN EARLY AGES AND THEIR RELATION TO OLD TESTAMENT FAITH. 8vo. 6s.

SERMONS PREACHED BEFORE THE UNIVERSITY OF OXFORD, and on Various Occasions. *Crown 8vo.* 3s. 6d.

SERMONS, PAROCHIAL AND OCCASIONAL. *Crown 8vo.* 3s. 6d.

A REVIEW OF THE BAPTISMAL CONTROVERSY. *Crown 8vo.* 3s 6d.

Newbolt.—Works by the Rev. W. C. E. NEWBOLT, M.A., Canon and Chancellor of St. Paul's Cathedral.

THE GOSPEL OF EXPERIENCE; or, the Witness of Human Life to the truth of Revelation. Being the Boyle Lectures for 1895. *Crown 8vo.* 5s.

COUNSELS OF FAITH AND PRACTICE: being Sermons preached on various occasions. *New and Enlarged Edition. Crown 8vo.* 5s.

SPECULUM SACERDOTUM; or, the Divine Model of the Priestly Life. *Crown 8vo.* 7s. 6d.

THE FRUIT OF THE SPIRIT. Being Ten Addresses bearing on the Spiritual Life. *Crown 8vo.* 2s. 6d.

THE MAN OF GOD. Being Six Addresses delivered during Lent and the Primary Ordination of the Right Rev. the Lord Alwyne Compton, D.D., Bishop of Ely. *Small 8vo.* 1s. 6d.

THE PRAYER BOOK: Its Voice. and Teaching. Being Spiritual Addresses bearing on the Book of Common Prayer. *Crown 8vo.* 2s. 6d.

Newman.—Works by JOHN HENRY NEWMAN, B.D., sometime Vicar of St. Mary's, Oxford.
    PAROCHIAL AND PLAIN SERMONS. *Eight Vols. Cabinet Edition. Crown 8vo.* 5s. *each. Cheaper Edition.* 3s. 6d. *each.*
    SELECTION, ADAPTED TO THE SEASONS OF THE ECCLESIASTICAL YEAR, from the 'Parochial and Plain Sermons,' *Cabinet Edition. Crown 8vo.* 5s. *Cheaper Edition.* 3s. 6d.
    FIFTEEN SERMONS PREACHED BEFORE THE UNIVERSITY OF OXFORD *Cabinet Edition. Crown 8vo.* 5s. *Cheaper Edition.* 3s. 6d.
    SERMONS BEARING UPON SUBJECTS OF THE DAY. *Cabinet Edition. Crown 8vo.* 5s. *Cheaper Edition. Crown 8vo.* 3s. 6d.
    LECTURES ON THE DOCTRINE OF JUSTIFICATION. *Cabinet Edition. Crown 8vo.* 5s. *Cheaper Edition.* 3s. 6d.
    ** *A Complete List of Cardinal Newman's Works can be had on Application.*

Norris.—RUDIMENTS OF THEOLOGY: a First Book for Students. By JOHN PILKINGTON NORRIS, D.D., late Archdeacon of Bristol, and Canon Residentiary of Bristol Cathedral. *Cr. 8vo.* 3s. 6d.

Osborne.—Works by EDWARD OSBORNE, Mission Priest of the Society of St. John the Evangelist, Cowley, Oxford.
    THE CHILDREN'S SAVIOUR. Instructions to Children on the Life of Our Lord and Saviour Jesus Christ. *Illustrated.* 16mo. 2s. 6d.
    THE SAVIOUR KING. Instructions to Children on Old Testament Types and Illustrations of the Life of Christ. *Illustrated.* 16mo. 2s. 6d.
    THE CHILDREN'S FAITH. Instructions to Children on the Apostles' Creed. *Illustrated.* 16mo. 2s. 6d.

Overton.—THE ENGLISH CHURCH IN THE NINETEENTH CENTURY, 1800-1833. By the Rev. JOHN H. OVERTON, D.D., Canon of Lincoln, Rector of Epworth, Doncaster, and Rural Dean of the Isle of Axholme. *8vo.* 14s.

Oxenden.—Works by the Right Rev. ASHTON OXENDEN, formerly Bishop of Montreal.
    PLAIN SERMONS, to which is prefixed a Memorial Portrait. *Crown 8vo.* 5s.
    THE HISTORY OF MY LIFE: An Autobiography. *Crown 8vo.* 5s.
    PEACE AND ITS HINDRANCES. *Crown 8vo.* 1s. *sewed*; 2s. *cloth.*
    THE PATHWAY OF SAFETY; or, Counsel to the Awakened. *Fcap. 8vo, large type.* 2s. 6d. *Cheap Edition. Small type, limp,* 1s.
    THE EARNEST COMMUNICANT. *New Red Rubric Edition.* 32mo, *cloth.* 2s. *Common Edition.* 32mo. 1s.
    OUR CHURCH AND HER SERVICES. *Fcap. 8vo.* 2s. 6d.

[continued.

Oxenden.—Works by the Right Rev. ASHTON OXENDEN, formerly Bishop of Montreal—*continued*.

>FAMILY PRAYERS FOR FOUR WEEKS. First Series. *Fcap. 8vo.* 2s. 6d. Second Series. *Fcap. 8vo.* 2s. 6d.
>>LARGE TYPE EDITION. Two Series in one Volume. *Crown 8vo.* 6s.
>
>COTTAGE SERMONS; or, Plain Words to the Poor. *Fcap. 8vo.* 2s. 6d.
>THOUGHTS FOR HOLY WEEK. *16mo, cloth.* 1s. 6d.
>DECISION. *18mo.* 1s. 6d.
>THE HOME BEYOND; or, A Happy Old Age. *Fcap. 8vo.* 1s. 6d.
>THE LABOURING MAN'S BOOK. *18mo, large type, cloth.* 1s. 6d.

Paget.—Works by FRANCIS PAGET, D.D., Dean of Christ Church.

>STUDIES IN THE CHRISTIAN CHARACTER: Sermons. With an Introductory Essay. *Crown 8vo.* 6s. 6d.
>
>THE SPIRIT OF DISCIPLINE: Sermons. *Crown 8vo.* 6s. 6d.
>
>FACULTIES AND DIFFICULTIES FOR BELIEF AND DISBELIEF. *Crown 8vo.* 6s. 6d.
>
>THE HALLOWING OF WORK. Addresses given at Eton, January 16-18, 1888. *Small 8vo.* 2s.

PRACTICAL REFLECTIONS. By a CLERGYMAN. With Prefaces by H. P. LIDDON, D.D., D.C.L., and the BISHOP OF LINCOLN. *Crown 8vo.*

THE BOOK OF GENESIS. 4s. 6d.	THE MINOR PROPHETS. 4s. 6d.
THE PSALMS. 5s.	THE HOLY GOSPELS. 4s. 6d.
ISAIAH. 4s. 6d.	ACTS TO REVELATIONS. 6s.

Percival.—THE INVOCATION OF SAINTS. Treated Theologically and Historically. By HENRY R. PERCIVAL, M.A., D.D., Author of 'A Digest of Theology,' 'The Doctrine of the Episcopal Church,' etc. *Crown 8vo.* 5s.

Prynne.—THE TRUTH AND REALITY OF THE EUCHARISTIC SACRIFICE, Proved from Holy Scripture, the Teaching of the Primitive Church, and the Book of Common Prayer. By the Rev. GEORGE RUNDLE PRYNNE, M.A. *Crown 8vo.* 3s. 6d.

Pullan.—LECTURES ON RELIGION. By the Rev. LEIGHTON PULLAN, M.A., Fellow of St. John's College, Lecturer in Theology at Oriel and Queen's Colleges, Oxford. *Crown 8vo.* 6s.

Puller.—THE PRIMITIVE SAINTS AND THE SEE OF ROME. By F. W. PULLER, M.A., Mission Priest of the Society of St. John Evangelist, Cowley, Oxford. *Crown 8vo.* 7s. 6d.

Pusey.—LIFE OF EDWARD BOUVERIE PUSEY, D.D. By HENRY PARRY LIDDON, D.D., D.C.L., LL.D. Edited and prepared for publication by the Rev. J. O. JOHNSTON, M.A., Principal of the Theological College, Vicar of Cuddesdon, Oxford, and the Rev. ROBERT J. WILSON, D.D., Warden of Keble College. *With Portraits and Illustrations. Four Vols.* 8vo. Vols. *I. and II.*, 36s. Vol. *III.*, 18s.

Randolph.—THE LAW OF SINAI: being Devotional Addresses on the Ten Commandments delivered to Ordinands. By B. W. RANDOLPH, M.A., Principal of the Theological College and Hon. Canon of Ely. *Crown* 8vo. 3s. 6d.

Sanday.—Works by W. SANDAY, D.D., Margaret Professor of Divinity in the University of Oxford.

INSPIRATION: Eight Lectures on the Early History and Origin of the Doctrine of Biblical Inspiration. Being the Bampton Lectures for 1893. *New and Cheaper Edition, with New Preface.* 8vo. 7s. 6d.

THE ORACLES OF GOD: Nine Lectures on the Nature and Extent of Biblical Inspiration and the Special Significance of the Old Testament Scriptures at the Present Time. *Crown* 8vo. 4s.

TWO PRESENT-DAY QUESTIONS. I. Biblical Criticism. II. The Social Movement. Sermons preached before the University of Cambridge. *Crown* 8vo. 2s. 6d.

Strong.—CHRISTIAN ETHICS: being the Bampton Lectures for 1895. By THOMAS B. STRONG, M.A., Student of Christ Church, Oxford, and Examining Chaplain to the Lord Bishop of Durham. 8vo. 15s.

Tee.—THE SANCTUARY OF SUFFERING. By ELEANOR TEE, Author of 'This Everyday Life,' etc. With a Preface by the Rev. J. P. F. DAVIDSON, M.A., Vicar of St. Matthias', Earl's Court; President of the 'Guild of All Souls.' *Crown* 8vo. 7s. 6d.

Williams.—Works by the Rev. ISAAC WILLIAMS, B.D.

A DEVOTIONAL COMMENTARY ON THE GOSPEL NARRATIVE. *Eight Vols. Crown* 8vo. 5s. *each. Sold Separately.*

THOUGHTS ON THE STUDY OF THE HOLY GOSPELS.
A HARMONY OF THE FOUR GOSPELS.
OUR LORD'S NATIVITY.
OUR LORD'S MINISTRY (Second Year).
OUR LORD'S MINISTRY (Third Year).
THE HOLY WEEK.
OUR LORD'S PASSION.
OUR LORD'S RESURRECTION.

FEMALE CHARACTERS OF HOLY SCRIPTURE. A Series of Sermons. *Crown* 8vo. 5s.

THE CHARACTERS OF THE OLD TESTAMENT. *Crown* 8vo. 5s.

THE APOCALYPSE. With Notes and Reflections. *Crown* 8vo. 5s.

SERMONS ON THE EPISTLES AND GOSPELS FOR THE SUNDAYS AND HOLY DAYS. *Two Vols. Crown* 8vo. 5s. *each.*

PLAIN SERMONS ON CATECHISM. *Two Vols. Cr.* 8vo. 5s. *each.*

Wordsworth.—Works by the late CHRISTOPHER WORDSWORTH, D.D., Bishop of Lincoln.

THE HOLY BIBLE (the Old Testament). With Notes, Introductions, and Index. *Imperial 8vo.*
    Vol. I. THE PENTATEUCH. 25*s.* Vol. II. JOSHUA TO SAMUEL. 15*s.* Vol. III. KINGS to ESTHER. 15*s.* Vol. IV. JOB TO SONG OF SOLOMON. 25*s.* Vol. V. ISAIAH TO EZEKIEL. 25*s.* Vol. VI. DANIEL, MINOR PROPHETS, and Index. 15*s.*
    Also supplied in 12 Parts. Sold separately.

THE NEW TESTAMENT, in the Original Greek. With Notes, Introductions, and Indices. *Imperial 8vo.*
    Vol. I. GOSPELS AND ACTS OF THE APOSTLES. 23*s.* Vol. II. EPISTLES, APOCALYPSE, and Indices. 37*s.*
    Also supplied in 4 Parts. Sold separately.

LECTURES ON INSPIRATION OF THE BIBLE. *Small 8vo.* 1*s.* 6*d.* *cloth.* 1*s.* *sewed.*

A CHURCH HISTORY TO A.D. 451. *Four Vols. Crown 8vo.*
    Vol. I. TO THE COUNCIL OF NICÆA, A.D. 325. 8*s.* 6*d.* Vol. II. FROM THE COUNCIL OF NICÆA TO THAT OF CONSTANTINOPLE. 6*s.* Vol. III. CONTINUATION. 6*s.* Vol. IV. CONCLUSION, TO THE COUNCIL OF CHALCEDON, A.D. 451. 6*s.*

THEOPHILUS ANGLICANUS: a Manual of Instruction on the Church and the Anglican Branch of it. 12*mo.* 2*s.* 6*d.*

ELEMENTS OF INSTRUCTION ON THE CHURCH. 16*mo.* 1*s.* *cloth.* 6*d.* *sewed.*

ON UNION WITH ROME. *Small 8vo.* 1*s.* 6*d.* Sewed, 1*s.*

THE HOLY YEAR: Original Hymns. 16*mo.* 2*s.* 6*d.* and 1*s.* Limp, 6*d.*
    ,,   ,,   With Music. Edited by W. H. MONK. *Square 8vo.* 4*s.* 6*d.*

MISCELLANIES, Literary and Religious. *Three Vols.* 8*vo.* 36*s.*

ON THE INTERMEDIATE STATE OF THE SOUL AFTER DEATH. 32*mo.* 1*s.*

Younghusband.—Works by FRANCES YOUNGHUSBAND.

THE STORY OF OUR LORD, told in Simple Language for Children. With 25 Illustrations on Wood from Pictures by the Old Masters, and numerous Ornamental Borders, Initial Letters, etc., from Longmans' New Testament. *Crown 8vo.* 2*s.* 6*d.*

THE STORY OF GENESIS, told in Simple Language for Children. With Frontispiece. *Crown 8vo.* 2*s.* 6*d.*

THE STORY OF THE EXODUS, told in Simple Language for Children. With Map and 29 Illustrations. *Crown 8vo.* 2*s.* 6*d.*

www.ingramcontent.com/pod-product-compliance
Lightning Source LLC
Chambersburg PA
CBHW031431230426
43668CB00007B/494